Values and Ideals of

American Youth

Edited by ELI GINZBERG

WITH A FOREWORD BY *John W. Gardner*

Essay Index Reprint Series

BOOKS FOR LIBRARIES PRESS
PLAINVIEW, NEW YORK

Library of Congress Cataloging in Publication Data

Ginzberg, Eli, 1911-   ed.
    Values and ideals of American youth.
    xii, 338p. : ill. ; 23 cm.
    (Essay index reprint series)
    Includes bibliographical references.
    1. Children in the United States--Addresses, essays,
lectures. 2. Youth--United States--Addresses, essays,
lectures. I. Title.
[HQ792.U5G5 1972]   301.43'1'0973   72-6798
ISBN 0-8369-7252-X

FOREWORD

John W. Gardner

SIXTEEN-YEAR-OLD Julia was boasting of the way in which she had exploited a thirty-year-old married man. "That's the way to do," she said, "When you get a sucker, bump his head."

That merciless bit of youthful cynicism, reported by Allison Davis and John Dollard in *Children of Bondage,* is the sort of thing that leads some adults to wring their hands in despair, and others to devote their lifetimes to study and action concerned with the values and ideals of youth. In the latter category are the contributors to this volume.

A concern for the attitudes and values of youth is not new—and not unique to the kinds of people who contributed to this volume. Surely since the dawn of history every adult has been an unlicensed, self-appointed expert on the subject.

Adults in our time have not abdicated their ancient responsibility in this matter. The sheer volume of talk and writing on the subject is awesome. Unfortunately, most of it isn't worth listening to. Much of it is produced by adults who have a wholly distorted (and idealized) memory of their own childhood. A good deal of it comes from people whose true source of anxiety is not the morals of youth but the rapidity of change in the world. Most of it is lacking in any discriminating grasp of what the problem is all about.

An observer of military affairs once said that in time of war fanaticism is most intense among those who are a long way from the front lines.

John W. Gardner is President of the Carnegie Corporation of New York.

Similarly, the most violent views about youth are apt to be held by those not directly concerned with youth. The closer one gets to those who are devoting their lives to the problems of young people, the less one hears harsh judgments, oversimplified diagnoses, and shrill cries of alarm.

Alarm is not absent from this book. But it is alarm tempered by depth of understanding, tested against facts, and seasoned by lifelong observation.

If one accepts the contributors to this volume as reasonably representative of the best thinking on this subject today, one might be inclined to ask how they would compare with a similar cross-section taken ten, twenty, or thirty years ago. In my opinion, the heartening answer is that they compare more than favorably. The years have not been wasted. For example, these authors exhibit a balanced approach to some questions that have not always enjoyed such an approach.

Most of them have an intimate grasp of the extent to which attitudes and values are conditioned by environment; yet they do not slide off into the glib environmental determinism which was not uncommon a few years ago.

They reject the stern authoritarianism of an older day; but they have seen the undisciplined permissiveness which succeeded it, and they reject that too.

They know they can never retreat to the complacent and unexamined beliefs of their grandparents; but neither can they accept the vogue of belieflessness that has reigned for a quarter of a century.

And above all, these authors understand, without affectation, that the problems of youth must be illuminated by searchlights from many directions. Thus they seek the varying perspectives provided by workers from many different fields. They are quite prepared to call on an anthropologist for help, to listen to the testimony of a physiologist, to borrow philosophical and legal concepts, to employ the techniques of psychological research, and to test all results against the seasoned judgment of the social worker.

The solid emphasis upon the values and ideals of youth as a major topic in the 1960 White House Conference on Children and Youth is in

itself significant. Some of the fields of investigation most intimately concerned with children and youth, e.g., psychology, sociology, and anthropology, went through a period in which they were extraordinarily wary of the word "values" and all that it connoted. For many, the very word suggested a lapse from the scientific attitude. We have outgrown that. We haven't yet learned how to talk about values in reliably meaningful terms; but we have learned not to be afraid to try.

This book is not a systematic treatment of the vast subject with which it deals. It is a collection of soundings by some of the ablest and most gifted workers drawn from all parts of the field. Some of the soundings go very deep, some are broader. To the professional thoroughly versed in one part of the field, they will provide interesting insights into other parts of it. To the interested citizen, they will provide a usefully broad and varied introduction to the whole subject.

PREFACE

This volume of distinguished papers and addresses is a by-product of the Golden Anniversary White House Conference on Children and Youth. While it is not an official publication of the Conference, it is the result of formal action taken by the Executive Committee of the Conference to encourage such a publication. The Executive Committee expressed the hope that a publisher could be found who would recognize the public service which would result from making available in book form a selection of some of the important papers and addresses that were prepared for the Conference.

In my capacity as Chairman of the Committee on Studies of the President's National Committee of the White House Conference I was charged to carry out this assignment. In this undertaking I had the advice and assistance of the following members of a small *ad hoc* committee: Dr. Philip Barba, Mr. Joseph Reid, Dr. Ruth Stout, and Dr. Ralph Tyler.

With the help of the Conference's Studies Staff, my associates and I made an initial screening of suitable materials. But the Columbia University Press made the final decisions as to the contents of this volume.

Included are six "Survey Papers," which were originally prepared for the guidance of Conference participants, and which were printed in *Children and Youth in the 1960's:* those by Mead, Loomis, Kagan, Axt, Lourie, and Granger.

Also included are seven "Reference Papers," which were included in a Conference publication entitled *Reference Papers on Children and Youth,* and which provided a probing analysis of selected themes around which the Conference's program was constructed: those by Bronfenbrenner, Clark, McFarland, Ehrmann, Patterson, Taba, and Warburton.

The remaining nine chapters are addresses which were delivered at the
Conference, seven at the Theme Assemblies and two at the Forums: those
by Dubos, Janeway, Parsons, Pope, Sittler, McGinley, Sachar, Josselyn,
and Smith. Each of these addresses was briefly summarized in the *Conference Proceedings* but they have not been previously generally available.

Dr. Joseph B. Margolin, Staff Coordinator of Studies of the Conference,
had the primary responsibility, under a broad directive from the Committee on Studies, for developing the two major collections of "Survey Papers"
and "Reference Papers." In this he had the advice and assistance of Dr.
Harold Orlans, the Staff Director of Studies of the Conference. Had it
not been for the superior manner in which Dr. Margolin and Dr. Orlans
carried out their assignment, the present volume could never have been
produced. The assistance of Mr. Herbert Fockler of the Conference staff
was also important. Theirs was the difficult task of working out with the
contributors coverage, emphases, and style. They were the initial editors
of the "Survey" and "Reference" papers that appear in this volume.

A word about the contributors and their contributions: Because of
the Conference's time schedule most of the contributors were forced
to prepare their papers under great pressure and had no opportunity to
edit them. Nor was it practical, after the Conference, to return the papers
to their authors for revision. In preparing the selections for press, I have
presumed to make minimum additional changes in form and content,
without in any way undertaking major revisions. In this I was assisted by
Ruth Szold Ginzberg.

Dr. John W. Gardner, a member of the President's National Committee, repeatedly served the Conference as its literary spokesman and
he graciously responded to the urging of the Executive Committee to do
so once again by writing a foreword to this collection.

ELI GINZBERG

Columbia University
March, 1961

CONTENTS

CONTENTS

PART ONE

Development and Adaptability

ADAPTABILITY FOR SURVIVAL
AND GROWTH

René J. Dubos

IN SEPTEMBER, 1959, the U.S. Air Force Academy conducted a conference on "Fitness of American Youth." It may be thought that fitness for combat has little to do with the qualities we want to cultivate in children living in a world of peace. However, some of the facts brought out in the 1959 discussions illustrate a most fundamental difficulty of today—our ignorance of the problems that the youth of today will face when they reach adulthood in tomorrow's society.

At the Air Force conference, Colonel Kossuth of the Medical Corps wisely emphasized that there is no such thing as fitness *per se*. Because fitness must always be defined in terms of a particular situation, the Armed Forces find it necessary frequently to revise their standards of physical health to keep them in tune with the changing requirements of military duty. With propeller-driven aircraft, for example, there were many situations in which survival depended on strength of arm and limb. Moreover, the pilot of a fighter airplane in World War II had to watch for enemies in the sky by direct visual perception. His head swiveled from side to side as he scanned the sky, and for this reason calisthenics to develop neck muscles were part of training.

Today, power controls have lessened physical requirements for aircraft operators, and with electronic vision the fighter pilot never need

René J. Dubos is member and professor, Rockefeller Institute.

look to the rear. In any case, direct vision would be of little help in modern combat now that aircraft approach each other at terrific speeds. At 600 miles per hour—and this is now considered moderate speed—half a mile is covered in little more than a second, which is clearly not enough time for the pilot to see, to react, and to change the direction of his aircraft. As a result, keenness of vision no longer means the difference between life and death for the fighter pilot; it has been superseded by keenness in ability to detect slight changes on electronic dials and gauges.

More generally, strenuous physical conditioning programs are no longer as relevant to performance in the Armed Forces as they used to be. And in fact, recent tests indicate that pilots at the peak of physical form do not score any better in difficult operations than do those of comparable groups who are less physically fit.

The changes in relevance of physical prowess to military performance have, of course, many counterparts in civilian life. Effectiveness in modern technology depends to a large extent on dial watching and on reading printed matter. Whereas physical stamina and distant vision were once extremely important, muscles are now called into play chiefly in leisure time, and nearsightedness has become almost an asset. Indeed, the present trends of life in the United States seem to provide justification for the child who does not want to walk because he considers it old-fashioned, and for his mother who dissuades him from exposure or physical exertion because modern existence should be air-conditioned and effortless. And yet, while this attitude appears logical on the surface, I believe that it may lead to disaster in the long run, and this is the theme of the present essay. I shall defend the view that the continued growth of man, indeed his very survival, demands that he cultivate powers of *adaptation* of a nonspecialized nature, even though the qualities thereby acquired appear of little use for daily life in the modern world.

The word adaptation is tricky. It can refer to the hereditary changes in genetic characters by which living things become progressively better adapted to their environment from one generation to the next—the processes involved in Darwinian evolution. Genetic forces operate in man just as they do in other living things, and there is no doubt that they have

been responsible during the course of millennia for the adaptive differentiation of human types in the various parts of the world. Clearly the Negro possesses genetic traits which make him better adapted to unprotected life in the tropics than is the fair-skinned, blue-eyed Scandinavian. But important as they are, these genetically controlled phenomena of very long duration are not the adaptive processes which I have in mind today. Instead, I should like to emphasize the fact that during the past century mankind in the Western world has become adapted to very new conditions of its own making, and that even more drastic alterations in the ways of life will soon demand further adaptations. One century is a short time on the evolutionary scale for man, and for this reason genetic changes cannot possibly account for the adaptations that have occurred during the past few decades and that will be needed in the near future. On the other hand, and fortunately, each individual has in reserve an enormous range of potential adaptive resources that can be called into play under demanding circumstances. These adaptive potentialities have made it possible for millions of people to move in one generation from life on an isolated farm to the tensions of Broadway and 42d Street, and we shall have to depend on these potentialities to survive the even more drastic and more rapid changes which are in the offing. Merely for the sake of illustration, let us consider some of the changes that have occurred in our communities during the past half century, and try to imagine what might happen during the lifetime of our children.

Disease from contaminated food or beverages was very common a few generations ago, and nutritional deficiencies were almost the rule. In contrast, laboratories now check on the safety of what we eat and drink. Furthermore, the nutritional requirements of man are well known, and in the Western world at least, we have the means to satisfy them. But all this theoretical and practical knowledge does not guarantee that nutrition will not present problems in the immediate future, even assuming that economic prosperity continues to grow.

On the one hand, modern agriculture and food technology have come to depend more and more on the use of chemicals to control pests and to improve the yields of animal and plant products. The costs of production would enormously increase without these chemicals and their use is

therefore justified, but unfortunately, and despite all care, several of them eventually reach the human consumer in objectionable concentrations. As more and more different types of substances are being introduced in agriculture and food technology every year, it will become practically impossible to test them all with regard to long-range effects on human health, and the possibility of toxic reactions must be accepted as one of the inevitable risks of progress.

Another potentially disturbing aspect of nutrition in the future arises from the fact that human food requirements have been formulated on the basis of a certain level of physical activity and of exposure to the inclemencies of the weather. But no one knows exactly what these requirements will be for the wheelborne, air-conditioned human being of the next decades. The well-fed child of today may prove to have been overfed in terms of the kind of life he will lead tomorrow.

Just as we have eliminated most physical overexertion from our life, and minimized exposure to heat or cold, so we have greatly decreased contact with infectious agents and learned to treat the diseases caused by some of those that we cannot yet escape. One needs only recall the toll exacted by infectious diseases in the past to appreciate the magnitude of the contributions made to human health by sanitation and drug therapy. But even this achievement may turn out not to be an unmixed blessing. True enough, certain acute infectious diseases are practically under control, but others are becoming more prevalent—paralytic poliomyelitis for example. And more than ever before, hospitals are crowded with patients suffering from chronic disorders which do not kill outright, but often blight life.

Fifty years ago, short-range transportation was by horse, and we had stables in every block. The stables constituted a fine breeding ground for flies and these, as well as other insects, acted as agents for the transmission of many diseases. Progressively, mankind managed to cope with this problem by developing certain kinds of natural immunities, and by introducing sanitary practices. Today the situation is different. Horses have been replaced by automobiles, and the diseases they brought about have disappeared. But unsought results of this advance have been the pollution of the atmosphere by automobile exhausts and 40,000 fatalities

each year on our highways. We are beginning to think constructively about these new problems, and may learn to do something about them, but we may expect that new difficulties will soon arise from further improvements in methods of transportation. Probably unexpected toxic manifestations will accompany the use of new fuels—or of atomic energy. Probably also a few more of our degrees of freedom will be eliminated by the enforcement of more drastic traffic laws, and this will contribute still further to the soul-destroying mechanization of our everyday life.

In any case, the rapid increase in population—the population explosion as it is properly called—will make it more and more difficult to avoid regimentation of life. Even though political freedom may survive in principle, individual activities will be increasingly restricted within any political system. The social structure is bound to become more rigid as the larger population becomes increasingly dependent on a more complex technology. Until we have learned to change our ways, restrictions of individual freedom are likely to increase the incidence of psychoneuroses.

In the same class belong the mental health problems caused by automation. While some look upon automation as the gateway to the golden age, others see it as the source of new social and medical difficulties. It is highly likely that purely automated work will fill the worker with a sense of inadequacy because he feels less useful in an effort he cannot appreciate, with anxiety because his efforts seem so abstract, and with strain because of new kinds of responsibility. Nervous strain will inevitably result from the need to give unremitting attention to irregularly intermittent signs of varying perceptibility, and all this without an opportunity for physical activity.

There is no possibility, in my opinion, that pills can prevent or cure these minor but important mental illnesses, or that medical personnel and services will ever be sufficient to deal with the large numbers of persons who will need psychiatric help in the regimented life that will characterize the first phases of the automation age. Adjustments will certainly be made, but we can anticipate a period when mental frustrations will have consequences worse than those that used to result from inclement weather or physical exertion.

It would be presumptuous and indeed impossible to try to predict what

precise effects the ever-changing social environment will have on the children who are growing up today. But the formulation of the problem might be facilitated by considering one particular aspect of it on which some concrete information is available. As anyone can observe, most children are now growing in size more rapidly than did those of one or two generations ago. Of special importance is the fact that this change affects not only size but other physiological characteristics, and that in general boys and girls are maturing physically and reaching puberty somewhere between six months and two years earlier than did their parents. It is probable that improvements in nutrition, control of infection, and other unidentified factors are responsible for this physiological acceleration, but of greater importance than the causes of acceleration are the problems that it poses for the management of young people.

It is indeed ironical that legislation and social mores tend to prolong the period during which young people are treated as immature and irresponsible precisely at the time when children are growing faster and physically maturing earlier. Vigorous and well-fed young people need rough physical activity, but our society urges on them a sheltered and effortless life. They are eager to show their worth and to function usefully, but labor laws bar them from employment. They crave an imaginative life and the chance to manifest initiative, but most forms of responsibility are denied them because they are regarded as children. It would be entertaining if it were not tragic to contrast the place occupied in our society by the modern fully developed six-foot teenagers with that occupied by their physiological equivalents in the past. Throughout history, young adults have acted effectively as leaders in warfare, active members of political parties, creators of business enterprises, or advocates of new philosophical doctrines—whereas modern young people are expected to find fulfillment in playgrounds, juvenile spectacles, and ice cream parlors!

Because I am convinced that our young people are potentially as able, enterprising, and worthy as those of the past, I find it pathetic that society does not offer them the challenges they deserve. I am afraid that present social attitudes render them more likely to yield to sexual impulses, become juvenile delinquents, or turn to philosophies of despair. Society must recognize that fully developed, well-fed young bodies need some

satisfying and worthwhile form of expression if they are to become creative and healthy human beings.

The facts and views that I have outlined imply that physical and mental disorders will exist in the world of tomorrow as they have in the past, but in different forms. By and large, we may assume that the gains derived from any advance are likely to be offset by new problems arising from this very advance. But recognition of this need not create a gloomy outlook for the future. For many millennia, mankind has moved forward and upward, though in an erratic and halting manner. It has taken all sorts of disasters and upheavals in its stride, often deriving from painful experiences the stimulus for more brilliant performances. While we cannot create for our children a world free of stresses—nor in my opinion should we do it if we could—there is no ground to believe that human nature will lose the resilience and creativeness that it has always displayed.

There is one aspect of the modern world, however, which has little historical precedent. In the past, most changes in the ways of life and in the physical environment occurred rather slowly, often taking several generations to reach their maximum before affecting large numbers of people. This slow rate of change permitted all sorts of progressive adjustments—at times through genetic mechanisms, more commonly through biological adaptations, and always through social devices. The fundamentally new aspect of the situation in our society is not that many changes are taking place, but rather that they occur so rapidly as to make orderly adjustments more difficult. Ambassador Kennan has forcefully stated the importance of this new situation. In his words: "Wherever the past ceases to be the great and reliable reference book of human problems, wherever, above all, the experience of the father becomes irrelevant to the trials and searchings of the son, there the foundations of man's inner health and stability begin to crumble, insecurity and panic begin to take over, conduct becomes erratic and aggressive. These, unfortunately, are the marks of an era of rapid technological or social change." Although Mr. Kennan's words referred to political and social issues, they are just as valid for the biological aspects of life. They apply to all the reactions of body and soul to the ever-changing environment.

The crucial consequence of this rapidity of change is that our children will have to meet emergencies without benefit of their forebears' help or experience. The best thing that we can do for them, perhaps the only thing worth doing, is to create an atmosphere in which they will develop such nonspecialized adaptive powers that they can respond rapidly and effectively to all kinds of new and unexpected threats for which they cannot be specifically prepared. The objection may well be raised, of course, that these are idle words, which correspond to a counsel of perfection without relevance to the facts of life. In part this is true, but in part only.

The reason that we know so little about how to make young people develop their own adaptive powers is that modern civilization has not concerned itself with this problem. Everywhere in the world, and in the United States in particular, the trend has been to control and modify the external environment for the sake of human comfort, with total elimination of effort as an ideal. We do little if anything to train the body and soul to resist strains and stresses. But we devote an enormous amount of skill and foresight to conditioning our dwellings against heat and cold, avoiding contact with germs, making food available at all hours of the day, multiplying labor-saving devices, minimizing the effort of learning, and dulling even the slightest pain with drugs.

Needless to say, I am not advocating a retreat from these practices which have made life so much easier and effective—although not necessarily very much happier. But I would urge that we also pay attention to another approach for dealing with the external world, namely the cultivation of the resources in human nature which make man potentially adaptable to a wide range of living conditions.

The field of adaptation has been so neglected and the knowledge concerning it is so scarce that it might be useful to illustrate its manifestations with two limited but concrete examples. The first example has to do with an experience common to all of us, namely our ability to withstand hot and cold weather. When the outside temperature falls to 50° in September, everyone feels cold and additional clothing is in order. In contrast, the same temperature in February evokes thoughts of summer and invites to a leisurely stroll. Clearly, the body becomes more or less

adapted to the prevailing temperature as the season advances, and this ability to adapt has helped mankind to make its home over vast areas of the globe despite wide climatic differences. In view of this, it is probably unwise to avoid *completely* exposure to inclement conditions, and thus prevent the temperature adaptive mechanisms of the human body to come into action.

The second example is more technical but worth describing nevertheless, because it is presently the subject of much experimentation. Modern laboratory techniques have made it possible to raise animals under such conditions that they do not come into contact with any microbes, either at birth or during the rest of their lives. These so-called germ-free animals grow well, and can reproduce normally, but it is a common finding that they succumb rapidly to infection as soon as they are removed from their sheltered environment and brought into contact with ordinary microbes. The reason for this great susceptibility is now fairly well understood. In brief, it resides in the fact that germ-free animals fail to develop properly the structures and functions which permit normal animals to respond effectively to the challenge of infection. These defensive structures and functions are part of the equipment by which the body can adapt itself to the microbial threats of the environment under normal conditions. There is no doubt that in man as well as in animals, natural defense mechanisms can either atrophy or develop properly, depending upon the circumstances of life. In the case of germ-free animals, failure to come in contact with ordinary germs during the early stage of life is responsible for the lack of development of the defense mechanisms.

Let me acknowledge once more that little is known scientifically of the mechanisms involved in adaptation and that this ignorance makes it difficult to formulate rational courses of training. In fact, hardly anything has been added to this subject since Bacon wrote in his essay *Of Nature in Men:* "Let a man either avoid the occasion altogether, or put himself often to it, that he may be little moved with it." While Bacon's aphorism is a picturesque statement of an important sociomedical problem, the solution that it offers hardly fits the modern world. Man cannot "put himself often to threats" the nature of which he cannot anticipate, but it seems to me that science can develop techniques compatible with

civilized life and yet conducive to the development of general vigor and resistance. There is some indication, for example, that training for life in the tropics can be achieved by repeated short-time performance in hot humid weather, and does not necessarily require *constant* exposure to unpleasant conditions. I have no doubt that techniques of adaptation could be developed for all sorts of strains and stresses if we were to devote our attention to the problem, instead of relying exclusively on protection and escapism.

In the absence of precise scientific knowledge, we must resort for the time being to empirical wisdom in advising young people to develop their adaptive potentialities, so as to help them deal successfully with the unpredictable challenges and emergencies that they will encounter throughout life. If this is not done, the alternative for mankind will be to run frantically like a hunted beast from one protective and palliative measure to another, trying to escape effort and disease at the cost of sacrificing the wholeness of life and many of its values.

Because of the nature of my subject, I have dealt almost exclusively with some biological aspects of the problem of adaptation. And yet I believe that the same point of view applies to many other aspects of human life—to education for example. It is assumed in many groups that the best pedagogic formula is to encourage the student to specialize as early and as completely as possible in some field of learning—particularly in regard to technology, science, or economics. And yet it is probable that this specialized formation has many drawbacks, for in a world where everything changes rapidly, the practical facts learned in school soon become obsolete. The techniques and equipment which are the most up-to-date expression of knowledge during the school years are usually outmoded by the time the student enters practical life. The only knowledge of permanent value is theoretical knowledge, and the broader it is the greater are the chances that it will prove useful in practice because it is applicable to a wider range of conditions. The persons most likely to become creative and to act as leaders are not those who enter life with the largest amount of detailed, specialized information, but rather those who have enough theoretical knowledge, critical judgment, and discipline

of learning to adapt rapidly to the new situations and problems which constantly arise in the modern world.

These qualifications are not acquired without effort, and may even demand painful effort. In fact, I doubt if it is wise to make learning passive and effortless because one of the most important aspects of education should be to instill the willingness to engage in difficult intellectual work. Like health, learning cannot be acquired passively. It is an active process and the measure of its success is the extent to which it permits the individual to adapt to the unpredictable circumstances of life and thereby to meet them successfully.

Biologists have long known that the less specialized a species of animal or plant, the greater are its chances to spread over wide areas of the world and to survive by adaptation when the environment changes. Mankind is no exception to this rule. It is because man is endowed with a huge range of biological and mental potentialities that he has been able to function under so many different conditions and to raise his status through creative undertakings. Man can continue on his ascending course only if he remains able to adapt rapidly to the unpredictable circumstances that he will encounter. For our children, and for the human race as a whole, adaptability is the price of survival and growth.

A PHYSICIAN'S VIEW OF CHANGE

Charles A. Janeway, M.D.

EACH OF US tends to be biased by his own background and training. As a physician, I am going to attempt to approach my formidable topic from a biologic point of view. The key word in my theme is "adaptation." Adaptation is the process whereby an animal species responds successfully to its environment and thus is able to survive. Survival of a species depends upon several factors: first, reproduction at a rate at least equal to the death rate; second, successful nurture of the young during their period of growth and maturation; third, acquisition of sufficient food from the environment; and fourth, adequate defense against natural enemies or disease.

Man is subject to the same biological laws as other animals. His life span as a species in terms of geologic time is very brief, but in that short period he has proved eminently successful in the struggle for survival: he has wrested control of a large part of the land mass of the earth from most other animals except possibly the insects; he has spread over areas with widely differing climatic conditions; and, although a creature of the land, he has learned to utilize the seas and the air for his own purposes. His success in reproducing himself, in raising his young, in obtaining sufficient food, and in defending himself against his natural enemies has been shown by a slow, steady increase in human population

Charles A. Janeway, M.D., is Thomas Morgan Rotch Professor of Pediatrics, Harvard Medical School and Physician-in-Chief, Children's Hospital Medical Center, Boston, Massachusetts.

until recent times. This has continued, despite a comparatively slow rate of reproduction, a very long interval between birth and maturity, and a high rate of death from disease (throughout the world nearly one out of every two children born die by the age of twelve from natural causes).

During the past fifty years, medical knowledge has been widely applied to the prevention of disease, particularly those epidemic diseases, such as plague, cholera, and malaria, which can be prevented by simple sanitary measures and those which yield to effective immunization procedures, such as diphtheria and smallpox. The result has been dramatic and has resulted in the world-wide phenomenon of the "population explosion." The institution of spraying with DDT to eradicate malarial mosquitoes in Ceylon, for example, cut the total death rate in that country in half in eighteen months. Since the beginning of time, population has been held in balance with environmental resources by deaths from war, starvation, and pestilence. These have balanced a very high birth rate in all but a few countries. Now suddenly pestilence is being brought under control, and mankind is faced for the first time in his history with the necessity for a conscious choice between adopting a sensible program for lowering the birth rate or allowing the population in many areas of the world to increase to a point where starvation or war become unavoidable.

What has been the key to man's evident fitness to survive in a world inhabited by many more powerful animal species? The answer lies in one organ—the key organ of adaptation—the brain. The human brain, which controls the voluntary movements of the body and regulates many of its unconscious functions, has been most highly developed in its capacity for thought, memory, and learning. This means that whenever the individual is faced with a new situation—receives a stimulus from the environment, in psychological language—that stimulus evokes the memory of previous similar experiences, and the choice of one of several alternative responses is made on the basis of these memories. Thus learning becomes possible. The human brain not only has an infinitely greater capacity for learning than the brain of any other mammal but is capable of abstract thought and imagination.

With these intellectual qualities, developed through the slow processes

of evolution, Western man has created the science and technology which have shaped the modern world in which we find ourselves. The vast changes which have been wrought in the conditions of human life in Western society during the past few hundred years, and which exceed in magnitude all those which preceded them, are the products of the most powerful tool of adaptation yet forged by the human brain—the scientific method. In fact, in a sense, science and its technological consequences have changed the meaning of the term adaptation. For, although modern man cannot avoid the biological necessity for adaptation to his natural environment, he is in the unique biological position of being increasingly able to mold his physical environment to suit his own needs. The modern world, as we know it, is to a large extent the product of science and technology, a world in which the forces of nature are being harnessed to serve the needs of man, and in which, as a result, the necessity is not so much for adaptation to the natural world as to the new world created by human ingenuity.

WHAT ARE SCIENCE AND TECHNOLOGY?

Since science and technology have revolutionized the world in which we live and probably will continue to do so at an ever accelerating pace, it is important to understand what these powerful forces are and what they are not:

Science is the product of man's curiosity about the natural world around him. It is the attempt to understand natural phenomena so that they can be described by some rational law and consequently predicted. Science is systematized knowledge. The driving force of science is curiosity; the essence of science is its method, which consists of a constantly repeated series of steps, as follows:

1. Observation and recording of data. Wherever possible, this is done quantitatively, that is, in numbers.

2. Formulation of a theory or law—a conceptual scheme, which permits a generalization about the myriad observed details. Where data is quantitative, this law may be formulated as a mathematical equation.

3. Testing of the theory by further observations and, if possible, by experiment.

4. Reformulation of the theory to fit the new observations or experimental results, and so on, *ad infinitum.*

This method has proved enormously successful in dealing with the phenomena of the physical world. It has made them increasingly predictable and thus susceptible of control.

Science is not religion or morality, although its dedication to verifiable truth and its merciless exposure of false interpretations have a definite moral value. Although the scientific method is systematic, disciplined, and rational, when it is used to explore the world around us, the scientist, in the formulation of new theories and experiments, and in his ability to see new relationships, must exercise originality, imagination, and wonder—the very qualities of mind which characterize the gifted poet, artist, or seer.

Technology, on the other hand, is the application of scientific knowledge to the achievement of practical goals. Technology is remaking the modern world. It is often confused with science in the popular mind; but the atomic bomb, the Salk vaccine, Pioneer V, hybrid corn, the jet airplane—these are triumphs of technology. They would not have been possible without the scientific knowledge accrued over many years through repeated cycles of painstaking observation, formulation, and experiment by curious and imaginative men with little thought for the future applications of their discoveries.

Although science and technology have been distinct in the past, they are tending to merge in the modern world. Scientific advance depends both upon creative imagination and upon the development of new techniques to extend the range of possible observation or experiment. These new techniques require increasingly complex instruments. Today's scientists are able to look far beyond the visible world around them, thanks to satellites probing the vastness of space, to the bathyscaph exploring the ocean deeps, to the electron microscope exposing the mysteries of the cell, to isotopes tracing the intricacies of chemical reactions, and to atom smashers with which the physicists are penetrating ever deeper into the nature of matter. These new techniques of scientific research

depend upon technology of a high order—often too expensive for one man to use or too complex for one man to understand. More and more, such research is a matter of team rather than individual effort, and requires governmental support because of its expense. Nevertheless, behind even the most complex space probe lies the imagination and curiosity of only a few scientists.

I lay great stress on this point, because imagination and curiosity are rare qualities, enormously valuable to the human race. Imagination involves the capacity to look at things in new and unorthodox ways; it implies freedom to observe, to think, and to challenge accepted viewpoints. When so much of our scientific research is carried out under government auspices, the temptation for well-meaning individuals in positions of political power to demand various guarantees of secrecy and conformity to orthodox views becomes an increasing danger. If our scientists are placed in a strait jacket of political and intellectual conformity, we may lose our capacity for adaptation to an ever-changing environment and, like the dinosaurs, become extinct. This is the mortal danger to which McCarthyism and its backwash have subjected us.

For survival still depends upon successful adaptation. Man has mastered the major problems of his physical environment to a very large extent. Food production has so increased that, in the United States, which has less than 10 percent of its population engaged in farming, as compared with 80 percent in the underdeveloped countries where many people still go hungry, agricultural surpluses are piling up and present a grave national problem. Climatic changes have been overcome through better housing, heating, and air conditioning. Disease has been brought sufficiently under control so that the life expectancy at birth of the average American is nearly seventy years, as contrasted to about thirty years in Asia.

Nevertheless, each technological advance brings its own unexpected problems. The automobile, available at prices which the vast majority of Americans can afford, has created wholly new opportunities for family living and recreation, but at the same time it has become our greatest killer, exceeding all but the diseases of old age as a cause of death. The elimination of hunger has made obesity a major health problem in Amer-

ica. And the amount of leisure in our society seems connected in some obscure way with the rising rates for mental illness and juvenile delinquency. Moreover, modern man is threatened, as he has never been threatened before, with extinction; like primitive man he lives in perpetual insecurity, not from enemies with whom he can grapple in physical combat nor from diseases which he interprets as the visitations of malevolent gods, but from his own kind, armed with the dreadful weapons of annihilation which his own science and technology have provided for him. He has conquered most of his old enemies except himself. Technology based on the physical sciences has given him fantastic power over his environment. Application of the biological sciences has led to far better utilization of the land, increased crop yields, control of many plant parasites, and to sanitation and immunization which have brought the great epidemic scourges under control and enormously decreased the hazards of childbirth, infancy, and childhood.

But the social sciences, concerned with the complex phenomena of human behavior, have lagged far behind. The social and cultural aspects of our environment present a new frontier of knowledge which desperately requires exploration by the scientific method adapted to its peculiarly subtle and difficult problems. It is precisely in the formative stage of this new field of the social sciences that imagination and unorthodox thinking are most urgently needed if we are to develop the understanding of individual and group behavior so essential for successful adaptation to our human environment. And yet it is precisely in this young field of science, which touches all aspects of human life and its institutions, religion, medicine, law, business, politics, and international relations, that emotion and fear are most readily aroused by the attempt to make objective observations and accurate interpretations of individual and group behavior.

We must remember that science is neither religion nor politics, it is knowledge; it is the search for verifiable general laws governing all the phenomena which can be observed. Scientific knowledge can be used for either good or evil purposes; how it is used must be decided by all citizens in a democracy, in line with their goals and system of values, hence their need to know more about science, its methods, and its technological and social implications. But, attempts to interfere with the acquisition

of knowledge or with freedom in its interpretation can only cripple the potential of humanity for adaptation and survival in an ever more rapidly changing world.

THE IMPACT OF TECHNOLOGY IN THE NEXT DECADE

Now that we have seen how vital is the role of science as a mechanism of adaptation and how rapid are the changes being wrought in our total environment by technology, let us examine a few of the changes which seem most important for the coming decade.

First, we are entering a new phase of the industrial revolution. The essential phenomenon of the industrial revolution thus far has been the increase in productivity per worker. In a peasant economy, a horse or a bullock is all a man possesses to increase what he can do by the sweat of his brow. In an industrial economy, the tapping of energy sources and conversion of their power into useful work by machines multiplies enormously the amount of work a man can do and at the same time lightens his physical labor. The introduction of nuclear power will certainly accelerate this trend. But we are in a new sort of industrial revolution, in which the science of electronics has put machines to work to multiply not so much man's physical strength as his intellectual power. In the next ten years automation of many industrial processes, and the introduction of computing machines into many tasks now performed laboriously by the human brain, should have a tremendous impact on our economy. It will mean a reduction in manual and clerical labor and an increasing demand for skilled technicians and engineers—with an even greater strain on our educational system. It seems certain that it will be associated with a further rise in the standard of living and a continuing increase in leisure time for the majority of the labor force.

Second, electric power, which has decentralized industry, the automobile, which has exurbanized our population, and the general rise in living standards, are all manifestations of the technological advances which are changing the face of America and thus altering the lives of its children. The village or small town, with its diversified population of various ages

and its large family groups of a few generations ago, as well as the urban slum with its well-knit ethnic groups, are both giving way to mushrooming suburban developments, where mass produced small houses and mass produced television sets purveying mass entertainment inflict a dull uniformity on our civilization. His status symbolized by the community where he sleeps and by the make of car in which he fights his way to work through streams of traffic, the father of the family uses up much of his precious leisure in commuting, while the young mother, in quarters too cramped to house the helpful grandmother of former days, strives to do her job as homemaker by day and may go out to work or to committee meetings at night.

Superhighways, supermarkets and developments eat up the vanishing countryside, and public planning commissions, where they exist at all, are engulfed by the sheer necessity of providing roads, utilities, and schools, and are unable to give time or thought to the conservation of the natural beauty of the countryside or the preservation of human values through provision of adequate facilities for creative recreation. Moreover, these developments spread over a multitude of political units—towns, counties, and even states—created to meet the demands on government in an earlier settled, more static era. These problems of a dynamic and mobile society are having important effects upon family life and hence upon children. It is urgent that we learn to plan the social arrangements of our affluent society in relation to human needs and values.

This affluent society, the by-product of technology, has long been an American dream. Now that it is within our grasp, it is turning out to be something less than the utopia we had hoped for. Our country developed many of its characteristics from frontier society. Hard work, courage, individual initiative, combined with the ability to cooperate with neighbors in time of need, these molded the American character— sturdily independent, idealistic, but practical. But now, the frontier gone, a continent won, and its wealth spread more widely among our people than ever before, our generation lives comfortably with an increasing amount of leisure for enjoyment. What are to be our goals and ideals now that the tasks which spurred on our forebears are largely completed?

Something seems to be missing. It is probably not an accident that

rates for suicide and juvenile delinquency are high in countries with the most widespread material prosperity, such as Sweden, Denmark, and the United States. The welfare state does not answer every human need. Man needs to be challenged, to lose himself in a struggle for something bigger than himself in which he believes deeply. War, which provided such a challenge in times past, is unthinkable. Purely intellectual challenges, such as the pursuit of science, technology, or scholarship, will suffice for a few, creative activity in the arts will satisfy others, but religion, family life and opportunities for service to others through volunteer organizations and community activities must provide for the majority of our citizens a sense of purpose and satisfaction, which is easy to achieve in times of crisis, but much harder to sustain when the economic and social system provides for our material needs so lavishly.

Third, the revolution in transportation and communication is bringing about tremendous changes not only in this country, but throughout the world. Recently I had the experience of having a leisurely breakfast in Paris and reaching my home fifteen miles outside Boston before lunch time. Soon most places on earth will be closer than Washington was to New York at the start of World War II. Moreover, modern means of communication can reduce these distances to nothing. In a few years, street scenes in Delhi or Moscow, voices in Buenos Aires or Hong Kong, could be commonplace sights and sounds in our homes and schools. Trade is apt to follow transport and communication. Thus, powerful forces unleashed by modern technology are in process of creating one world despite the cultural, religious, economic, and political differences which divide its inhabitants and the nations in which they are grouped.

POPULATION PRESSURES AND WORLD EVENTS

Transport and communication move in two directions. In his travels Justice Douglas often found the inhabitants of a remote village in the Middle East better informed about the world through the radio than many an American community. The rapid rise of the standard of living goes on in the industrialized West while most of the inhabitants of the

rest of the globe, where three-fourths of the world's children reside, continue to live in rural villages, tied to the soil, struggling with constant poverty and hunger. And yet the impact of technology upon them may have as profound effects for their future as it has already had on our own civilization. Few of the benefits of industrialization have yet reached the masses of Latin America, Asia, or Africa but they are determined to have them. This "revolution of rising expectations" is the most explosive force in the world today. It has shattered colonial empires and created a stream of new nations which are struggling to overcome the age-old problems of illiteracy, poverty, hunger, and disease in a generation while they learn the difficult art of self-government. Their problems are vastly magnified by the fact that the population pressure is steadily rising, as their high birth rate continues while modern medicine and public health cut sharply into the toll of disease which has held down their numbers in times past.

Now that the airplane and the radio have shrunk the size of our planet and ended the comfortable geographical isolation in which our country was able to conquer a rich and sparsely inhabited continental empire and to develop its own way of life, we Americans must face the prospect that we no longer are sole masters of our own destiny. We now live in a world which we cannot control, from which we cannot escape by isolation, and in which we cannot continue to raise our own standard of living without considering the desperate situation of the masses of Asia, Africa, and much of Latin America. We are citizens of the world, and, just as we cannot afford to have economically backward, dependent areas, or underprivileged groups in our own communities or our own country, so we cannot afford to allow differences between our high general standard of living and the low levels in many other parts of the world to increase.

How to narrow this gap, how to provide equality of opportunity and hope, not just for the youth of America but for all the world's youth, how to assist the people of other nations to help themselves with dignity and without loss of freedom, is the greatest challenge which faces us now and in the immediate future. It is a far greater challenge than the conquest of space, exciting and important as that may be! It will probably be a long time before we can colonize other parts of the universe

and thus reduce population pressures on this planet; meanwhile we are faced with the problem of adapting ourselves more successfully than we have so far to the human environment which presses in upon us ever more closely. The job for most of us is centered in our own homes and communities, but our responsibility extends to state, federal, and world levels. One may well ask, "Am I my brother's keeper?" There can only be one answer, "Yes, for if you are not, there is no future for mankind."

THE OLDER ADOLESCENT

Irene M. Josselyn, M.D.

THERE IS a popular concept that the nature of the adult personality is determined during the first six years of life. This concept oversimplifies the psychological process that eventually results in an adult personality format. Undoubtedly most of the essential components of the adult personality are shaped during that early period but the interrelationship of those early components, an interrelationship that makes the adult personality, is not finally established until late adolescence.

During childhood the components are aligned according to the capacities of the child and the demands and gratifications characteristic of childhood. This alignment is disrupted with puberty and what have been the psychological patterns of the child cease to govern effectively the behavior and the goals of the individual. Previous modes of response disappear. Previous concepts of the self and the world in which the self existed no longer suffice. Yet there is no immediate formulation of a new defined personality structure or of a new understanding of the world.

The psychological task for the individual following the disruption created by the onset of puberty, thus the task of the second phase of adolescence, is a realignment of the component parts of the psychic structure in preparation for adulthood. Before the individual can attain that level of maturation he must develop a new concept of himself and feel at ease in a world that is in many ways different from the one he has

Irene M. Josselyn, M.D., is known for her work on the faculty of the Chicago Institute for Psychoanalysis and is clinical professor, Department of Psychiatry, University of Illinois College of Medicine.

known. The adolescent dilemma is not just "Who am I?", but more importantly "Who am I to be?"; not just "Where am I?", but more importantly "Where am I going?" These themes appear together, sometimes in discord, sometimes in harmony. Perhaps during early adolescence, "Who am I?" and "Where am I?" predominate. During the second half of adolescence "Who am I to be?" and "Where am I going?" are asked more urgently. None is abandoned until in adulthood the individual can say, "I am, and I am here."

During childhood two important self-defining psychological characteristics develop. These are a concept of a self-ideal which the child strives to emulate and a conscience which provides a broad control of his behavior. Partly as a result of these, he has a basis for self-formulation. By them he defines his concept of his own personality and the goals of that personality. Both, however, define what to him is a desirable and lovable child. Both must be partially abandoned in order for him to become a desirable and lovable adult.

There are many areas in which this shift is required. Consider an everyday example. The "good" child goes to bed and is asleep at a certain time. The "good" adult, even if he is tired, meets those obligations he has assumed, regardless of fatigue; he is "good" here by staying up rather than by retiring at a predetermined hour. Many other examples could be cited.

One of the most significant shifts that must occur is in regard to sexual attitudes and sexual behavior. If acceptable sexual behavior in childhood were accepted as a standard for adult behavior it would cripple if not make impossible healthy heterosexuality. The abandonment of childhood sexual attitudes is fostered by the biological impact of puberty when the old standards become inapplicable, but new standards, new ideals do not immediately become integrated into the new self with sufficient effectiveness to give the sense of self-definition that was provided by the standards of childhood.

Thus the adolescent strives to formulate what he will do with his newly intensified sexual feelings and his more broadly encompassing striving for maturation. Childhood patterns will not suffice and if they did would arrest his psychological growth. Furthermore his fantasy of himself as an

adult is often frightening; its translation into reality frequently is anticipated as an achievement he cannot attain.

In reality the core of the individual's self-ideal and conscience remains intact, but that core is so overshadowed by his struggle to free himself of his childlike identity that it does not, for a time, answer his questions even though it usually governs important aspects of his behavior. His struggle to define a concept of himself as mature sexually as well as in other areas may, as we know, lead or threaten to lead to experimentation or to philosophical distortions that may prove extremely traumatic or disturbing. Fortunately the adolescent often seeks guidance, though his choice of a guide is not always a wise one.

Why do adolescents not turn more often to their parents to reveal their conflicts at this time? Some parents could not or would not help; others could and would. But even in the latter instance the adolescent usually cannot turn to his parents except in short bursts of confidence when overwhelmed by his own confusion. His failure to utilize an available parent is not necessarily due to a basically faulty relationship between himself and his parents. We are too quick to criticize parents for their failure to meet the needs of the adolescent without taking into account the adolescent's own contribution to difficult parent-child relationships. The reluctance of the adolescent to seek guidance from his parents is often related more significantly to another aspect of his changing self-ideal. To the adolescent, turning to a parent for help is often experienced as a reversion to being a child dependent upon his parents. His ideal image of himself that he wishes to bring to fruition is one in which he is an adult. His inherently determined striving for greater maturation and the achievement of a new identity for himself, an adult identity, is violated, in his eyes, if he accepts the support he wants from his parents whom, after all, he has known intimately only in the role of giving parental care to a child, a child whom he feels an urgency to exorcise!

Are we helping parents sufficiently to understand, tolerate, and remain available when needed during this period, which is one of crisis for them as well as for the adolescent?

More typically the adolescent, rather than turning wholeheartedly to his parents, turns to non-parental adults for help. If he turns to a per-

son of the same sex he does so primarily to explore the possibilities for a solution to his problems that another like himself has found satisfactory. If he turns to an adult of the opposite sex he may do so because he finds that person manifesting a peace with the world that he wants to understand. He also may do so in an attempt to evaluate the kind of person of the opposite sex who will ultimately be most lovable in his eyes. Irrespective of the sex of the recipient of his confidence he is fortunate if he relates to a person who has found an effective self-ideal, a person who does not demand that everyone follow his particular ideal, a person who does not need to be worshiped indefinitely by the adolescent, and a person who can tolerate the confusion of the adolescent.

This formulation of the type of adult from whom the adolescent will gain constructive support as he seeks a definition of his self raises an important question. Do we, in our school systems, our churches, and our recreational facilities, select staff who have a useful ideal through which they can find gratification for themselves, who are secure enough in their own philosophy to be tolerant of contrary philosophies, who have sufficiently satisfying relationships with others that they do not have to hold the adolescent for their own gratification, and who understand the adolescent well enough to know when to actively intervene and when to allow the adolescent to experiment with his own formulations? The answer to this question is "probably not." Too many adults to whom the adolescent is exposed in school, at recreational facilities, and in church activities, fail the adolescent. The adults may be unsure of their own self-image and self-goals and therefore only further confuse the adolescent. They may be so unsure of their own point of view that they seek support from others; they may therefore attempt to impose their ineffectual but rigid standards on the adolescent. They may have so little understanding of the adolescent state that they cannot offer guidance or freedom but attempt to force the young person into a personality structure long before such crystallization should take place. Lastly, they may need to hold on to the adolescent for their own balance and so are unwilling to allow him freedom to seek help from others.

The adolescent turns not only to adults for support. He turns to his own

age group. In common parlance the term gang has become synonymous with delinquency, but the delinquent gang is just one of the many examples of the efforts of adolescents to find a satisfactory self-image through an interchange with others struggling for the attainment of the same goal. The adolescent feels less threatened when he is with his own age group and particularly those of the same age group who have, in broad terms, the same problems in finding a self-identity. Thus in an adolescent group we see the same unresolved problems or the same experimental resolutions of the same problems in each of the individuals composing the group.

Again this adolescent characteristic invites a question. Have we tapped the potential benefits to be derived from utilizing the natural group formation at adolescence? A great deal of work has been done in utilizing delinquent gang structure to modify the behavior patterns of the individuals composing the group but, publicity to the contrary, delinquency is a relatively small fraction of the manifest disturbances of adolescents. Working with a natural group to help individual adolescents who are evidencing behavior that suggests that their final attainment of pseudo-adulthood will be reached by acceptance of psychologically unhealthy concepts is not widely done. Instead, often an attempt is made to alienate the individual from his group rather than to help the group to avoid ineffectual resolutions of the common problems of its members. Work with a natural adolescent group is still in its infancy.

Participation of an individual adolescent in a natural group has a further significance. The adolescent will soon enter an adult world in which he will assume or have imposed upon him a role in the social structure. Because he is unsure of himself and unsure of who he will become the group provides him with a trial run in preparation for an adult role in a social structure. During this period of development he has many experiences in the sub-culture of his own group that permit him to assume many roles. He may transiently be a leader and later a follower; he may transiently be a deviant, at another time a conformist. From such experimentation he learns what role he can most effectively play in the sub-culture of his own age group. A learning experience that provides

him with his own self-identity in a group will facilitate his ultimate conceptualization of himself in the culture of which he will become a part in adulthood.

This raises another question. Is our overall culture tolerant and understanding of the significance of the multiple roles an adolescent may play in his group or do we too readily suggest that he should conform if we like the conformity demanded or too readily encourage nonconformity if we question the demands made? And is it helpful to let the adolescent struggle with his intragroup relationship without giving well-timed guidance either to him or to the group?

The tendency to join a group during adolescence has another significance. Our culture is not a static one; it is constantly changing. The adolescent of today will find his adult identity in a cultural framework that will be in part a continuation of the culture of his childhood but it will also be a somewhat new culture. That new culture will be determined by his own age group. The impractical ideas of the adolescents of today will be modified by experience to become the new culture of tomorrow. Thus the adolescent is striving to find not only his own identity as a person and his identity as a part of a group, but also the identity of the culture of which he will be a part in adulthood. The adolescent wishes not only to leave childhood; he wishes to live in a world different from that of his childhood. His age group will determine the degree of modification that is achieved. The more he participates in the trials conducted by discussions and experimentation the sooner he will be prepared for the world of tomorrow.

Another question becomes pressing. Are we tolerant of the adolescents' exploration of cultural patterns other than those established by the adolescents of yesterday? Are we providing adequate tools for evaluating the merits of different social relationships as well as the values of current patterns so that the ultimate modification they will instigate will be, if possible, a valid growth from preceding patterns rather than an irrational, arrested growth or denial of any value of the previous structure? Furthermore, are we providing safeguards against premature crystallization and at the same time creating an atmosphere in which adolescents feel safe

to explore, at least theoretically, certain modifications without the threat of later retaliation for having ideas they themselves at a later date. will not respect? The punishment for the "sins" of the adolescent should not be visited upon the adult he will become.

During the latter part of adolescence the individual faces a very specific problem—that of determining his future role in the social structure, his career. Not only must he become identifiable to himself as a person, a person capable of being independent of the sheltering of his parents, a person with an adult self-image, a person who is related to his own age group, a person with a function in a social group, and a person prepared to participate in the modifications of his culture, he must also find a self-image which will enable him to play a role in the new family of which he may become a part. Irrespective of the other factors that make up psychologically healthy adulthood, vocational self-identity is an important part of adulthood. A vocational choice may be determined by neurotic needs and prove to be basically unsound even though it may gratify neurotic demands. However, an unfortunate vocational choice may also create neurotic problems in adulthood. During the latter part of adolescence vocational identity is imposed upon the adolescent. While immediate poor choices can often be rectified, much unhappiness as well as loss of time and money can be avoided if the initial choice is wise.

A question which is really a double one thus becomes significant. Are we doing as much as we can to aid the adolescent to find his career identity and are we creating an atmosphere that rewards the individual when he fulfills that identity? The first part must be answered by vocational guidance people as they perfect their diagnostic tools in order to be able to evaluate more adequately the significant requirements of any career format. Regardless of their contribution, however, it will remain only theoretical unless adequate vocational guidance personnel are available to advise the individual. On the other hand vocational guidance will never effectively establish a happy vocational identity for the individual unless that identity leads not only to self-fulfillment, but to recognition by others. As long as our culture considers the white-collar job, though dulling for a particular individual, superior to manual labor which may

offer a happy self-fulfillment for that individual but deprecation from others, vocational guidance will be handicapped in assisting the adolescent to discover who he really is.

Finally, the adolescent is preparing for his identity as a marital partner and as a parent. Marital rites do not create a marital relationship. Childbirth does not bring into existence parents. Both, it is true, are not attained until after the precipitating event. However, the adolescent can have experiences that will ultimately lead to self-identity in both roles. Relations with people of both sexes which invite mutual respect and prepare the way for acquiring self-identity in accordance with the sex of the individual and for respect for this self-identity by the opposite sex will provide the foundation upon which an identity as a marital partner in young adulthood can be built. Furthermore, teaching that leads to an understanding of others and guidance in translating that understanding into wisely meeting the needs of others not only paves the way for a meaningful marital relationship but also for an identity as a parent of the future. The question involved here is: Are we preparing the adolescent not only for earning a living but also for living with others and especially in an intimate relationship with a marital partner, and are we preparing him for his identity as a parent?

The individual, as he tries to formulate who he will be and where he will be, does so in the framework of the culture in which he lives. Our adolescents live in a democracy. Other adolescents have been studied who have grown up in a primitive culture, in a monarchy, or under a dictatorship, to list a few broad categories. It is easy to cite cultures in which certain adolescent problems are not found. Without doubt, for example, a dictatorship that does not permit any selectiveness in identity minimizes the struggle of the adolescent; a primitive society that predefines adult roles also removes the responsibility from the adolescent to find his own unique self. A democracy in which each person has a right to his own identity as long as that identity does not jeopardize that of others undoubtedly places the greatest burden upon the adolescent and the greatest burden upon those who live with him. Our national history, however, is the story of the growth of a nation which realized its individual self-identity in late adolescence and created leaders in adult life who

chose the methods of evolution rather than those of revolution. Many of the troubled adolescents of yesterday have become the progressive thinkers of today because they were allowed time to be adolescents and were permitted to become adults with an individual self-identity.

If one could wish for one gift to bestow on the adolescent as he struggles for his own self-identity in later adolescence, the author would ask for a better publicity agent for him. One final question evolves from this. In our public stress upon delinquency are we failing to give to the adolescent the public support he deserves as he seeks his self-identity, living as he does in a world of turmoil? To the author the adolescent of today, in view of all he faces in the real world, justifies a belief in the potentialities of the human species.

THE YOUNG ADULT

Margaret Mead

YOUNG PEOPLE today reach adulthood in a period of very rapid change. New standards of educational and vocational adjustment, earlier onset of puberty, earlier ages of marriage and parenthood, compulsory military service for many, great economic prosperity with economic opportunities for untrained workers, increasingly deep uncertainty about the future of mankind in general and of the United States in particular —all these conditions have altered the manner in which young people meet the age-old problems of shifting from the contradictions and unevenness of physical puberty, dependency upon parents and teachers, and juvenile status before the law, to the status of responsible adults.

EDUCATIONAL ENVIRONMENT

We may consider first the educational environment in which the onset of puberty takes place (1). The increasing number of young people attending high school has resulted in a high school population which is extremely heterogeneous in character, and which includes those who are capable of absorbing higher education and those who are impatient and incapable of profiting by education at the moment. In this latter group are boys who are chafing to become independent, and girls whose attention is focused primarily upon marriage.

Margaret Mead is Adjutant Professor of Anthropology, Columbia University and Associate Curator of Ethnology, American Museum of Natural History.

In large cities where the recent urban migrants are rural Mexicans, Puerto Ricans, and Negroes from the rural South—all with educational backgrounds which fail to fit them for urban schools, and with types of precocious maturity which make them especially intolerant of educational restraints and imposed dependencies—the American high schools have become quite different from the schools which remain the image, in the minds of the older teachers and high school graduates of an earlier age, of what high schools should be.

The rapid spread of junior high schools (2) has accentuated some of these qualities of the recent urban arrivals, isolating, as it does, groups of boys and girls who range from those with the physique of children to those who have fully attained the stature and physique of adults, and leaving them without the leadership and corrective example once provided by the older young people of the high school of former years. Here the anxieties about relative growth, forced association with the opposite sex at a period when it is not yet physiologically appropriate, the discrepant rate of maturation of boys and girls, are all intensified. The junior high school has become a forcing ground for inappropriate and socially maladjusted attitudes in both boys and girls, laying the basis for hostility to females on the boys' part and, on the girls' part, pressure toward marriage combined with contempt for males. Although these deficiencies are widely recognized, the temptation of using new junior high schools as a quick solution to the population pressures on the school system makes it probable that junior high schools will increase rather than decrease.

A presently available corrective is to locate junior high schools in close propinquity to senior high schools and community junior and senior colleges. These can provide models of late adolescent behavior on the one hand and, on the other, can relieve the pressure on the younger and less developed boys for precocious mating behavior.

CULTURAL AND SOCIAL TENSIONS

The past decade witnessed an increasing access on the part of juveniles to those mechanical aspects of urban and suburban living which make

the practice of antisocial behavior easier; they can range farther afield, acquire and manufacture weapons, and so forth. The spread of gang behavior into prepuberty, into a period in which the young are least accessible to ethical and moral appeals, has played a part in the establishment of styles of antisocial behavior characterized by heartlessness and impersonality.

Correctives here lie particularly in those educational and recreational institutions which can utilize the curiosity and activity patterns of the prepubertal boys, and which can give the girls accessibility to mimetic maternal behavior. There has appeared also, in many religious groups, an attempt to shift religious choice and membership downward to an age earlier than the traditional period of expected spiritual awakening at puberty. So, while the restraints and requirements of formal education have spread upward in the age range by increased pressure upon all young people to attend high school—which turns many schools into places where young people respond either as prisoners, or as the irresponsible members of a drafted peacetime army whiling the time away—many other behaviors have shifted downward in the age range. We therefore find high school combined with gainful employment. We find active mating behavior, organized antisocial behavior, and attempts on the part of religious and youth groups to create countervalues.

The pseudo-permissiveness of the last twenty years which has combined some recognition of the physical problems of puberty, a distrust of any absolute pedagogical or parental imperatives, a relaxation in school discipline very often unaccompanied by genuine changes in the content of classroom learning or in parental and pedagogical expectation, has encouraged the development of an adolescent generation more than usually dependent upon the mores of the peer group and unresponsive to the efforts of responsible elders. The commercialization of the styles and fads of various subcultural groups, and the continuous publicizing in the mass media of teenage behavior styles in their more extreme forms, have created a mass adolescent culture pattern, available to high school students, of a sort that was not available even to college students twenty years ago. Search for identity by means of special clothes, special vocabulary, and special attitudes towards the rest of the world, once confined to

deprived and semicriminal groups, now pervades the entire high school population.

The survival of adult expectations of an entirely different order, among adults to whom marriage while in high school appears as monstrously inappropriate, serves to confuse the issue further. Young people whose education will terminate upon leaving high school find themselves in a world in which they are treated, depending on regulations in various states, as mechanically incompetent to obtain a driver's license, liable to military service, excluded from those branches of industry in which more rapid advance is possible, and by child labor laws which also serve to restrict competitive membership in many occupations. They are forbidden to buy beer and cigarettes, tempted by the illicit traffic in narcotics, denied orderly information available to the same age group in the armed services about protection from venereal disease, pressured to display precocious mating behavior, and excluded from daytime education if they become parents (3).

CONFORMITY

The objection may be raised that it is inadvisable to stress first the negative side of our high school age mores. It may also be argued, however, that the increased conformity which is demanded of those high school students who will go on to post-high school education is in part a reaction against the high school styles that have been set by this newer group of young people who now attend high school. In this group, the immediate family background, previous educational training, neighborhood mores, and occupational goals contrast strongly with the more traditional image of high school students, for whom high school graduation was in itself either a desirable goal, voluntarily pursued, or a prelude to higher education.

So we have conferences on "nondelinquent youth," emphasis upon an unspotted school record even in elementary school, tremendous pressure on young people who are themselves ambitious or come from ambitious backgrounds to learn how to present a career line which shows even and

continuous conformity to existing educational and social standards (4). The kind of behavior in college undergraduates which twenty-five years ago was expected as evidence of high spirits is now cause for expulsion from our overcrowded colleges. Experimentation and pursuit of imaginative bypaths is discouraged. High school and college have become progressively vocationalized, and statistics on successes and failures in national contests for scholarships and for admittance to specially desirable institutions have increased the widespread sense that to succeed today it is necessary to conform and to compete in terms of national norms.

There are various counteractive forces here, also. Witness the frequency with which the children of college-bred parents rebel, not during puberty but during their college years, and the number of able young people who never look to higher education for themselves and are content with truncated, low-level goals, who later come to form the group that sees the American scene as a complex, bureaucratically controlled "rat race," in which the attainment of rewards is capricious and corrupt (5).

The image of the successful American has come to include the requirement of some post-high school special training. Models for this image are both those young people who acquire conspicuous and recognized forms of higher education—in liberal arts colleges and professional and technical schools—and also those hundreds of thousands who obtain educations in inferior colleges which are seen as symbolically the same—a college degree is a college degree wherever and whenever obtained—yet at the same time intrinsically different and inferior.

SHIFT FROM LONGTIME GOALS

There has been a marked shift throughout this generation from the pursuit of longtime goals, once regarded as characteristic of the educated portions of the community, to the "more, more, more now" philosophy once regarded as characteristic of economically underprivileged groups with an uncertain present and a dark and deprived future. Immediate sex gratification as represented by early marriage, early attainment of full adult status including parenthood, and the possession of the material at-

tributes of economic independence, such as house and car, TV, a full and complete way of life bought on the installment plan rather than saved for —this has become the style for young professional and business people. Postponement of sex gratification, postponement of parenthood, and curtailment of installment buying—these now occur, not as the normal and expected behavior of the upper- and middle-class groups, but as escape behavior for a selected minority of the urban proletariat who wish to flee from their environment into the suburbs.

The widespread dissemination of information on the preferred style of living which has been greatly accelerated by TV (as opposed to radio where words, no matter how persuasive, did not necessarily evoke a picture in the minds of the rural dwellers, the inexperienced, and the poor) has increased the extent to which all Americans live on a single scale of values. Each defines his success not in relation to his immediate neighbors alone, but in terms of a national image of the good life (6). While this condition increases productivity and prevents stagnation and plateaus (as in the United Kingdom) because of the image which differing classes and groups share of their consumption potential, it also tends to create an enormous group of people who may define themselves as failures, as "nobodies," as "people who don't count." These self-definitions are reflected throughout the country, in the way in which college students think of themselves as helpless to affect society in any way, and in the comments of many highly educated and highly placed persons on the hopelessness of attempting to influence anything as complex as the modern world. They are balanced by the efflorescence of institutions like high school bands, and local contests within a national pattern, in which positions of prestige and identity can be won within local communities.

With rapid social change, the remembered behavior of parents no longer provides a possible model. Instead, the conspicuous consumption patterns of young couples just a few years older and a few income notches higher, as pictured in the mass media, become the only recognized models.

As young people are made aware, by the distance between their parents and themselves, of the unprecedented nature of present-day life, their need to catch at the present is reinforced. They feel that there is no

other way of life except the here and now. The continued comment of their elders on how much better their lot is now—and yet how precarious it is, how subject to the sudden inroads of war and depression—combined with their experience of the shrinking lives of their parents with the coming of enforced retirement and inadequate pensions, further reinforces the emphasis on the present. They want to obtain and experience everything at once, within the first four or five years after finishing their formal education. Mortgaging their future in order to obtain the kind of house and furniture and car that will fulfill this dream reduces the picture of the far future to a period which will be spent "paying for dead horses."

Paralleling the shift to immediate goals and immediate economic gratifications has come a shift in attitudes towards sex which places an increasing burden on the late adolescent, especially the boy, at a time when his sex impulses are most urgent and he has least experience in managing them. While the American insistence upon marriage as the only moral and appropriate framework for sex gratification has not altered, the general acceptance of sex activity for everyone between puberty and senility, as conducive to normality, health, and adjusted personality, has enormously increased. Accompanying this is an uneasiness, a lack of faith in single blessedness, whether secular or religious.

Young people are confronted by an adult world which warily watches them lest they get in trouble and prods them towards the earliest possible establishment of permanent and suitable sexual ties. The social anxieties found in the poor and disorganized parts of our society a quarter of a century ago have spread upwards, and parents heave sighs of relief when both sons and daughters are "safely married."

The age at which marital choices are expected to be made makes the adolescent girl of fourteen to sixteen responsible for obtaining and holding a suitable mate, pushing him towards the amount of vocational education which will support early marriage and parenthood, subordinating abilities and ambitions of her own to further this marriage by foregoing advanced education herself, and working to facilitate his. The parents who place such great importance on their children's behaving normally have become increasingly willing to underwrite marriages in which the

young husband is unable to support his wife and children. This practice encourages two types of marriages: the one in which the young husband will later, when he feels more mature, desert because he will have come to classify his wife as part of the family on which he now no longer wishes to be dependent (7); and the one in which both husband and wife remain immature and dependent upon the previous generation (8).

These widespread patterns of early mate selection—parentally approved and supported "going steady" and dependent marriages—have other implications for the personality development of late adolescents. A sexual code has developed in which young men protect their own girls but regard all other girls as fair game, and in which girls, who have to protect themselves against the irresponsible advances of all casually met males, relax within the confines of a trusted and settled relationship.

These patterns of intersex behavior lead to a distrust among males and an increasing dependence by boy-girl pairs upon each other for social and intellectual companionship. The result is a decreasing amount of friendship within each sex.

Companionships of gang or group type without differentiation into pair relationships, and close, dependent, and demanding pair relationships across sex lines, produce new problems of identity formation. The friend who mirrored one's problems and shared one's identity struggles in an earlier type of male adolescent development is replaced by a girl, some two years more mature, with an undeveloped individuality, who is singlemindedly trying to promote one goal only: an early marriage having any sort of economic base that will support life. Where these marriages are successful, it seems to be through the permanent acceptance by the husband of domestic goals as primary goals, with his career and personal interests subordinated to the demands of house and children.

Rebellion against this all-demanding pattern of early domesticity takes a variety of forms: extreme and often brutal exploitation on the part of uncommitted males; reckless seductive behavior on the part of uncommitted females; and insistence on counter-mores sex behavior of both delinquent and "beatnik" patterns (9).

THE SEARCH FOR IDENTITY

In this context, it is not surprising that one of our chief concerns today is the search for identity, the difficulties of identity formation in a changing society, and the extent to which identity and meaningfulness are linked together (10). Whether we turn to studies of individual young people in psychological difficulties (11), to studies of the widespread articulate value systems of high school and college youth (12), or of the projective behavior of young people (13), or of the images of man or paths of life with which young people seek to orient themselves, the result is the same. Today's problem remains a search for a meaningful identity in a world which is seen as too large, too complex, too unpredictable, too likely to collapse into chaos to provide a framework for the individual life (14). As identity search becomes more acute and more persistent we become more conscious of our lack of provision for this search.

The search for the testing out and selection, and final acceptance, of a satisfying identity within which the individual personality can pursue a creative life with freedom and dignity is a task which is appropriate to late puberty (15). The adolescent becomes accustomed to the changes which have taken place within his body, to the new balance that must be established between his inner perceptions of an emerging adult self and the new responsibilities thrust upon him. It is here, during the rapid swing between a return to the dependencies of childhood and a precocious reach for the independence of adulthood, between impulse newly realized and controls only partly developed—it is in this period of shift and flux that ideals can be grasped and kept with an intensity which seldom appears at other stages of growth (16). The great, burning faiths of the past and blazing hopes for the future of mankind can be presented to the adolescent and embraced by him. Talents and special gifts can be tried out, tentatively, and some measure established of the amount of commitment that can be made to art or science, to politics or business or other vocation, without consideration of its simple economic value. This is the period in which a boy should be able to choose a career as an

astronaut or explorer of the ocean depths; it is here that commitments as poets or prophets should be made.

But such search and such commitments are possible only if the society is willing to extend to young people, in their late adolescence, a kind of psychological moratorium (as Erikson has called it) during which they can experiment without being called upon to succeed; an *as if* period in which heights of aspirations and depths of despair can both be experienced without final economic, social, or personal psychological consequences.

In those periods of history which we think of as golden ages, such a time of freedom from immediate consequences of any act was permitted to a small number of youth—at least to the males—of privileged classes. A few years without pressure, exposed to all the best that had been thought and said in the world, a chance to travel and to assay the world around them, freedom from insistent importunity to marry, to make a living, to settle down, was given them. There was time to form intense friendships with the like-minded of the same sex, time for strong teacher-student ties to develop, time for the growing mind to find models among the great of the past and of the emerging present, time to sleep, to grow, to experiment, to change, and to choose. In such periods the fiercest political idealism, the hardest religious choices, the acceptance of stringent artistic disciplines belonged to youth; and these demands upon the privileged were reflected in turn in a greater tolerance towards the young people with less education, who were expected to sow their wild oats even while settling down to a life of premature toil.

During the past quarter century we have enormously widened the possibilities offered by society to all children: medical care to save them from disease, crippling, and early death; free education to a later-and-later age; opportunities for a comfortable and self-respecting way of life. But at the same time there have been certain losses. One of the most striking is the loss of a period when youth can find itself. Instead we have a society organized to push each individual directly from childhood into adulthood. The educational period which was once tentative and experimental is now quite as directly functional as the life of a weaver's apprentice in the Middle Ages.

The armed services have come to provide, in a somewhat haphazard and accidental way, a refuge for the boy who has embarked on an uncongenial educational path, who finds himself at odds with the world around him, lacking the training or the motivation or the certainty for the next step. If he also has the necessary qualifications for the armed services he is able to buy time, to gain some experience of a different world, to repair educational deficiencies, to experiment with new skills. But this is done within a framework which is only incidentally devoted to such gains—a very inadequate substitute for the kind of moratorium once provided by a liberal arts education. For those who can take advantage of it, however, this period sometimes provides a priceless surcease from conflict. Boys wholly uncertain of who and what they are may emerge matured and decided upon some new vocational choice, or may return to the earlier one now certain of themselves and their aims. But the armed services as organized at present provide this refuge only for a selected number; some of our specially gifted young people lack the physical requirements for enlistment; many of them lack the kind of tolerance for mass living which makes it possible to treat military life as a moratorium. For girls this is not an available solution. It increases the pressure on them (and thereby on the boys) to settle for an early marriage and a premature acceptance of adulthood as solutions to the questions of identity and meaningfulness.

Meanwhile, the studies made of the values and goals of high school and college students are almost uniformly disturbing. It is true that young people have wider knowledge, larger vocabularies, greater ability to speak on their feet than previous generations; they acknowledge membership in religious organizations, and there seems to be an arrest in the trend towards secularism. But the special degree of great questioning, high dedication, uncompromising search for something greater than mankind has yet attained, a willingness to search and wait and search again— these are lacking. Instead, among a certain proportion of those who would, in other generations and in other periods, have provided the questing edge of life, we find a most conspicuous countertrend; the "beat generation," with its nihilism, substitution of immediate sensation for any other meaning, and outright contrapuntal rejection of the domestic, rou-

tine virtues of the bulk of our young people (17). The expected marriage style of this latter group, this "beatnik-rejected" majority, was described in a recent study as marriage to a social duplicate, assiduous cultivation of other families resembling themselves in every respect, and equally assiduous avoidance of families with problems of any sort, even of families broken by death (18). Opposition between, on the one hand, the carefully domestic who look only for safety for themselves and the "beatnik" on the other, between the conforming, vocationally obedient student and the juvenile delinquent—this opposition runs through the world of youth, where specially gifted young people, pursuing an interest in art or music, risk being caught in narcotics squad operations by operatives disguised as poets.

The intellectually gifted, generous, and idealistic adolescents of the 1930s risked compromising alignments with the politically suspect. The penalties incurred for even the most juvenile sympathies with politically disapproved groups have led today's adults to discourage the formation of groups of political idealists and to warn young people against joining anything. This penalizing of experimentation and insistence on conformity to average adult norms has led to activities of a form different and more dangerous than those of the 1930s, as the experiments of the gifted verge directly, not upon political dissent, but upon crime. Just as the identification of adolescent political idealism became increasingly difficult to distinguish from treason after World War I, thus discouraging even mild forms of idealistic social commitment in youth, so the present narrowing line between the arts and crime or mental disorder may be expected to discourage a future group from asking those questions about themselves for which they can find only bizarre and unacceptable answers.

Those who lament the loss of deep political and social idealism in present-day youth do not take enough account of the difference between the period before World War I when the forms of utopianism which were later identified as Communism, Fascism, and Nazism, were not yet identified with any major state in the Western world. Young people could experiment with extreme ideas and risk personal martyrdom without the additional accusation of treason to their own country. Today,

for young people in the Free World and the Communist World alike, any deviation is almost immediately identified not as merely quixotic and extreme, but as giving aid and comfort to the enemy. Those whose generosity and sympathy with the underdog might lead them towards forms of social collectivism in the Free World, and advocacy of greater individual freedom in the Communist World, are both given pause when it is treason, not martyrdom, that is involved.

RESEARCH AND REMEDIES

It would seem worthwhile at this point to mention some outstanding research results relevant to late adolescence which have not yet been utilized in our social practices (19).

The first of these establishes the wide range of difference in physical, emotional, and intellectual maturation within each sex, and the definite discrepancy between the maturation of boys and girls during puberty which places girls some one and one-half to two years ahead of boys of the same age. Insistence upon classifying adolescents for all activities by chronological age means a disregard of these findings, creates serious anxieties (especially in the most slowly maturing boys and the most rapidly maturing girls), exposes the boys to premature pressures towards heterosexual behavior, and prevents young people of either sex from following their own individual pace of development by forcing them to adjust to externally imposed, chronologically determined norms. Failure to adapt our educational and social system to this range of differences may be held responsible for some of the sense of self-alienation, search for negative identities, and so forth, characteristic of this present group of young people.

The second body of research establishes the unevenness of maturation within the individual. It includes intensive depth psychology studies of individuals, such as those reported by psychoanalysts and other clinicians, and chronologically oriented surveys. The weakness of the ego, the overwhelming strength of impulse, the shifting ability to concentrate and identify the fluctuations in quality, which seem to be characteristic of

adolescents in our culture and which result from complex outer pressures coinciding with a period of rapid growth—these demand more rest, more leisure, more time to stabilize these labile trends, and more material upon which the imagination can feed than are at present provided in a system which is hurrying young people towards adulthood (20).

Finally, recent work of Piaget and Inhelder has stressed the extent to which intellectual development, particularly of those capabilities most needed in scientific work, occurs *after* puberty (21). The old stereotypes introduced by the earlier testing norms have tended to persist; they obscure the possibility that failure to provide the necessary environment in post-puberty may result in inhibiting, stunting, or shunting aside many of our most valuable human capacities. There is a further possibility that premature domesticity may itself be a factor in preventing the development of the higher mental capacities both in males and females.

Most of the conspicuous attempts to alter our present system of induction into adulthood recognize, at least implicitly, the need to provide a period in late adolescence for more fruitful identity development. These programs cover a broad range: work camps with meaningful and dangerous tasks like forest-fire fighting for identified juvenile delinquents; supervised part-time work for high school students; proliferation of high school programs to provide diversified experience in summer institutes or in summer internships or abroad; new kinds of colleges and new kinds of freshman courses in traditional colleges. All these are directed towards providing conditions for growth, for experience upon which choice can be better based, for an exploration of the relationship between a presently unstable, emerging self and the possibilities presented by a world which I recently heard described as "difficult because never before have there been so many available forms of goodness."

But goodness, to make an appeal to the late adolescent, must be cast in a heroic mold. If it is not, many of the most gifted will find all the ideals of their generation meaningless; they will develop "work blocks," relax into apathy and fantasy, leave school, and permit their gifts to fester and decay. So far very little participation has been offered to young people in the major task of our time, the absolute necessity of saving the human race from eradication. The shortened time-perspective within

which we are asking them to live is a thin disguise for a growing and un-faced realization on the part of adults that this is indeed the responsible generation on which rests the task of assuring the continuance of the human experiment.

CHANGING SEXUAL MORES

Winston Ehrmann

IN THE UNITED STATES a central interest of those who are directly or indirectly involved in the welfare of adolescents and young adults is the premarital heterosexual behavior and attitudes of these young people. An increasing number of young unmarried adolescents are engaging in heterosexual activities, primarily in activities short of intercourse, and secondarily in coitus. Public confusion and private anxieties have been greater about the sexual behavior of youth than about most other areas in which equally radical changes have occurred because the traditional mores of right and proper conduct of generations past do not offer sufficient guidance in this day of great individual freedom. There is a great conflict between the cultural values of "Sex is sinful, especially outside the marriage relation" and of "Individualism, romance, and love glorify and justify sexual expression." Even though these statements are an oversimplification of a very real conflict, they nevertheless epitomize the dilemma of youth and sex in American society.

No implication is intended here that masturbation, homosexuality, prostitution, and other sexual problems are not matters of grave personal and social concern, but rather that they are in general peripheral and secondary in importance to heterosexual activities in the social existence of most male and female adolescents. In marked contrast to the attitudes of only a few decades ago, today masturbation is usually accepted with-

Winston Ehrmann is Professor, Department of Sociology and Anthropology, University of Florida; on leave, was Professor, Colorado State University.

out undue alarm and anxiety as a nonpathological manifestation of sexual striving and development.

Premarital heterosexual behavior among peers on the one hand and homosexuality and prostitution on the other are fundamentally separate public issues because of the different value judgments held about each one. Most Americans would do away with prostitution and homosexuality if this could be done humanely through education, psychotherapy, and social welfare measures, and without disastrous consequences to other realms of life. But one of the last things we would be willing to abolish is all forms of premarital heterosexual relations between young people.

Some lovemaking, when not carried to excess, is considered a normal activity of young people and an integral part of the courtship process leading to marriage. If premarital heterosexual relations were confined within these limits, sexual problems would still occur, but they would undoubtedly be less severe and less numerous than they are now. Problems are created for parents because they fear that their daughters might "get into trouble," or that their sons, or especially their daughters, might get bad reputations because of sexual excesses, or that their children might be drawn into unfortunate marriages because of irresistible sexual attractions. Adolescents are also plagued by these same problems, but in somewhat different ways, because they are the actors and not the audience in this human drama.

In our examination of what young people are doing, we may find some things which are disconcerting. But before becoming too alarmed, we should remember, first, that we can find disturbing aspects in any realm of human behavior, and second, that young people are not drifting willy-nilly through their sexual problems, but with and without the help of concerned adults they have already reached at least a partial solution to a new way of life. Furthermore, a sympathetic understanding of the complex world of the adolescent should alleviate some of our own anxieties and hence enable us to be more wise, charitable, and just in the aid we extend to youth.

CULTURAL AND HISTORICAL SETTING

All societies regulate heterosexual behavior primarily through marriage and its preliminaries. Preliterate and civilized societies alike vary from being very restrictive to very permissive in the control of premarital and extramarital relations, the restrictive societies being in the minority. In a minority of societies, adults attempt to prevent children from engaging in or observing any sexual activity. A majority of societies tolerate or permit sex expression in childhood, such as masturbation, mutual fondling, and premarital sexual intercourse in postadolescence, under prescribed rules and regulations of the society. Again, and contrary to popular opinion, if premarital sexual relations are permitted, it does not follow that adulterous relations are sanctioned after marriage. Although some societies allow the male—and even a very few the female as well—to have adulterous relations, the more usual combination is some sexual permissiveness prior to marriage and sexual fidelity to the spouse after marriage.

Within the stream of our own cultural heritage, the treatment of sex has fluctuated considerably in time and place between a rigid adherence to a general taboo on all sexual activity except marital heterosexual coitus, as among some early Christians and, later, among the Puritans of New England and some groups during the Victorian period, and a liberal permissiveness as among the Elizabethans and, with adequate social safeguards, among the contemporary northern Europeans. Furthermore, there has been considerable confusion about sexuality not only because there has sometimes been a marked divergence between what people did and what they were supposed to do; but also because there has been a conflict among the ideals that people have held about sex, especially premarital coitus. It might be said that the soul of Western man has been truly tormented and fascinated by the dilemma of sex.

The religious tradition of our culture, stemming from Orthodox Jewish codes and Christian precepts, has been a strict single standard which has consistently forbidden premarital coitus, and any sexual activity other than marital coitus for both males and females. The tacit or overt ac-

ceptance of some premarital heterosexual expression for both males and females, the liberal single standard, has occurred to a greater or lesser extent among small and large segments of the population. At the same time, however, there have existed in the religious traditions and in the folk culture undertones of a double standard which, while formally prohibiting premarital intercourse for both sexes, have meant in reality strong condemnation of female sexual transgressions, but only mild condemnation or toleration, and even at times encouragement, of male sexual exploits (1, 2).

THE SEXUAL REVOLUTION IN THE UNITED STATES

The remarkable series of changes in sexual behavior and attitudes in the United States, and in many other parts of the world as well, during the first part of the twentieth century and especially since World War I, are with justification called a sexual revolution.

The traditional authority of family, community, and church declined. Individual freedom of decision and action in male-female associations increased, and the status of women rose rapidly. Furthermore, women became less dependent economically upon men than ever before. The newer theories of human personality and individual freedom and the older ideals of romanticism which blossomed again in present times encouraged sexual expression. And the opportunity for sexual expression was made possible in the anonymity of the city or the automobile. Thus, eroticism could be pursued and pregnancy usually avoided either by the use of contraceptive techniques with coitus or, more often, by petting without coitus. The most extreme representatives of this revolt were the free love advocates of the 1920s.

Three great value systems which grew with this revolution are: First, marital sexual adjustment is not just a hoped-for byproduct of marriage, but a right of both men and women, an end to be purposefully sought. Second, premarital heterosexual behavior, usually as petting and less frequently as coitus, is an end in itself, a way of establishing one's identity as male or female, a form of expressing love, and in part a means of eventu-

ally selecting a mate. Third, as a corollary of the foregoing, there is a consuming public interest in sex and a willingness and readiness to discuss it. This interest finds extensive expression in the mass media, education, counseling, church programs, and public welfare activities.

The social situation after World War I created the "great sex dilemma" for youth. On the one hand the traditional mores enjoined them to abstain from sexual activities and on the other the new freedom enticed them to violate this taboo. The two principal social inventions which were made by youth in response to this social situation were dating and petting. Being together on dates became the context within which the social intercourse of the sexes took place. Petting was the compromise between the erotic demands of the new relationship and the strong prohibition against sexual intercourse. Dating and petting are not uncomplicated acts of just being together or just making love. They are a complex set of interrelationships in which the social and psychological nature of male-female relations are established. The traditional controls imposed in previous generations through the mores and the close scrutiny of parents and community did not reach effectively into this new, private world of the adolescent. Youth, therefore, was forced to develop a different kind of social control within this new social order.

With the new freedom following World War I young people developed a form of promiscuous dating in which popularity was sought by having as many different partners as possible. Some girls rebelled against the Victorian mores of their mothers and became sexually promiscuous. Most girls, however, in the face of male opposition or with the cooperation of their boy friends began to evolve elaborate codes of conduct for channelizing and controlling sexual activities.

The great depression and World War II brought a sobering effect to the hectic trend of the twenties. Dating became more a basis for companionship and less a means for status striving, and the "battle of the sexes" grew less sanguinary. Instead of the social whirl and the thrill of always doing something new, boys and girls sought understanding, friendship, love, and emotional security. Thus, "going steady" which had been largely limited to "old engaged couples" now became a common custom of all ranks of adolescents and young adults. Males and females learned

to understand and to have more confidence in themselves and in one another. The new codes of conduct seem to be better solutions to the dilemma of youth and sex than were those of the preceding generation, because they provide more safeguards against the exploitation of one sex by the other (3, 4).

DATA ON PREMARITAL SEX EXPRESSION

The interested laymen must realize that all of the published works on the systematic study of sexual behavior could be placed on a single bookshelf of a few feet in length. This paucity of scientific knowledge about sex would not be appalling or even ridiculous if there were not now a great public clamor and demand for sex education programs, advice to the lovelorn, marriage manuals, and solutions to many pressing sexual problems. The many excellent clinical studies of youthful sexuality have been useful in developing a better understanding of the psychodynamics of human behavior and more effective psychotherapeutic techniques and mental health and educational programs. They do not, however, reveal patterns of sexual behavior with respect to social structure and interrelations. The innumerable, anecdotal observations contained in the mass media may reveal keen insights into human motivation and behavior, but many of them are contradictory, and there is frequently a confusion about "what ought to be" and "what is."

The entire field of systematic research into human sexual behavior is published in about 20 monographs, some of which deal only incidentally with sex, and a few dozen articles in professional journals (5). Since World War II, there have appeared six major studies which present systematically collected data on the sexual behavior of American youth. Three of these works are by the members of the Institute for Sex Research, Indiana University: Kinsey, Pomeroy, and Martin on the male, 1948 (6); Kinsey, Pomeroy, Martin, and Gebhard on the female, 1953 (7); and Gebhard, Pomeroy, Martin, and Christenson on pregnancy, birth, and abortion, 1958 (8). These volumes contain more data on sexual be-

havior than all other published works combined. The study by Locke, 1951, gives the incidence of premarital sexual intercourse for a divorced and a happily married group (9). Burgess and Wallin, 1953, in their analysis of factors influencing engagement and marriage adjustment, include extensive data on sexual behavior and attitudes (10). The study by Ehrmann, 1959, deals entirely with youthful sex expression in the dating situation (11). The principal systematic studies of sexual behavior published prior to World War II are those of Exner, 1915; Davis, 1929; Hamilton, 1929; Terman, 1938; Bromley and Britten, 1938; and Landis, 1940 (12–17).

Most of the data on youthful sex expression come from sample populations of white, urban, high school and college educated, Protestant groups. Considerably less data, or none at all, have been obtained from other segments of the population.

SEXUAL BEHAVIOR OF YOUTH

Preadolescent

One of the many contributions of Kinsey and his associates is the systematic description of a wide variety of sexual expression from infancy to puberty (18). In the Kinsey sample, 27 percent of the females recalled that they had been sexually aroused and 14 percent that they had experienced an orgasm before adolescence. By fifteen years of age, 92 percent of the boys had had an orgasm, but only about 20 percent of the females. The first and most frequent sexual activity in childhood of both sexes was masturbation. About one-half of the males and females had engaged in some sort of sociosexual play with members of the same or opposite sex. Although these forms of childish sex play are, technically speaking, both heterosexual and homosexual, they do not have the same personal and social significance for the preadolescent as they do for the adolescent and adult. The most frequent form of sex play was exhibitionism, and second was manual exploration and fondling. Only a very small percentage had engaged in coitus.

Adolescence and Young Adulthood

One of the principal ways in which the data of Kinsey and his associates (1948 and 1953) are analyzed is in terms of educational level, the number of years of school completed by the individual: those who never went beyond grade school; those who went to high school, but not beyond; and those who went to college. All males who had one or more years of college and the females with one to four years are classified as college level. The females with more than four years form a separate postgraduate level group. This classification is also an approximate index of social class position. Total sexual outlet is the proportionate distribution of orgasm achieved through the different kinds of sexual behavior. The percentages of adolescents and young adults involved in each of these activities are given in the following sections.

In the Kinsey sample at ages sixteen to twenty years, masturbation was the major source of orgasm for females of all educational levels and for college level males, but sexual intercourse was the principal outlet for grade school and high school level males. The percentages by sex, source of outlet, and educational level are given in Table I.

TABLE I. PERCENTAGE OF TOTAL OUTLET, BY SOURCE, IN ACTIVE SAMPLE OF SINGLE MALES AND FEMALES, AGES 16–20, BY EDUCATIONAL LEVEL

	Educational Level					
Sexual Outlet	Grade School (male)	High School (male)	(female)	College (male)	(female)	Post-Graduate (female)
Masturbation	29	37	44	67	65	66
Nocturnal orgasm	5	6	2	16	4	4
Petting to orgasm	2	2	21	5	18	16
Coitus	57	44	29	10	10	8
Homosexual	7	11	4	2	3	6
Total	100	100	100	100	100	100

Source: Kinsey 1948:378, Table 96, and Kinsey 1953:563, Table 172. "Active sample" refers to those experiencing orgasm from any source.

For the males, the percentages for intercourse with companions and with prostitutes are combined under coitus; and the very small percentages of sexual activities with animals (1 percent or less) are omitted, and the remaining percentages are rounded to equal 100.

Between the ages sixteen to twenty years, 88 percent of the males and 41 percent of the females in the Kinsey sample had masturbated. Among males both the number who masturbated and the frequency of masturbation decreases after the teens, whereas among females the number increases to middle age although frequency remains relatively unchanged.

Homosexuality means sexual activity with persons of the same sex and heterosexuality with persons of the opposite sex regardless of the kinds of activities. As has been pointed out by innumerable writers in the field of psychology and psychiatry and conclusively demonstrated statistically in the Kinsey studies, heterosexuality-homosexuality is a continuum ranging from those persons who are exclusively heterosexual in their responses to those who are exclusively homosexual. Using the Kinsey data as the basis of some broad generalizations, it can be said that if a person were classified as a homosexual on the basis of any homosexual experience—childish exploration, adolescent searching, or adult preference—then between about one-quarter of all females and one-half of all males would be homosexuals. Considered from the other extreme, only about 4 percent of adult males and a smaller percentage of adult females are exclusively homosexual throughout their lives. Between the ages sixteen to twenty, 22 percent of the single males and 3 percent of the single females in the Kinsey sample had experienced orgasm in a homosexual experience.

Petting is heterosexual activity without coitus. Light petting, or necking, generally denotes holding hands, kissing, and embracing, whereas heavy petting usually means more intimate caressing and fondling. Orgasm may be reached by one or both parties in petting, but in most instances some erotic stimulation without orgasm is the usual result.

Several researchers have obtained data on the incidence of petting and Kinsey and associates obtained data on the incidence of petting experiences, erotic arousal in petting, and petting to orgasm. The proportion of college level subjects who had engaged in premarital petting reported by different investigators ranges between 90 and 99 percent for both sexes. Nearly 100 percent of the females in the Kinsey sample who had married had had some petting experience prior to marriage. The inference to be drawn from the findings of all researchers is that all but a few individuals have petted prior to marriage.

Interestingly enough, although coitus is more severely condemned than is petting, much more data have been collected on coital than on petting activities of adolescents and young adults. The incidence figures on premarital coitus, often reported as the number of nonvirgins, varies considerably among the sample populations of single persons, but they are relatively consistent among the samples of married persons. One reason for this greater consistency of data on premarital histories among the married is that they have completed the cycle of premarriage whereas the single persons have not. For example, among predominantly college and high school level subjects the range in the incidence of premarital coitus in 6 samples of married males is between 54 and 98 percent and in 12 samples of single males is between 32 and 93 percent; whereas in 5 samples of married females the range is between 27 and 50 percent and in 8 samples of single females is between 7 and 26 percent. The data from the married samples suggest that most men and between one-third and one-half of all women had experienced coitus prior to marriage (19–23).

SOCIAL AND CULTURAL ASPECTS

The dramatic change in the premarital heterosexual experiences of American youth in the last forty years is characterized by the marked increase in social dating and going steady and in petting and coitus among social equals, especially among engaged couples. Thus, there has been a decrease in the activities of males with prostitutes and an increase in premarital petting and coital experience with other girls and women.

Most young people begin to date shortly after puberty, and some even before, and they continue to date until marriage, a period of 5 to 10 years. Except for carrying out the daily routines of life and going to school, dating is the most time-consuming activity of youth. Although petting does not occur on all dates, it does on most, and even when there is no physical lovemaking, the relationship between the couple is very often predicated on the supposition that it might. In a study of several hundred collegians, Ehrmann found that there was no petting on only 15 percent of the dates of males and 27 percent of the dates of females. Petting oc-

curred on 73 percent of the dates of males and on 71 percent of the dates of the females. The males experienced coitus on 12 percent of their dates and the females on 2 percent. In this sample most of the males did not date coeds, but most of the females dated fellow male students.

Youth has evolved, and is continuing to evolve, quite elaborate codes of conduct for channelizing and controlling sexual behavior. Since these activities take place within the dating situation, one of the most effective means is the acceptance or rejection of one sexual expression rather than another or the acceptance or rejection of a date with a particular partner.

Traditionally, the initiation of sexual activities was usually considered to be a male prerogative, and the restraint of such activity primarily a female responsibility. Ehrmann found that, although this supposition is generally true, there is considerable variation according to the kind of personal relation existing between the couples, such as being or not being in love. In his sample, the males initiated sexual activity on about three-quarters of all dates and the female on about one-quarter.

On most dates sexual activity was limited either by the female's refusal or by the male's attitude toward her. On about one-half of all dates neither partner attempted to go beyond a certain point in petting, usually by a tacit agreement. The male does not press his demands beyond this point usually because he respects the girl or he knows from past experience that she will rebuke him if he tries to go farther, and sometimes because he is timid. On about three-tenths of the dates no sexual activity took place or it did not go beyond a certain stage of intimacy (i.e., beyond light petting to heavy petting; or beyond heavy petting to coitus) because of overt refusal or resistance by the female. On about two-tenths of all dates sexual intimacies were limited by the inappropriateness of the situation. And on a very small number of dates the male would not go farther even though the female was willing.

Morals, respectability, religious beliefs, family training, fears, and a desire to wait for marriage are the most important individual reasons given for restraints in sexual activities as reported by several investigators in the last thirty years (27). There may have been an actual shift in the attitudes of young people in the last two decades. For example, fear of pregnancy was cited more often as a reason for not having intercourse in

the earlier than in the latter studies. Recent studies have also indicated the importance of "lack of opportunity" or "inappropriateness of the situation." Kinsey and his associates were the first to indicate that sexual unresponsiveness among many young females is also a significant deterrent, and Ehrmann that this is a primary reason for sexual restraints of females with boys they did not love, but not with boys they loved.

Sexual activities are also channelized by standards of sex conduct which vary considerably from group to group. Since World War I, it appears that the strict single standard and especially the double standard are decreasing in importance, while the permissive single standard is increasing in importance (24–26).

Religion and Church Attendance

The research findings indicate that the degree of religious devoutness as measured by regularity of church attendance or nonattendance is more uniformly related to patterns of premarital sexuality than is membership in one of the three major religious groupings. According to Burgess and Wallin, Ehrmann, and especially Kinsey and associates, the less devout males and females were sexually more active and had higher proportions of nonvirgins than the most devout. Furthermore, the difference among Protestants, Catholics, and Jews of the same degree of devoutness was generally much less than the difference between the more and less devout of any one religious group (28).

Rural-Urban Residence

According to Kinsey and associates the urban male as compared to the rural male, and the urban female after age twenty as compared to the rural female of the same age group have slightly higher incidence rates of premarital petting and coitus. The difference between the rural and urban groups was much smaller than had been anticipated in view of comments made by previous writers on this subject. The reasons for this unanticipated finding may be: 1) the presumed difference was more apparent than real ("city youth are more wild than country boys and girls"); and 2) rural life is becoming more like city life (29).

Race

Hohman and Schaffner found among a large sample of male army inductees that a great majority of the whites and most of the Negroes had experienced premarital coitus (27). Gebhard and associates report that although the Negro females have higher incidence rates of premarital sexual intercourse than the white females, they show the same variation according to educational level, the more educated having lower rates than the less educated.

The actual and assumed difference between the sexual mores of Negroes and whites must be viewed in the historical perspective of what happened to the Negro in the United States. Under the conditions of slavery, the Negro was unable to develop any semblance of a stable marriage and family life. Sexual activities became transitory, and the Negro family became centered around the mother. The social situation was further complicated by the white males of the planter class taking Negro concubines while jealously guarding the chastity of their white females. After emancipation, the mass movement of Negroes to southern cities and later, during and after the two world wars, to northern cities as unskilled laborers of a minority group who suffered from extreme discrimination, perpetuated the unstable and insecure conditions under which they lived. A new trend, however, may be developing. The patterns of sexual behavior of Negroes and whites of the same social level appear to be becoming more alike. It is quite possible that in the near future the ethnic differences may be less than the social class differences (30).

Decade of Birth

The general supposition that the marked liberalization of premarital sex practices occurred during the period of World War I and shortly thereafter is substantiated by research findings. Furthermore, this change was considerably more pronounced among females than males. In the studies of Kinsey and his associates, among females born after 1900 (those who reached sexual maturity around World War I and later) there were proportionately 2 to 3 times as many nonvirgins at marriage as among those born before 1900. Among the males, however, there was only a

small difference in this respect. The same trend was also reported earlier by Hamilton, Terman, and Locke. Subsequent studies, including those of Kinsey and associates, Burgess and Wallin, indicate, however, that the trend has not continued and that there has been a leveling off in that the proportion of males and females with premarital coital experience seems to have remained relatively constant in the last two decades (31).

Social Level

The findings of Kinsey and associates indicate that the male patterns of sexual behavior vary markedly according to social class as measured by the educational level, but that the female patterns show only limited variations in this respect. Many more high school level and especially grade school level males than college level males engaged in premarital coitus, as indicated in a previous section. Masturbation, nocturnal emissions, and petting to climax are much more characteristic of the college level males, but homosexuality occurs more frequently among the grade school and high school level males.

Some information on the comparative social class of companions is supplied by Hollingshead and Ehrmann. Hollingshead observed among a group of high school students that boys of a higher social class exploit girls of a lower social class for sex purposes. In a sample college population, Ehrmann found that most males and females have their sexual experiences with persons of the same social class; but when class lines are crossed, the highest rate of premarital intercourse occurs between males of a higher and females of a lower social class (32, 33).

Nearness to Marriage

Kinsey and his associates demonstrate that female, but not male, premarital sexual behavior is more significantly associated with nearness to marriage than any other matter which they investigated. Furthermore, although the female patterns are associated somewhat with social class difference, but much less so than the male, this association depends primarily upon the age at marriage and nearness to marriage. The data indicate that: 1) the sexually most active period of single females is the one or two

years prior to marriage; 2) females in the lower educational levels marry at an earlier age than those in the higher one; hence, the girls in the lower levels are more active sexually at an earlier age and those in the higher levels at a later age (34).

Number of Partners

The limited statistical evidence on the number of petting partners prior to marriage confirms the general impression that petting is the most promiscuous of all premarital activities. The data of Kinsey and associates indicate that over one-half of married females had engaged in premarital petting with six or more partners. In the collegiate sample of Ehrmann over one-half of the girls and one-third of the boys were dating three or more different persons a month and petting occurred among most of these. Women are somewhat more monogamous than men in their premarital sexual intercourse relationships. One-half or more of all women who are nonvirgins had coitus with their future spouse only, whereas a majority of men had this experience with both their future spouse and other women (35).

Going Steady and Being in Love

According to Ehrmann, the patterns of sexual expression of the female much more than of the male are related to going steady or being in love. Three times as many of the females who were going steady or were in love, as compared to those who were not, had experienced coitus. They also petted more frequently, and they initiated the sexual activity more often. Love also tended to equate the actual sexual behavior of males and females and also many other aspects of the heterosexual relation. There was considerably more mutuality in the sexual attitudes between those who were in love than between those who were not. How far to go in sexual activities was decided more often by a consensus of partners in love and less often by overt final refusal by one partner (36).

Juvenile Delinquency

The relationship between sexual behavior and delinquency has not been established. Sexual delinquency like other forms of delinquency may rep-

resent manifestations of emotional problems, rebellion against the mores, or accepted behavior of the gang. Some of the sexual practices of male gangs seem to be essentially extremes of the same kind of behavior existing among other youths (37). Although exploitation of one sex by the other sex occurs in all groups, the principal difference between the gang member and the nongang member seems to be that the former's behavior may be more openly and frankly exploitative and less subtle and sympathetic toward the female.

Pregnancy, Abortion, and Illegitimacy

An inference from the data compiled by the Kinsey researchers is that one-tenth or more of American females experience a premarital pregnancy (38). The Statistics Committee of the Conference on Abortion in the United States of the Planned Parenthood Federation of America reports that "a plausible estimate of the frequency of induced abortions in the United States could be as low as 200,000 and as high as 1,200,000 per year" (39). Probably more than one-half of these are performed on married women. Official statistics indicate that about 4 births in 100 in the United States are illegitimate (40). As reported by Gebhard and associates, ultimately one-tenth of the Kinsey sample of white, nonprison females had a premarital pregnancy. Of the premarital pregnancies that ended before marriage, almost nine-tenths were induced abortions and the other one-tenth were either spontaneous abortions or live births.

Although the incidence of premarital conceptions of grade school and high school educated single females is considerably higher among the Negro than the white female samples, the incidence percentages for the college educated, single females of Negroes and whites are comparable. Among the 202,000 babies born out of wedlock in 1957, about 40 percent were born to mothers under twenty years of age (41). The Kinsey researchers found an interesting inverse relationship between illegitimacy and abortion. Out of wedlock births are much higher among Negro than white females, but induced abortions are much higher among white than Negro females.

CONCLUSION

Although it is specifically not the purpose of this paper to make recommendations, certain implications from this presentation should be taken into consideration.

Even this brief sketch indicates that sexual expression is an exceedingly complex process. Few behavior patterns and codes of conduct in other areas reveal as many variations as do those pertaining to sex. The differences between groups and within groups are frequently very great.

The growing belief that women, as well as men, have a right to participate in sexual activities before marriage, and to expect sexual satisfaction in the marriage relation has meant the democratization of sex behavior and codes and the development of a new cultural tradition. There is undoubtedly more public approval of sexual expression in, than before, marriage. Much of what parents and others attempt to teach youth makes this distinction quite explicit.

Attaining this result, however, is not easy for at least two reasons. In the first place great personal freedom gives young people the opportunity for sexual activities, and the stimulus of romanticism encourages rather than restrains them. In the second place, the married and the unmarried see the transition from the single to the married state in quite a different way. Married people realize by hindsight that a great transformation occurred when they entered marriage. Single persons, however, see marriage as the end stage and a glorious fulfillment in a gradual transition from random dating, going steady, becoming engaged, and getting married. As they proceed through this evolution, they more and more see themselves as being married.

The greater freedom also means the greater chance of exploitation of one sex by the other, such as a girl enticing a boy into a marriage he does not wish or is not prepared to enter and a boy seducing and abandoning a girl. The best protection against exploitation thus far perfected is actually the elaborate codes of conduct and rituals that youth have developed in the last half century.

And last, but not least, the lovemaking of young people should not be

viewed as a simple set of mechanical acts in which young people engage solely to have "fun." It is one of the most significant ways in which male-female relations are channelized. It is a means of expressing chivalry and exploitation, altruism and egoism, permissiveness and authoritarianism, romantic ideals and elementary sex urges, denial and fulfillment, and hence maleness and femaleness. In fact, it is a way of reaching identity and of growing up.

THE CHANGING AMERICAN CHILD

Urie Bronfenbrenner

IT IS NOW a matter of scientific record that patterns of child rearing in the United States have changed appreciably over the past twenty-five years (1).

Middle class parents especially have moved away from the more rigid and strict styles of care and discipline advocated in the early 1920s and '30s toward modes of response involving greater tolerance of the child's impulses and desires, freer expression of affection, and increased reliance on "psychological" methods of discipline, such as reasoning and appeals to conscience, as distinguished from more direct techniques like physical punishment.

At the same time, the gap between the social classes in their goals and methods of child rearing appears to be narrowing, with working class parents beginning to adopt both the values and techniques of the middle class.

Finally, there is dramatic correspondence between these observed shifts in parental values and behavior and the changing character of the attitudes and practices advocated in successive editions of such widely read manuals as the Children's Bureau bulletin on *Infant Care* and Spock's *Baby and Child Care*. Such correspondence should not be taken to mean that the expert has now become the principal instigator and instrument of social change, since the ideas of scientists and professional workers

Urie Bronfenbrenner is Professor of Child Development and Family Relationships, Cornell University.

themselves reflect in part the operation of deep-rooted cultural processes. Nevertheless, the fact remains that changes in values and practices advocated by professional figures can be substantially accelerated by rapid and widespread dissemination through the press, mass media of communication, and public discussion.

Given these facts, it becomes especially important to gauge the effect of the changes that are advocated and adopted. Nowhere is this issue more significant, both scientifically and socially, than in the sphere of familial values and behavior. It is certainly no trivial matter to ask whether the changes that have occurred in the attitudes and actions of parents have been such as to affect the personality development of their children, so that the boys and girls of today are somewhat different in character structure from those of a decade or more ago. Or, to put the question more succinctly: has the changing American parent produced a changing American child?

Do we have any basis for answering this intriguing question? To begin with, do we have any evidence of changes in the behavior of children in successive decades analogous to those we have already been able to find for parents? If so, we could take an important first step toward a solution of the problem.

Unfortunately, in contrast to his gratifying experience in seeking and finding appropriate data on parents, the present writer has, to date, been unable to locate enough instances in which comparable methods of behavioral assessment have been employed with different groups of children of similar ages over an extended period of time. Although the absence of such material precludes any direct and unequivocal approach to the question at hand, it is nevertheless possible, through a series of inferences from facts already known, to arrive at some estimate of what the answer might be.

Specifically, although as yet we have no comparable data on the relation between parental and child behavior for different families at successive points in time, we do have facts about the influence of parental treatment on child behavior at a given point in time; that is, we know that certain variations in parental behavior tend to be accompanied by

systematic differences in the personality characteristics of children. If we are willing to assume that these same relationships obtain not only at a given moment but across different points in time, we are in a position to infer the possible effects on children of changing patterns of child rearing over the years. It is this strategy that we propose to follow.

THE CHANGING AMERICAN PARENT

We have already noted the major changes in parental behavior discerned in a recent analysis of data reported over a twenty-five-year period. These secular trends may be summarized as follows: 1) Greater permissiveness toward the child's spontaneous desires; 2) Freer expression of affection; 3) Increased reliance on indirect "psychological" techniques of discipline (such as reasoning or appeals to conscience) vs. direct methods, such as physical punishment, scolding, or threats; 4) In consequence of the above shifts in the direction of what are predominantly middle-class values and techniques, a narrowing of the gap between social classes in their patterns of child rearing.

Since the above analysis was published, a new study has documented an additional trend. Bronson, Katten, and Livson (1) have compared patterns of paternal and maternal authority and affection in two generations of families from the California Guidance Study (2). Unfortunately, the time span surveyed overlaps only partially with the period covered in our own analysis, the first California generation having been raised in the early 1900s and the second in the late 1920s and early '30s. Accordingly, if we are to consider the California results along with the others cited above, we must make the somewhat risky assumption that a trend discerned in the first three decades of the century has continued in the same direction through the early 1950s. With this important qualification, an examination of the data cited by Bronson et al. points to still another secular trend—a shift over the years in the pattern of parental role differentiation within the family. Specifically: In succeeding generations the relative position of the father vis-a-vis the mother is shifting with

the former becoming increasingly more affectionate and less authoritarian, and the latter becoming relatively more important as the agent of discipline, especially for boys.

In pursuing our analytic strategy, we seek next for evidence of the effects on the behavior of children of variations in parental treatment of the type noted in our inventory. We may begin by noting that the variables involved in the first three secular trends constitute a complex that has received considerable attention in recent research in parent-child relationships.

Within the last three years, two sets of investigators, working independently, have called attention to the greater efficacy of "love-oriented" or "psychological" techniques in bringing about desired behavior in the child (3). The present writer, noting that such methods are especially favored by middle-class parents, offered the following analysis of the nature of these techniques and the reasons for their effectiveness.

Such parents are, in the first place, more likely to overlook offenses, and when they do punish, they are less likely to ridicule or inflict physical pain. Instead, they reason with the youngster, isolate him, appeal to guilt, show disappointment—in short, convey in a variety of ways, on the one hand, the kind of behavior that is expected of the child; on the other, the realization that transgression means the interruption of a mutually valued relationship.

These findings mean that middle class parents, though in one sense more lenient in their discipline techniques, are using methods that are actually more compelling. Moreover, the compelling power of these practices is probably enhanced by the more permissive treatment accorded to middle class children in the early years of life. The successful use of withdrawal of love as a discipline technique implies the prior existence of a gratifying relationship; the more love present in the first instance, the greater the threat implied in its withdrawal (1).

It is now a well-established fact that children from middle-class families tend to excel those from lower-class families in many characteristics ordinarily regarded as desirable, such as self-control, achievement, responsibility, leadership, popularity, and adjustment in general (4). If, as seems plausible, such differences in behavior are attributable at least in part to class-linked variations in parental treatment, the strategy of inference we have adopted would appear on first blush to lead to a rather optimistic

conclusion. Since, over the years, increasing numbers of parents have been adopting the more effective socialization techniques typically employed by the middle class, does it not follow that successive generations of children should show gains in the development of effective behavior and desirable personality characteristics? Unfortunately, this welcome conclusion, however logical, is premature, for it fails to take into account all of the available facts.

SEX, SOCIALIZATION, AND SOCIAL CLASS

To begin with, the parental behaviors we have been discussing are differentially distributed not only by socioeconomic status but also by sex. As we have pointed out elsewhere, girls are exposed to more affection and less punishment than boys, but at the same time are more likely to be subjected to "love-oriented" discipline of the type which encourages the development of internalized controls (5). And, consistent with our line of reasoning, girls are found repeatedly to be "more obedient, cooperative, and in general better socialized than boys at comparable age levels." But this is not the whole story. "At the same time, the research results indicate that girls tend to be more anxious, timid, dependent, and sensitive to rejection. If these differences are a function of differential treatment by parents, then it would seem that the more 'efficient' methods of child rearing employed with girls involve some risk of what might be called 'oversocialization'" (5).

One could argue, of course, that the contrasting behaviors of boys and girls have less to do with differential parental treatment than with genetically based maturational influences. Nevertheless, two independent lines of evidence suggest that socialization techniques do contribute to individual differences, within the same sex, precisely in the types of personality characteristics noted above.

In the first place, variations in child behavior and parental treatment strikingly similar to those we have cited for the two sexes are reported in a recent comprehensive study of differences between first and later-born children (6). Like girls, first children receive more attention, are

more likely to be exposed to "psychological" discipline, and end up more anxious and dependent, whereas later children, like boys, are more aggressive and self-confident.

A second line of evidence comes from our own current research. We have been concerned with the role of parents in the development of such "constructive" personality characteristics as responsibility and leadership among adolescent boys and girls. Our findings reveal not only the usual differences in adolescents' and parents' behaviors associated with the sex of the child, but also a striking contrast in the relationship between parental and child behaviors for the two sexes.

To start on firm and familiar ground, girls are rated by their teachers as more responsible than boys, whereas the latter obtain higher scores on leadership. Expected differences similarly appear in the realm of parental behavior: girls receive more affection, praise, and companionship; boys are subjected to more physical punishment and achievement demands.

Quite unanticipated, however, at least by us, was the finding that both parental affection and discipline appeared to facilitate effective psychological functioning in boys, but to impede the development of such constructive behavior in girls. Closer examination of our data indicated that both extremes of either affection or discipline were deleterious for all children, but that the process of socialization entailed somewhat different risks for the two sexes. Girls were especially susceptible to the detrimental influence of overprotection; boys to the ill effects of insufficient parental discipline and support. Or, to put it in more colloquial terms: boys suffered more often from too little taming, girls from too much.

In an attempt to account for this contrasting pattern of relationships, we proposed the notion of differential optimal levels of affection and authority for the two sexes.

The qualities of independence, initiative, and self-sufficiency, which are especially valued for boys in our culture, apparently require for their development a somewhat different balance of authority and affection than is found in the "love-oriented" strategy characteristically applied with girls. While an affectional context is important for the socialization of boys, it must evidently be accompanied by and be compatible with a strong component of parental

discipline. Otherwise, the boy finds himself in the same situation as the girl, who, having received greater affection, is more sensitive to its withdrawal, with the result that a little discipline goes a long way and strong authority is constricting rather than constructive (5).

Available data suggest that this process may already be operating for boys from upper middle-class homes. To begin with, differential treatment of the sexes is at a minimum for these families. Contrasting parental attitudes and behaviors toward boys and girls are pronounced only at lower-class levels, and decrease as one moves up the socioeconomic scale (7). Thus our own results show that it is primarily at lower middle-class levels that boys get more punishment than girls, and the latter receive greater warmth and attention. With an increase in the family's social position, direct discipline drops off, especially for boys, and indulgence and protectiveness decrease for girls. As a result, patterns of parental treatment for the two sexes begin to converge. In like manner, we find that the differential effects of parental behavior on the two sexes are marked only in the lower middle class. It is here that girls are at special risk of being overprotected and boys of not receiving sufficient discipline and support. In the upper middle class the picture changes. Girls are not as readily debilitated by parental affection and power; nor is parental discipline as effective in fostering the development of reponsibility and leadership in boys.

All these trends point to the conclusion that the "risks" experienced by each sex during the process of socialization tend to be somewhat different at different social class levels. Thus the danger of overprotection for girls is especially great in lower-class families, but less so in the upper middle class because of the decreased likelihood of overprotection. Analogously, boys are in greater danger of suffering from inadequate discipline and support in the lower middle than in the upper middle class. But the upper middle-class boy, unlike the girl, exchanges one hazard for another. Since at this upper level the more potent "psychological" techniques of discipline are likely to be employed with both sexes, the boy, as well as the girl, presumably now runs the risk of being "oversocialized," and of losing some of his capacity for independent aggressive accomplishment.

Accordingly, if our line of reasoning is correct, we should expect a changing pattern of sex differences at successive socioeconomic levels. Specifically, aspects of effective psychological functioning favoring girls should be most pronounced in the upper middle class; those favoring boys in the lower middle. A recent analysis of some of our data bears out this expectation. Girls excel boys on such variables as responsibility and social acceptance primarily at the higher socioeconomic levels. In contrast, boys surpass girls on such traits as leadership, level of aspiration, and competitiveness almost exclusively in the lower middle class. Indeed, with a rise in the family's social position, the differences tend to reverse themselves, with girls now excelling boys (8).

The implications for our original line of inquiry are clear. We are suggesting that the "love-oriented" socialization techniques, which have been employed in increasing degree by American middle-class families, may have negative as well as constructive aspects. While fostering the internalization of adult standards and the development of socialized behavior, they may also have the effect of undermining capacities for initiative and independence, particularly in boys. Males exposed to this "modern" pattern of child rearing might be expected to differ from their counterparts of a quarter century ago in being somewhat more conforming and anxious, less enterprising and self-sufficient, and, in general, possessing more of the virtues and liabilities commonly associated with feminine character structure (9).

At long last, then, our strategy of inference has led us to a first major conclusion. The term "major" is appropriate since the conclusion takes as its points of departure and return four of the secular trends which served as the impetus for our inquiry. Specifically, through a series of empirical links and theoretical extrapolations, we have arrived at an estimate of the effects on children of the tendency of successive generations of parents to become progressively more permissive, to express affection more freely, to utilize "psychological" techniques of discipline, and, by moving in these directions, to narrow the gap between the social classes in their patterns of child rearing.

FAMILY STRUCTURE AND PERSONALITY DEVELOPMENT

But one other secular trend remains to be considered: What of the changing pattern of parental role differentiation during the first three decades of the century? If our extrapolation is correct, the balance of power within the family has continued to shift with fathers yielding parental authority to mothers and taking on some of the nurturant and affectional functions traditionally associated with the maternal role. Again we have no direct evidence of the effects of such secular changes on successive generations of children, and must look for leads to analogous data on contemporaneous relationships.

We may begin by considering the contribution of each parent to the socialization processes we have examined thus far. Our data indicate that it is primarily mothers who tend to employ "love-oriented" techniques of discipline and fathers who rely on more direct methods like physical punishment. The above statement must be qualified, however, by reference to the sex of the child, for it is only in relation to boys that fathers use direct punishment more than mothers. More generally,

The results reveal a tendency for each parent to be somewhat more active, firm, and demanding with a child of the same sex, more lenient and indulgent with a child of the opposite sex. The reversal is most complete with respect to discipline, with fathers being stricter with boys, mothers with girls. In the spheres of affection and protectiveness, there is no actual shift in preference, but the tendency to be especially warm and solicitous with girls is much more pronounced among fathers than among mothers. In fact, generally speaking, it is the father who is especially likely to treat children of the two sexes differently (5).

Consistent with this pattern of results, it is primarily the behavior of fathers that accounts for the differential effects of parental behavior on the two sexes and for the individual differences within each sex. In other words, it is paternal authority and affection that tend especially to be salutary for sons but detrimental for daughters.

But as might be anticipated from what we already know, these trends are pronounced only in the lower middle class; with a rise in the family's

social status, both parents tend to have similar effects on their children, both within and across sexes. Such a trend is entirely to be expected since parental role differentiation tends to decrease markedly as one ascends the socioeconomic ladder. It is almost exclusively in lower middle-class homes that fathers are more strict with boys and mothers with girls. To the extent that direct discipline is employed in upper middle-class families, it tends to be exercised by both parents equally. Here again we see a parallelism between shifts in parental behavior across time and social class in the direction of forms (in this instance of family structure) favored by the upper middle-class group.

What kinds of children, then, can we expect to develop in families in which the father plays a predominantly affectionate role, and a relatively low level of discipline is exercised equally by both parents? A tentative answer to this question is supplied by a preliminary analysis of our data in which the relation between parental role structure and adolescent behavior was examined with controls for the family's social class position. The results of this analysis are summarized as follows:

Both responsibility and leadership are fostered by the relatively greater salience of the parent of the same sex. . . . Boys tend to be more responsible when the father rather than the mother is the principal disciplinarian; girls are more dependable when the mother is the major authority figure. . . . In short, boys thrive in a patriarchal context, girls in a matriarchal. . . . The most dependent and least dependable adolescents describe family arrangements that are neither patriarchal nor matriarchal, but equalitarian. To state the issue in more provocative form, our data suggest that the democratic family, which for so many years has been held up and aspired to as a model by professionals and enlightened laymen, tends to produce young people who "do not take initiative," "look to others for direction and decision," and "cannot be counted on to fulfill obligations" (5).

In the wake of so sweeping a conclusion, it is important to call attention to the tentative, if not tenuous, character of our findings. The results were based on a single study employing crude questionnaire methods and rating scales. Also, our interpretation is limited by the somewhat "attenuated" character of most of the families classified as patriarchal or matriarchal in our sample. Extreme concentrations of power in one or another parent were comparatively rare. Had they been more frequent,

we suspect the data would have shown that such extreme asymmetrical patterns of authority were detrimental rather than salutary for effective psychological development, perhaps even more disorganizing than equalitarian forms.

Nevertheless, our findings do receive some peripheral support in the work of others. A number of investigations, for example, point to the special importance of the father in the socialization of boys (10). Further corroborative evidence appears in the growing series of studies of effects of paternal absence (11). The absence of the father apparently not only affects the behavior of the child directly but also influences the mother in the direction of greater overprotectiveness. The effect of both these tendencies is especially critical for male children; boys from father-absent homes tend to be markedly more submissive and dependent. Studies dealing explicitly with the influence of parental role structure in intact families are few and far between.

Papanek, in an unpublished doctoral dissertation, reports greater sex-role differentiation among children from homes in which the parental roles were differentiated (12). And in a carefully controlled study, Kohn and Clausen find that "schizophrenic patients more frequently than normal persons report that their mothers played a very strong authority role and the father a very weak authority role" (13).

Finally, what might best be called complementary evidence for our inferences regarding trends in family structure and their effects comes from the work of Miller, Swanson, and their associates on the differing patterns of behavior exhibited by families from bureaucratic and entrepreneurial work settings (14). These investigators argue that the entrepreneurial-bureaucratic dichotomy represents a new cleavage in American social structure that cuts across and overrides social class influences and carries with it its own characteristic patterns of family structure and socialization. Thus one investigation contrasts the exercise of power in families of husbands employed in two kinds of job situations, those working in large organizations with three or more levels of supervision and those self-employed or working in small organizations with few levels of supervision (15). With appropriate controls for social class, equalitarian families were found more frequently in the bureaucratic

group; patriarchal and, to a lesser extent, matriarchal in the entrepreneurial setting.

Another study shows that, in line with Miller and Swanson's hypotheses, parents from these same two groups tend to favor rather different ends and means of socialization, with entrepreneurial families putting considerably more emphasis on the development of independence and mastery and on the use of "psychological" techniques of discipline (16). These differences appear at both upper and lower middle-class levels but are less pronounced in higher socioeconomic strata. It is Miller and Swanson's belief, however, that the trend is toward the bureaucratic way of life, with its less structured patterns of family organization and child rearing. The evidence we have cited on secular changes in family structure and the inferences we have drawn regarding their possible effects on personality development are on the whole consistent with their views.

If Miller and Swanson are correct in the prediction that America is moving toward a bureaucratic society that emphasizes, to put it colloquially, "getting along" rather than "getting ahead," then presumably we can look forward to ever-increasing numbers of equalitarian families who, in turn, will produce successive generations of ever more adaptable but unaggressive "organization men." But recent signs do not all point in this direction. In our review of secular trends in child-rearing practices we detected in the data from the more recent studies a slowing up in the headlong rush toward greater permissiveness and toward reliance on indirect methods of discipline. We pointed out also that if the most recent editions of well-thumbed guidebooks on child care are as reliable harbingers of the future as they have been in the past, we can anticipate something of a return to the more explicit discipline techniques of an earlier era.

Perhaps the most important forces acting to redirect both the aims and methods of child rearing in America emanate from behind the Iron Curtain. With the firing of the first Sputnik, achievement began to replace adjustment as the highest goal of the American way of life. We have become concerned—perhaps even obsessed—with "education for excellence" and the maximal utilization of our intellectual resources. Already,

ability grouping, and the guidance counsellor who is its prophet, have moved down from the junior high to the elementary school, and parents can be counted on to do their part in preparing their youngsters for survival in the new competitive world of applications and achievement tests.

But if a new trend in parental behavior is to develop, it must do so in the context of changes already under way. And if the focus of parental authority is shifting from husband to wife, then perhaps we should anticipate that pressures for achievement will be imposed primarily by mothers rather than fathers. Moreover, the mother's continuing strong emotional investment in the child should provide her with a powerful lever for evoking desired performance. It is noteworthy in this connection that recent studies of the familial origins of need-achievement point to the matriarchy as the optimal context for development of the motive to excel (17).

The prospect of a society in which socialization techniques are directed toward maximizing achievement drive is not altogether a pleasant one (18). As a number of investigators have shown, high achievement motivation appears to flourish in a family atmosphere of "cold democracy" in which initial high levels of maternal involvement are followed by pressures for independence and accomplishment (19). Nor does the product of this process give ground for reassurance. True, children from achievement-oriented homes excel in planning ability and performance, but they are also more aggressive, tense, domineering, and cruel (20). It would appear that education for excellence, if pursued single-mindedly, may entail some sobering social costs.

But by now we are in danger of having stretched our chain of inference beyond the strength of its weakest link. Our speculative analysis has become far more speculative than analytic and to pursue it further would bring us past the bounds of science into the realms of science fiction. In concluding our discussion, we would reemphasize that speculations should, by their very nature, be held suspect. It is for good reason that, like "damn Yankees," they too carry their almost inseparable sobriquets: speculations are either "idle" or "wild." Given the scientific and social importance of the issues we have raised, we would dismiss the first of these labels out of hand, but the second cannot be disposed of so easily.

Like the impetuous child, the "wild" speculation responds best to the sobering influence of friendly but firm discipline, in this instance from the hand of the behavioral scientist.

As we look ahead to the next twenty-five years of human socialization, let us hope that the "optimal levels" of involvement and discipline can be achieved not only by the parent who is unavoidably engaged in the process, but also by the scientist who attempts to understand its working, and who—also unavoidably—contributes to shaping its course.

HIGHER EDUCATION

Richard G. Axt

IN 1970 there will be more than 6 million young people in American colleges, almost twice as many as today's 3.4 million college students. This predicted "rising tide" poses the central issue in college and university education for youth: Can 6 million students be educated ten years from now at a level of quality equal to or higher than that existing today? Or will the colleges fail to meet what has been called the "dual mandate" of quality and quantity?

The expected doubling of college enrollments is the main factor to consider in looking at the college curriculum, teaching methods, college teachers, and the financing of higher education. And how effectively and energetically we work for adequate curricula, teachers, teaching methods, and financial support for these students will determine whether or not the dual mandate of quality and quantity is fulfilled.

The prospect of 6 million college students raises these kinds of questions:

How many people should we educate in college? If we have 6 million college students in 1970, will it be those youth who could best profit from a college education?

Will students be helped to choose the most appropriate kind of college and courses?

Can we have enough well-trained college teachers for this enrollment increase? Will we have adequate buildings to house them?

Richard G. Axt is Research Administrator at Stanford University, Stanford, California.

Will teaching methods, courses, and student personnel services be adequate for a heterogeneous group of students, with differing aptitudes and aspirations?

Will the college curriculum adequately serve a complex and rapidly changing society?

And will the American people provide enough financial support to undergird a high quality educational enterprise?

We will look at some alternative courses of action on such questions after we have looked more closely at some of the important trends, predictions, facts, and practices in American colleges and universities.

How do we know that there will be 6 million or more students in American colleges and universities by 1970? We cannot, of course, be absolutely certain. A war or a serious economic depression could change the trends. But aside from such a major catastrophe, all the facts point to just such large numbers.

The young people who will attend college between 1970 and 1975 are already born and counted. We do not have to guess at the size of the eighteen- to twenty-one-year-old group in 1970. It will consist of 15 million persons (1). There are now 3.4 million persons (of all ages) in college; this includes about 35 percent of the eighteen- to twenty-one-year-old age group. If the same proportion of the 1970 college-age group were to enter college, there would be 5.4 million college students in 1970. All trends suggest that the proportion of youth who enter college will continue to increase.

In 1939, the number of persons enrolled in college represented only 14.3 percent of the eighteen- to twenty-one-year-old group (2). For recent years, the comparable proportions have been as follows:

Year	Percent
1955	30.9
1956	33.2
1957	34.0
1959	35.6

If about 40 percent of the college age group actually sought a college education in 1970, the forecast of 6 million students would be correct. Actually, if the proportion of youth attending college rises at the same

rate in the 1960s as it did in the 1950s, there would be about 7 million college students in 1970!

According to a recent Roper poll, about 70 percent of the parents of school-age youth in this country expect their children to enter college, a truly astonishing proportion (3). It can be seen from the figures given above that if even 60 percent of these college-aspiring parents succeed in attaining this goal, our college enrollments will double.

The reasons for this drive to attend college, which is not even approached in intensity in any other country except Russia, are not hard to find. First, as Ralph Tyler has pointed out, is the practical reason. A college education is essential for an ever-increasing proportion of the available jobs (4). A college degree is the step toward a "successful" career and a higher income. It has been estimated that a college graduate earns at least $150,000 more in his lifetime, on the average, than a high school graduate. Second, there is the sociological reason. Charles Frankel has stated it thus:

From a sociological point of view, the American college has one primary meaning. It is the great social escalator of contemporary American society, the major avenue by which the members of a mobile society are enabled to move upward on the social scene. Young Americans come to college to learn how to behave and how to dress; they come to college to meet—and to marry—the right people; they come so that they can leave labeled "college graduate." For the college degree is one of the few symbols of status that exists in the United States, and its social importance is all the greater as a result (5).

These central facts about the economic and the social role of a college education (not to mention the related technological need for trained personnel) add up to one unescapable conclusion. The question is not whether we will or should have 6 million college students, close to half the age group, in 1970. Barring disaster, we will. The question is, how well, how effectively, how appropriately for the student and for society will they be educated?

A distinguished group of Americans, in a recent report on *The Pursuit of Excellence* in education has said this:

Not only must our educators handle a huge increase in the number of students, they must offer higher quality in education. From time to time one still

hears arguments over *quantity* vesus *quality* education. Behind such arguments is the assumption that a society can choose to educate a few people exceedingly well *or* to educate a great number of people somewhat less well, but that it cannot do both. But a modern society such as ours cannot choose to do one *or* the other. It has no choice but to do both. Our kind of society calls for the maximum development of individual potentialities *at all levels* (6).

Our task is to seek ways to do this for youth in colleges and universities.

SOME FACTS ABOUT AMERICAN HIGHER EDUCATION

The two key facts about American higher education are its size and its diversity.

The 3.4 million college students in this country attend more than 2,000 different institutions classified as colleges or universities. These institutions employ more than 200,000 faculty members and have a total payroll of about twice that number (7).

We have more college presidents in America than there are full professors in England.

Expenditures by colleges on educational programs and plant construction are more than $4 billion annually.

The number of degrees granted by American colleges is another useful index of the size of the higher educational enterprise. In 1950, the colleges granted 498,500 earned degrees; this reflected the postwar bulge in enrollments made by veterans. This number dropped to 354,000 in 1955 and rose back to 470,000 in 1959.

Of the 470,000 degrees granted in 1959, 390,000 were bachelor's and first professional degrees (e.g., the M.D. degree), 70,700 were master's and second professional degrees, and 9,300 were doctoral degrees (8).

The diversity of American colleges has sometimes been overemphasized. A recent statement by the three major associations of private and public colleges notes: "No two are precisely alike in their sense of purpose, scope of activity, method of operation, sponsorship, financial support, or system of governance" (9). Having been saved from overstatement by the word "precisely," the statement goes on to note, quite prop-

erly, that among both private and public colleges there are both large and small institutions, two-year and four-year schools, general and specialized programs, and high quality and lesser quality performance. About 1,400 grant bachelor's or higher degrees; almost 600 offer less than four years of college work.

There are fairly large groupings of colleges and universities which are quite similar to one another and quite different from other groupings. The public junior colleges are, by and large, quite similar in their programs and in the makeup of their student bodies, although they differ in size. There is a national "Ivy League" of high quality, private colleges which consistently recruit a high proportion of the brightest high school graduates and have very similar educational objectives. The "Big Ten" universities tend to emulate one another in the scope of their programs, and to compete for good faculty members as well as star athletes.

Colleges and universities can be grouped by sponsorship; there are almost 400 state-controlled institutions, 300 district or city (mostly junior) colleges, 700 church-related colleges, and 500 private, nondenominational schools. There are 1,500 coeducational colleges; the other 500 are equally divided between those for men only and those for women (10).

It is more difficult to group institutions by the kinds of programs they offer, but this can be done in an approximate fashion. Almost 600 are junior colleges or offer terminal (no bachelor's degree) occupational programs. Of the 700 four-year colleges, a third or more strongly emphasize the training of elementary and secondary school teachers; most of the rest are "liberal arts" colleges with varying admixtures of professional curricula. Almost 500 schools offer both the bachelor's degree and the master's degree; about a third stress education curricula, the rest could be called "complex" liberal arts colleges with a good many professional curricula.

About 150 institutions have attained the status of universities in fact—not in name only—by offering the doctoral degree and having several professional schools (law, medicine, and so forth) attached to them. Another 40 or 50 schools grant the doctoral degree, but are highly specialized in, say, engineering, education, or theology.

Within each of these groupings, there are large qualitative differences

among institutions. How are these measured? One criterion is whether a college is accredited by a regional and/or professional accrediting association. Another is whether it has a Phi Beta Kappa chapter. The American Association of University Women issues a list of colleges "approved" for membership eligibility. Until 1948, the American Association of Universities, an elite group then numbering 36 members, "approved" colleges as being likely sources of good graduate students.

By such criteria, how many excellent or good colleges are there? More than 1,300 institutions (including junior colleges) have regional accreditation by one of the 6 regional associations. A number of additional specialized schools have professional accreditation, so about three-fourths of our colleges and universities are accredited. The Association of American University Women presently lists 446 colleges on its list of approved schools. There were 216 "approved" colleges in the AAU list in 1948 when the practice was discontinued; of these, 105 had Phi Beta Kappa chapters as well. Currently, 164 schools have Phi Beta Kappa chapters.

These various listings use much the same criteria, although obviously they are more stringently applied in some listings than in others. The factors looked at are the very ones at the heart of this work group's agenda: curriculum, class size, quality of staff, level of ability of students, and adequacy of financial support and library facilities.

If we consider schools with Phi Beta Kappa chapters as group "A," the AAU schools without such chapters as group "B," and the accredited schools on neither list as group "C," we would find at least two major kinds of differences. The median scores of students on a test like the Graduate Record Examination would be highest in group A and lowest in group C. It is also very likely that a higher proportion of the teachers in group A colleges would have doctoral degrees and have them from graduate schools in the American Association of Universities, which now has 41 members (11).

But qualitative comparisons are more complicated than such groupings would suggest. Students differ widely in their aptitudes and in the fields they wish to study. Within a given institution, schools and departments will vary greatly in quality at any given time. So the problem of "matching" the student to the school remains a very difficult one.

CURRENT PRACTICES AND TRENDS

We will look at current practices and trends under seven headings: curriculum, teaching methods, student personnel services, staffing the colleges, facilities, admission and retention practices, and cost and finance.

Curriculum

One way to look at the curriculum is in terms of the fields of study in which bachelor's degrees are granted. In 1958, the Office of Education listed 160 different fields in its survey of earned degrees. Here are some of the major groups as a proportion of the total:

Field	Percent	Field	Percent
Education	23	English	5
Business	14	Physical Sciences	4
Social Sciences	13	Biological Sciences	4
Engineering	10	Arts	3
Health Professions	7	All other (each less than 3 percent)	17
		Total	100

While there have been some minor shifts in the proportion of degrees granted in each field over the past decade, like the much discussed but rather slight decline in degrees in engineering, generally the pattern shown above has changed little since 1950.

Two trends should be singled out, one recent and the other of longer duration. The first is the trend to emphasize "general education," which means, in essence, a core of "liberal" subjects for all students, regardless of their "special," major field of study.

The goal of general education has been defined as the development in students of the ability "to think effectively, to communicate thought, to make relevant judgments, to discriminate among values" (12). The courses in general education cover the humanities, the social studies, and science and mathematics; they tend to be given in the first two years of college, before the student has heavily "majored" in, say, business or engineering. The main new element in this is specially designed general survey courses for the nonmajor in a field; e.g., a science course for those who do not intend to major in science.

The second trend, which goes back a good many years, is the increasing addition of professionally oriented courses to the liberal arts curriculum. This can best be seen in the following table of the professional and preprofessional curricula offered in 26 liberal arts colleges in 1900 and in 1957 (13).

TABLE I. PROFESSIONAL AND PREPROFESSIONAL CURRICULA OFFERED IN
26 LIBERAL ARTS COLLEGES IN 1900 AND IN 1957

1900

Preprofessional

Law		Medicine

Professional

| Civil engineering | Commercial law | Electricity |
| Commerce | and banking | Teaching |

1957

Preprofessional

Predental	Premedical	Preosteopathy
Preengineering	Preministerial	Prepharmacy
Prelegal	Prenursing	Prephysical therapy
Prelibrary science	Preoptometry	Presocial work

Professional or Vocational

Agriculture	Government service	Radio
Business	and foreign service	Recreation
Accounting	Homemaking	Speech therapy
Business adminis-	Hospital education	Teaching
tration	Journalism	Business adminis-
Merchandising	Library science	tration
Retailing	Medical technology	Christian education
Secretarial work	Microbiology	Elementary educa-
Chemistry	Military science	tion
Christian service	Ministry	Music education
Civil engineering	Music	Physical education
Commercial art	Nursing	Secondary educa-
Dietetics	Occupational and	tion
Engineering	physical therapy	Television
Forestry	Psychology	Theater (stagecraft,
	Public relations	etc.)

Teaching Methods

Teaching methods in colleges and universities (lectures, recitations, demonstrations, laboratory work, discussion groups, and tutoring) have remained essentially unchanged over the past decade (and over the past several decades).

To be sure, there has been extensive research and experimentation with audio-visual aids, educational television, "honors" programs for gifted students, more self-study by the student, larger classes, and so forth. This has been done both in an effort to make teaching more effective and to better utilize available teaching resources (14).

With the possible exception of honors programs (special courses, seminars, and tutorial work for excellent students) little of this experimentation seems to have taken root. Despite much experimentation and research with educational television and large expenditures for equipment, for example, relatively few college courses for credit are taught by this means (15).

Student Personnel Services

American colleges have always accepted a much greater responsibility for the total welfare of their students than have colleges in other countries. Thus, a variety of noninstructional services to students developed between 1910 and 1950. These include the admission process; detailed personnel records; educational, vocational, and personal adjustment guidance; physical and mental health services; remedial work in reading, speech, and study habits; supervision of student housing and food service; supervision and encouragement of student group activities; administration of student employment and financial aid; and, of course, overall discipline of the student body (16). To these were added, during the 1950s, marriage counseling and the advising of foreign students.

The general trend was away from faculty handling of noninstructional problems toward "professional" handling of such problems by deans and a corps of trained counselors of various kinds. While this trend has continued, in recent years the dichotomy between instruction and student personnel work has been questioned. Some now hold that the two should

be brought closer together on such matters as the modification of the curriculum and the improvement of methods of instruction.

Staffing the Colleges

Colleges recruit their teachers directly from the graduate schools. They prefer to hire persons with a doctoral degree or who soon expect to receive one. (There is a well-known informal degree, A.B.D.—"all but dissertation.") Colleges are not always successful in obtaining fully qualified teachers. Several recent reports show that the proportion of newly hired teachers who have the doctoral degree has been steadily dropping, from 31 percent in 1954 to 24 percent in 1959. In 1955, 40 percent of all college teachers had the doctoral degree, 50 percent the master's degree, and 10 percent less than the master's degree. The proportion with the doctorate has declined since 1955 (17).

During the 1950s the graduate schools came under increasing criticism for not turning out enough college teachers and for emphasizing research rather than training the graduate students to be college teachers (18). The graduate schools replied that they were the only type of institution that could, and had to, emphasize research. Many graduate schools have, however, given increased attention to preparing their students for college teaching, although method courses are still a rarity.

Facilities

Colleges and universities are increasing their investment in their physical plant at the rate of $750 million annually. About 50 percent of current construction is for instructional buildings, 30 percent for residential buildings, and the rest for general research and auxiliary buildings. Relatively few private colleges are actually expanding their plants, although many are replacing old buildings. Most public institutions have extensive building programs under way, and many of them are hard pressed to keep pace with increasing enrollments.

Three current trends can be noted. One is to make better use of existing and planned instructional space through space-utilization studies and better scheduling of classes. Until recently it was not uncommon to find up to half of the classrooms unused several afternoons a week. A second

trend is toward housing a large proportion of full-time students on campus. A third is to provide permanent facilities for housing married students (19).

Admission and Retention Practices

Enrollments in public institutions have increased at a greater rate over the past decade than in privately controlled institutions. This in part reflects the fact that the public institutions have had funds for expansion. But it is also related to the fact that private colleges have maintained a closer control over admissions than public colleges have been able (or have wanted) to do.

Many private colleges have long been very selective about whom they will admit. There is evidence that the prestige colleges are becoming even more selective (20).

Most publicly supported institutions historically have admitted any state resident with a high school diploma. In recent years, a few have introduced stricter admissions requirements, and many are moving into the "persuasive counseling" of poor students, advising them not to come to the particular institution (21).

Another way of selecting students is to do it in the freshman year by dropping those who do not make the grade. A recent survey showed that 28 percent of all freshmen drop out by the end of the first year and that only half of those who enter four-year colleges receive a degree four years later. While it is clear that both academic and financial problems contribute to this dropout rate, its full significance, and whether it is a matter for great alarm, is in dispute (22).

Costs and Finance

In 1957–58, colleges and universities received and spent for current educational operations about 3.7 billion dollars. (This does not include funds for new buildings or for self-supporting enterprises such as dormitories.) Of this amount 25 percent came from tuition fees, 48 percent from government (state, local, and federal), 16 percent from endowment income and gifts, and 11 percent from other sources (23).

The long-term trend has been the decreasing importance of endow-

ment income in college finance and the increasing importance of student fees. Over the past decade tuition fees have risen in both public and private institutions. These fees are presently averaging about $600–$700 in private colleges and $200 in public colleges.

However, the proportion of income received from student fees, for all colleges, has not changed much in the past few years because of the increasing importance of other sources of funds. The biggest of these is the federal government, which ten years ago financed about $200 million in research and development at universities; currently, this federal support exceeds $700 million.

There have also been significant increases in corporate and alumni contributions to higher education.

PROBLEMS AND ALTERNATIVES

The doubled college enrollments discussed earlier clearly will bring with them problems. In this concluding section we will mention some of the major ones, and some alternative courses of action, under the same seven headings used in the last section.

Curriculum

Two major questions are raised about the college curriculum. Has it "proliferated" too much into many specialized courses? And are students allowed to specialize too much and too early, to the detriment of their general education? These are economic as well as educational questions, because a great many small, specialized courses cost a great deal of money, although more often than not such courses fill a real educational need.

The idea that the content of the curriculum should be left entirely to the faculties and the professional accrediting groups is more and more questioned. College administrations, through the National Commission on Accrediting, have begun to examine the requirements of professional accrediting groups that a large part of the total available curriculum be devoted to professional courses. A proposal has been made that liberal arts

colleges severely prune their curricula, move to larger classes and fewer teachers and thereby be able to pay higher faculty salaries (24).

And while state legislatures are properly reluctant to delve into curricula, more and more states have set up coordinating boards which try to work out a rational division of majors and courses among the public colleges and universities in a state. One leading scholar suggests we need more "planned diversity" of this kind (25).

It seems likely that laymen, both as alumni and as taxpayers, will increasingly find themselves involved in questions about the college curriculum.

Teaching Methods

It was noted earlier that despite considerable research and experimentation, there has been relatively little change in teaching methods at the college level. Faculty members have been quite reluctant to adopt new educational media, such as educational television, or to experiment with larger-sized classes and with placing more responsibility upon the student to do independent reading and research.

While college and university administrations can try to encourage further improvement in college teaching methods, it seems likely that the general public will have little effect on this matter. In all likelihood, it will take the combined effects of greatly increased enrollments over the next few years and an increasing shortage of qualified faculty members to stimulate changes in teaching methods. Initially, at least, these are likely to be adopted more for their economic and manpower implications than for the direct improvement of the students' learning; a matter on which most faculty members are rather well-satisfied.

Student Personnel Services

Training programs for specialized workers in the student personnel services have developed rather rapidly, and more and more colleges and universities have set up adequate student services.

There are two major problems that lie ahead. The first appears to be the recruitment of adequate numbers of student personnel workers to

handle the increased enrollments. Secondly, there will be a need to double, or more than double, expenditures on student personnel services, again because of increased enrollments. This need for increased expenditures will come, of course, at a time when all aspects of higher education need more financial support. If funds are not unlimited, parents and taxpayers may well be tempted to weigh the relative importance of student personnel services as compared with the direct instructional programs of the institutions.

Staffing the Colleges

By all odds, obtaining sufficient numbers of qualified teachers in the next decade is the most crucial problem facing higher education. Even if proposals are adopted which would result in increasing the effectiveness of the individual teacher and decreasing the number of teachers in proportion to the number of students, the need for additional teachers will still be enormous. It has been estimated that colleges will need to add between 15,000 and 20,000 new teachers each year over the next decade. This number compares with the present number of less than 10,000 doctoral degrees granted each year, some to specialists, of course, who do not enter college teaching as a career.

One estimate is that the proportion of faculty members who hold the Ph.D. degree will drop from the current 40 percent or a little less to only 20 percent. In any case, it seems clear that many liberal arts colleges will have to rely largely on holders of the master's degree for their faculty. Already many junior colleges are recruiting faculty members from the high schools.

The key issues facing the educational community are these. Should the graduate schools place greater stress on training college teachers? Should two doctoral degrees be developed; one for teachers and one for researchers? Should an intermediate degree between the present master's and doctor's, especially designed for college teachers, be developed, or should the present master's degree be "rejuvenated"?

The key questions for the public and for the taxpayers are these. To what extent should an expansion of the number of graduate students and

an increase in financial support for graduate students (particularly those who wish to become college teachers) be encouraged? This in turn becomes primarily a question of finance. It raises the question whether programs like the Woodrow Wilson Fellowship program and the federal fellowship program under the National Defense Education Act should be expanded. The remaining policy question here, and probably the most important one, is whether college faculty salaries should be doubled as suggested by the President's Committee on Education Beyond the High School. This would certainly do more than any other single thing to recruit qualified faculty members despite the increasing competition of business and government, but it would cost a great deal of money.

Facilities

The present trend toward much better utilization of instructional laboratory and library space means that the physical plant of our colleges and universities will not have to be doubled to handle twice as many students. It will, however, have to be increased substantially.

Some college facilities such as dormitories, student unions, and dining halls are essentially self-supporting and present no particular problem other than the availability of low interest funds for borrowing.

Instructional facilities, on the other hand, are not self-supporting, and many billions of dollars will have to be spent on them over the next decade. Private institutions have been particularly hard-pressed to find the funds they need for this purpose, and states have had to spend increasing amounts out of current funds and to float larger bond issues to meet the rapidly accelerating need for buildings.

Admission and Retention Policies

The problem of handling greater numbers of students has led to more and more proposals to restrict admission to both public and privately supported institutions and thereby cut down the number of students. Proponents of this view point to the high dropout rate and to other evidences that many persons enter college who are not capable of completing the bachelor's degree program. Others take the view that American society

needs every person trained to the highest level for which he can qualify and that therefore the proportion of college age youth who enter college should continue to increase.

It was suggested earlier that this is likely to happen in any case. However, there is a real question whether in most cases students are attending the colleges most appropriate for them and are taking the courses and programs best suited to their talents.

There appears to be an increasing consensus that regardless of what specific decisions are made at given institutions and at given times on admissions standards, it is particularly important that through guidance and counseling in the high schools and through the development of a true diversity of institutions running from the local, junior college to the highly specialized graduate schools and universities, students be helped to find the college best suited to them.

Costs and Finance

Many, perhaps most, of the problems and alternatives discussed thus far turn out finally to have important financial implications. It seems clear that current expenditures on higher education, presently about $3.5 billion annually, will have to increase to $9 billion by 1970 (26). This estimate is based on the assumption that economies which accrue from larger classes, better use of facilities, and so forth, will be more than offset by the need greatly to increase faculty salaries. (Average faculty salaries in colleges and universities are about $4,700 annually for beginning instructors and $8,000 annually for full professors.)

This kind of increase in expenditures on higher education would, among other things, mean spending 1.2 percent of the gross national product on higher education rather than the present 0.8 percent. These apparently small percentage figures actually add up to this: if we spend $9 billion on higher education in 1970, we would be spending a 50-percent greater share of the gross national product for this purpose than we now do.

The key question is, of course, where such large sums of money would come from. While it is true that monies for higher education from corporations, alumni, and foundations have been given in increasing

amounts, scarcely anyone expects these sources to assume a significantly greater role. This leaves two major sources for the expected increase, namely, tuition fees and government funds. And in the category of government funds, the two major sources are state governments and the federal government.

The major current controversy is whether the larger portion of the increased expenditures for higher education should come from student fees or from government funds. And among those who believe that more government funds should be spent in preference to substantial increases in student fees, there is a controversy over whether such funds should come primarily from the state governments, as they now do, or whether an effort should be made to increase greatly the federal contribution to the operating expenses of colleges and universities.

Many facts could be cited to support either view on these policy questions.

It can be shown, for example, that median family incomes have greatly increased and that families have a greater ability to pay for higher education. It can also be shown that 50,000 to 100,000 high school graduates of college ability annually do not enter college primarily for financial reasons.

Another issue is whether college students should finance a college education through long-term loans on the assumption that a college education will increase their earning capacity. While statistics might well prove this a good idea for physicians, the same might not turn out to be true for, let us say, elementary school teachers and social workers, who are in a lower salary group.

Proponents of reliance on state financing of higher education can cite greatly increased state expenditures for this purpose and the fact that higher education has in recent years maintained its past proportion of total state expenditures. On the other hand, it can be shown that the federal government is the most effective unit of tax collection in the country and that rather substantial federal contributions to higher education would add only a small amount to the total federal budget.

We can conclude by suggesting that facts shed light on such basic issues in the cost and financing of higher education but do not settle

them. Such questions will be settled by the American people on the basis of the values they hold and the choices they make about how they wish to spend their ever increasing income and through which channels, private or public, they wish to spend that portion of the national income they deem vital to higher education.

How these questions are answered will in large measure decide whether the dual mandate of quality and quantity, for 6 million or more college students in 1970, will be met.

THE SIGNIFICANCE OF RELIGIOUS DEVELOPMENT

Earl A. Loomis, Jr., M.D.

DOES RELIGION MEAN anything to children? How does it come to have meaning for them? Is the decline, increase, or change in religious interests among children, youth, and adults at all related to their earliest experience? What is the nature of early religious experience? These questions and a great many more deserve the attention of researchers from both the side of religion and that of the behavioral sciences. There is much that we do not and cannot know. However, it may be worthwhile to examine, evaluate, and eventually to test a thesis that may do justice both to the child and to the adult community.

First of all, this thesis proposes that the religion of the child is not simply a watered-down version of adult religion tacked onto the growing child. Such religious caricatures exist, but they do not meet the criteria of genuine religious experience: 1) a response to what is experienced as ultimate reality; 2) a total response of the integrated person; 3) an intense and serious concern; and 4) a commitment toward imperatives for practical action. These criteria, proposed by Wach (1), will be explored in terms of their implications for children's religion and the development and meaning of religion in childhood.

Secondly, it is proposed that while the roots of religious experience,

Earl A. Loomis, Jr., M.D., is Professor and Director, Program in Psychiatry and Religion, Union Theological Seminary, and Chief, Division of Child Psychiatry, St. Luke's Hospital.

just as those of all deep-seated experiences of man, lie in infancy and childhood, the early religious experience of the child is constantly interacting with both the overt and covert religious life of the adults who are significant for the child.

Thirdly, it is in this very interaction of the religion of the child with the inner reaches of the religion of the adult, including his components of childlikeness, that basic religious communication takes place.

What we are attempting to study and understand is the place of religion in the life of the child, rather than determine the ultimate source of religion, its ultimate meaning, or its absolute truth. Therefore we need not concern ourselves here with the many knotty problems related to the differences between religions, but rather we can concentrate on the common elements and their common meaning for children.

Three elements in the development of infants and children are coming more and more to be recognized as indispensable. I am referring to trust, responsibility, and relationship. These three words touch upon the three developmental needs or tasks which are among the absolute minimum basic emotional and interpersonal requirements for the growing infant and young child.

TRUST

By trust we mean a constancy of expectation based on a constancy of experience. This constancy must begin early. In fact, it begins with conception. Through the long period of gestation, during which the regularities of her biology assist his regularities to develop, the physiological being of the mother speaks to the physiological being of the child. Not even at birth is the human organism to be self-regulating to any great degree. Therefore, the mother as a more-than-biological partner comes immediately into play. First by feel and smell, then by voice and sight the child comes to recognize the mother and be reassured by her presence, even at a distance. Her joy in his fulfillment of her expectations, her satisfaction in her own body's having participated in both an act and a

process akin to creation, are communicated initially through her caring concern for the newborn.

She cannot tell him that she will and wants to meet his needs, help him live and grow. She can give him this experience. Or rather, together they can create the experience for both of them. The experience comes first, and gradually the child becomes aware of the fact that he does expect confidently that his needs will be fulfilled. This calls itself to our attention sometimes through the surprise and anger of some children whom we observe in states of disappointment. In a sense, they could not be disappointed if they did not already have an expectation of being gratified. Rather, they would simply continue to be confirmed in their belief or expectation that satisfaction would be withheld. But physical and emotional survival and growth of the helpless human infant is dependent upon a certain irreducible minimum of gratification, and initially this gratification is very primitive: the alleviation of discomfort due to hunger, coldness, wetness; the providing of stimulation in the form of rocking, singing, "playing" with the baby; the providing of protection against pain and danger; and the doing of all the foregoing, initially at least, in such a way that the infant's needs are anticipated and that he suffers a minimum of frustration at the very beginning of life. It is communicated to the child not only by tenderness, but also by the assurance and confidence of the mother that she knows what she is doing.

The trust that Erikson calls "basic trust" emerges from a basically gratifying first year, and this kind of trust is the foundation which must be built in order to guarantee a background of security for the healthy personality that is to come. This trust will have to be strong enough to survive many testings, many disappointments, and many trials and temptations—particularly temptations to suspect that one is no good oneself, or that "people are no damn good." There has to be a certain minimum trust in the trustworthiness of the world and the worthiness of the self in order for growth, learning, and mature forms of love to develop, and these, of course, are the kinds of tasks the child faces in the years that follow.

The child comes to experience all this long before he has the words to

describe it. And, unfortunately for us researchers, by the time he has the words, he all too often has lost the memories of the experiences we are seeking to explicate. Yet from inference and observation it is quite clear that the earliest communications are nonverbal, as may indeed be the deepest ones.

If it is true that we learn to love by being loved, and that we learn to trust by being cared for, it is also true that we learn to become responsible through being responded to as a separate person. This separateness through which the child learns that the good self which gained its sense of goodness through intimate, almost fused, closeness with the good mother is gained through gradual differentiation and progressive discovery that the child can do things for himself. Doing things for himself on a small scale begins, of course, within the first year of life, as soon as the child begins to reach out selectively for things or persons, but by and large the ideal first year can seem to adults to be a simple, uncomplicated state in which the happy baby is rewarded just for being. He comes to feel and believe that he is good when he is comfortable and loved, probably because he is comfortable, lovable, and loved. Basic trust is always an experience of mutual goodness between mother and child.

A child learns to trust through experiences and in communication. Experiences with the trustworthy adult show him that there are persons upon whom he can depend. And relationships with adults whose words can be trusted lead him to believe in and respond to the words of the faithful parent. "Mommy is coming back," or "Daddy will fix it," come to mean more than statements of fact; they are promises whose sincerity can be counted upon. These experiences of trust have of course been long preceded by others in which words and language played little part. The substance of trust long precedes its vocabulary and in some sense always transcends its vocabulary. We sense this when we use phrases such as "empty words" to describe a statement without substance or meaning.

Parents usually intuitively use the most helpful words to represent to the child the substance of trust. These may take the form of "I am here." These may be seen as having something of the same connotation as the religious expression, "God is here," or "God is." The idea of God as a presence, One to whom the child's presence is meaningful, comes to be

attached to the child's early attitudes toward the person who matters to him, the person who accepts him, who can relieve his tension and discomfort. At one stage of growth this person, without ever saying so, may provide for the child those portions of his ego (that central integrating core of his personality) which he has not yet developed; at another stage the caring person may "kiss it and make it better"; still later it may be this same person who will explain that it was not made well by kissing (even though in a deep sense it really was).

It is more than the mother's recognition of the needs of the child; it is the mutual recognition by mother and child that contributes to the growing sense of selfhood of the infant and the confirmation of the mother's sense of true motherhood. Moving from the music in the voice to the saying of the word, it is the mother, and later the father too, who come to bring to the child the conviction that the words bear real meaning. As the child moves on to this stage the tying together of the words and the meaning make for semantic conviction. If this fails to come about, the "music" or the "words" lack conviction.

RESPONSIBILITY

In the second year of life, maturation of the child's tissues and the development of his personality cry out for an activity which will come more and more to replace the passive bliss of simply being comfortable and cuddled, the beloved recipient of attention and love from adoring and competent parents. This transition, however, expresses itself through the child's gradually taking over his own functions, many of which up until now had been performed for him by his mother. To feed himself, to transport himself, and to communicate through language become tasks which he tackles with periodic vigor when the time comes, tasks for which his mother and father must as readily shift gears in order to allow him to discover himself in action. Up until now there has been a sense that if he was uncomfortable he could do nothing about it except cry, emitting the simplest kind of signal of generalized distress. It has been, up until now, his mother's responsibility to hear the cry, discover and re-

move the source of discomfort, or—better yet—anticipate the discomfort and prevent it.

In this new stage the child for the first time has real means of directly getting his own gratifications and directly removing or avoiding distress. Now he can speed or slow his rate of eating; now he can go from place to place, standing on his own two feet; now he can vocalize his comments and requests; and now for the first time he can really say "No." Now he has the beginnings of power, to do all this, and with it the power to fall, the power to fail, and the power to disagree. This power is ambiguous because it causes both gratification and new distress. Its gratification is a wonderful new experience of active mastery of being a "going concern," of being no longer the totally passive victim or recipient of others' actions. But this power also introduces the capacity to fail oneself or others, to frighten oneself and others, and literally "to fall down and go boom." In a sense everyone of us pays the price of leaving Eden, when he finds himself to be a separate being and claims this capacity. With this separation comes the first possibility for responsibility —which always involves response-ability (openness to respond to another person or situation); and accountability (taking on oneself the consequences of one's behavior and claiming them as one's own).

One of the stages in the discovery of our selfhood is being recognized and treated as a separate self. This emerges from both our readiness to do things for ourselves and the readiness of the significant persons around us to allow us to prove ourselves in action. The movement from passivity to activity, from simply receiving to giving is part of our pilgrimage of self-definition. As religion has put it, we love (actively) because we were first loved (passively). But we must be allowed and encouraged to love at the time when we become ready. This means that after the experience of receiving, when we are ready to give, our gifts should be received and that we can thus learn the joys of doing and giving as well as those of having things done to and for us. Yet the ability to give freely is based upon the experience of having received freely. To force the child to give may evoke resistance or else a compliance which is insincere. To deny the opportunity to give may destroy the first flush of eager enjoyment of the newly discovered function. To overreact to the growing child's need to re-

fuse before he obeys may be to miss the crucial stage of his defining himself as one who can say no as well as yes. To be courageous enough to differ is essential to being a separate self. To be unafraid to tell the truth means to have lived through being respected even when one defies, even when the message of truth about oneself is an angry one.

RELATIONSHIP

The child moves inescapably to the next stage of development as he builds autonomy upon the foundation of trust and now must learn how to build mutuality upon independence. Having learned that he is loved, he has next to face the fact that love can be conditional as well as un-conditional—that no matter how much she wants to love her child all the time, his mother will find him less lovable and he will find himself less acceptable from time to time. In a child with basic security this shame or guilt will represent simply a normal emergence of self-regula-tion which gradually comes to replace external controls. Without that undergirding of basic trust, an excessive dependence upon external ap-proval for a sense of worth may lead the child both to over-value the outer world and to under-value his own being. He will not therefore be able to trust his own impulses, his own judgments and his own evalua-tions. He will not feel "good." Perhaps much later he will be an easy prey for group pressures and can ill afford to risk very much energy in attempts to modify his environment.

However, assuming the best, the young child has learned that he is good at least some of the time—good because he is given to, and good because he can do things on his own. He has received and he has begun to give—that is, in doing things to please (and displease) his parents and himself. But he has yet to learn to exchange. Mutuality implies exchange and comprehension—and on two levels. First of all, there is the exchange between adult and child that must be mastered in this period and this means a discovery of the meaning of the generations, that is, the dif-ferentiation between grownups and little children, between parents and offspring. It is a time of alternating rebellion and submission, of alternat-

ing intimacy and distance, and of fear of both. The second level of tasks has to do with the mystery of the sexes, with the fact that not only are parents large and children small, but that there are two kinds of people in the world. These two kinds, male and female, are so similar and so different—and in such mysterious and interesting (and sometimes frightening) ways.

To grasp the mystery of the first level is forcibly to be brought abreast of the reality of time, of birth and of death, of development and of aging. Each of these has religious overtones. The reality of the second level is grasped partly through physical observation and sensation, partly through the reflexive mysteriousness and secrecy of grownups and partly through the urgent and almost inescapable drama of relationships which intrudes into every family and every culture—into each in its own way. It is this drama in which the confusion of generations is still evident through the child's attempt to transcend time. It is in this drama that a sense of the mystery that is reality and the reality that is still mysterious may reach its peak of wonder and of curiosity. And wonder is a basic component of religion.

The urgency of this phase will pass, but hopefully out of its quest will emerge an eagerness for learning and an openness for friendship, games, and groups. Yet if the wonder is lost altogether and the curiosity satisfied or suppressed (and these two may mean the same thing), a loss has probably occurred. Whether this lack will make its claim in years ahead and whether its possibility for correction is now or never, we do not know. Some authorities feel that it is precisely at these periods of his life when the child is asking the insistent "why" questions—when "why" still means neither the strictly casual, the strictly logical, nor the strictly motivational, but rather an inextricably intertwined set of strands leading from the earliest precausality to the most sophisticated logical clarity. It is in these periods that attitude is as much a part of the answer as are words, that strict rationalism in response is seen more as threat than as helpful. (The threat of the adult's use of reasoning is reflected in the tirade of one preschool child against another: "I'll hit you! I'll cut you up in little pieces! I'll—I'll—I'll explain it to you!") (2).

Only a global and multilevel response can be fully satisfying. It may

not be enough when the dead fly is found beside the window screen to have an explanation that runs either along biological, philosophical, or religious lines. A feeling-tone response which includes the awareness of the child's participation in the life and death of the fly, his empathic awareness of the implied sense of loss, and his glorious childish capacity to meld whimsy with the utmost seriousness—all these are part of his question. And maybe all these are claims of his question upon the adult who would really be available to him. What I have said implies that the stages of child development each produce sequential readiness in children for certain modes of understanding. What is often forgotten is that they make claims upon an environment—the average expectable environment, to use Hartmann's term—to provide a context of responsive words and actions, feelings and meanings, around which the child can integrate his becoming both a separate person and a member of his family, clan, tribe and nation. While we may well recognize the vast profusion of diversified and differing responses to the questioning child which mothers and fathers of different times and locales and in different stages of their own development may give, an underlying core of conversation is necessary.

There may be a developmental readiness for religious conversation even as there is for walking, talking, reading, and writing, even as there is for the emergence of the logic of physical causality, social conventions, and personal motivation. It would seem to me that if this be the case, then certain consequences follow: the way in which the global conversations with the child from three to six encourage and accept his curiosity, his wonder, and his search for meaning and values; the way in which the child asks in words or actions whether or not he is good—all of him, body, mind, and sexuality, even imagination; the ways in which these discourses progress or are stunted by frightened or intimidated grown-ups, the way they are over-channeled through the precocious intrusion of dogma before myth and ethics before relationship. All these varieties of twisting may leave the child relatively undamaged in body, in general learning ability, and even in capacity for socialization. Yet may he not, through failure to exercise and practice the life of an emerging function, have lost the capacity for creative, imaginative, and global conceptualiza-

tion of the universe, of his own life, and of the meaning of time and eternity?

The delicate mystical and esthetic thread will be easy to lose and difficult to recapture if before it can be experienced and assimilated it is prematurely codified by the child under the influence of tradition, church, humanism, or "freethinking." Moreover, if the adults who matter hide their faith, are embarrassed by it or (perhaps even worse) deny their questionings and the mystery which it still constitutes, the child is ill equipped to integrate faith with life and faith with personal identity. It will tend to become either an alien appendage, tacked on tightly but isolated and irrelevant, or an intrusive foreign body that rankles within but cannot be dislodged without untold anguish. The former case leads to a facile but hollow use of logic; the latter to a logical primitivity which leaves the new person unable to move beyond the most infantile concepts of the sources of ultimate security.

This is the hypothesis. How can it be studied? Or perhaps putting it more concretely, what are the ways in which the spontaneous religion of childhood and the religion of parents may meet, interact, and be mutually fructifying? These statements assume that the investigator respects childhood and its phenomena as having importance in their own right and not simply as constituting a necessary evil that must be endured temporarily and then cast off as completely as possible as the price of maturity. The investigator rather would assume that each stage has its own validity and meaning as well as validity and meaning for those stages which are to come. He assumes that while each new stage has its own new tasks and demands which are made both by the child and upon the child, yet something of the preceding stages is forever a part of the full person as long as he lives. Hence the infantile, the childish, and the adolescent continue to be components of adulthood which must both submit to the dominance of adult identity and at the same time continue to be accessible through periodic normal regression in which the adult ideally can have access to the fruits and joys of the earlier stages—through dreams, fantasies, play, and worship.

Living with their own growing children constitutes a major source of stimulation for adults who experience the revival of certain aspects of

their own development. On some occasions these reawakenings may be frightening—on others they may be heartening. The inner action of the child's spontaneous religious ideas, feelings, and behaviors may well prove to be the occasion for some of the most richly rewarding inter-action. It may even disclose to the adult something of religion which he has forgotten and needs to know. This may be part of what Jesus meant when he stated in regard to children that "of such is the Kingdom of Heaven," or when on another occasion he told his disciples that "unless ye become as little children, ye cannot see the Kingdom of Heaven." In the Old Testament we have the examples of David and Samuel who in their youth demonstrated a wisdom and spiritual understanding il-lustrative of the child's deep potential for religious comprehension.

If the foregoing theses be accepted as working hypotheses or as part of a model for the re-examination of the relation of the religion of child-hood to adult religion and for the possibilities of interaction between the spontaneous religion of the child and the inward childlikeness of the adult, a number of possibilities can be traced out in more detail. Referring back from time to time to the sketch of child developmental stages which take us up to roughly age six or seven, we might ask to what extent the religion of the child meets the criteria for recognition as full-fledged religious experience.

We have already said that the religion of childhood and the function of childhood religious experience can be viewed both from the side of the children and of the adults themselves. These can also be viewed from the side of the function of religion as a social phenomenon or force.

THE FOUNDATION OF RELIGIOUS EXPERIENCE

Using the categories set forth at the outset we shall see what emerges. The first ingredient of genuine religious experience is expressed in adults through some kind of orientation toward a supreme being or beings who are defined as having superior or perfect attributes and nature. It is often postulated that before the infant can distinguish himself from

others or from the world, he goes through a stage of "omnipotence feelings" and that this stage is fostered initially by two features of his development: his initial inability mentally to distinguish himself from others, and the presence of the caring adult who anticipates his needs and hence gives him the illusion that they are self-fulfilled.

It is only later on, when he comes to distinguish satisfaction from nonsatisfaction (actually in part through the inevitable frustrations of life, even early life—the best of mothers sometimes cannot provide warm milk as promptly as the child would like to have it!), that he may transfer the omnipotence theme to the all-good, all-supplying parent, recognizing for a time perhaps his own helplessness and dependence. Later, he strives for his own independence in beginning to do things for himself. However, he still continues to regard his parents as omniscient and all-good, even if not fully omnipotent. He has then a model in his earliest developmental stages for the expectation that there is somewhere, somehow a source of perfect power, goodness, and love.

What is done with these expectations as he grows older will contribute significantly to his natural religious history. The fact that he has had a special quality of his experiences in relation to these parents lends to them special characteristics which will be difficult, if not impossible, to replicate later. What happens very often is that the attributes of the parents soon become fused with the growing god-image or its equivalent. If they are not later separated it may well be that some elements of his adult religion will carry with them some components which psychiatrists would call neurotic. However, initially, the confusion of parent and god is probably all but inevitable, if not indeed both necessary and providential. There are other examples in child development of similar necessary stages of fusion of functions which come gradually to become differentiated.

Whether the action and attitude of the child toward the proximate and later ultimate source of power, goodness, wisdom, and love is truly "a response to what is experienced as ultimate reality" seems to me to be self-evident. Whether or not the reality to which the child responds is indeed the deity is of course a theological rather than a psychological question. But as researchers we must ask what is the nature of the ex-

perience in which the child feels and responds to something that represents for him an active reality viewed as divine or as supremely good and as a source of good.

This restlessness or inner search for the source of meaning, of value and of security is the lifetime undertaking of each person which will serve as a driving impetus toward effective working through of the stages of development which lie ahead and which also, viewed from the standpoint of religion, can be interpreted as a drive to transcend the possibilities of everyday science, work, and relationships, at least to the extent that they are viewed as these and nothing more. This leads of course to the second criterion: Is the child's response to what he apprehends as ultimate reality a total response? Does it involve not only his intellect but his affections as well? Does it involve him as an integrated person?

Here again our searching for the answer will lead us back to the pilgrimage of becoming that constitutes childhood. Here again we will be reminded that the earliest, primal responses are likely to be global. Later the child begins to differentiate responses and functions. For a long time the function of integration is at least partially a borrowed one. In psychoanalytic parlance the mother must loan to the child, through her care of and relationship with him, her various ego functions, especially that of integration. As Winnicott, an English child psychiatrist, suggests, the mother has to put together the pieces of the child until he can see himself as a unified whole (3). To the extent, then, that the child is integrated either through his early lend-lease relationship with his mother or later in his own right (to the extent that any of us ever is) he will be laying the groundwork for response with his total being to "ultimate reality."

Yet the foundation should not be confused with the total structure. New relationships and new contents must be experienced in the years to come. Most of this will come about through the presence of persons through whom we receive the gifts of education, friendship, and good parental care. The power of these later gifts truly to affect us depends in large measure upon the degree to which they speak to our deepest inner condition. This means that they resonate with the "givens"—that which we are and have come to be in the period of the earliest development of

and definition of the self. The Psalms spoke of this metaphorically as "Deep calling unto deep." St. Augustine may have been speaking of its spiritual analogy when he prayed, "Thou hast made us for Thyself, O God, and our hearts are restless until they find their rest in Thee." The physiological counterpart of this is that babies have sucking mouths with which they seek food—mothers have feeding breasts that need a nursing infant in order to fulfill their function of giving milk. "Givens" and "gifts" are interlocked from the beginning and all along.

Next we must ask if the child's religion is a sufficiently intense experience involving profound concern and utter seriousness. Here many observers would be tempted to suggest that the infant and child are incapable of either profound concern for anything but themselves and of the kind of seriousness that a truly religious commitment would demand. They would base this objection on the ego-centricity of the child or his self-centeredness in thought, feeling, and action and also upon the fact that so much of his life is devoted to play which is presumed to be frivolous and unserious.

On the first count, the infant must of course plead guilty. He is indeed egocentric—more so than he will be later if he develops normally. However, the intensity of his concern actually may be greater, as a result of his lack of distraction and the narrowness of his focus. In regard to the second problem, any experienced student of the child's play must come to recognize its profound depth and intensity, as indeed any thorough investigator of religion will avoid overlooking the vitality which religious experience derives from the spontaneity and freedom represented in its play components. The absence of these components in much of adult religion is one source of the deadly, fossilized character which it sometimes tends to assume. This tendency has threatened all three of the major American faiths, but time and again they have been revivified through the rediscovery of their play-components. To cite examples, one can remind Judaism of the Chassidic movement, Protestantism of both Luther and Fox, and Catholicism of the Liturgical Revival and of Romano Guardini's classic chapter, "The Playfulness of the Liturgy."

In responding to the fourth criterion of genuine religious experience,

we must ask, "Is the religious concern of the child practical? Does it involve a commitment to action?" Again our answer leads us back to the modes of expression of the child through his various stages of development. Viewing the child through this lens, who can deny that his earliest means of expression and response are physical and actional, rather than simply ideational and verbal? Observation of the child's first signs of trust (or distrust) indicates that they take the form of muscular relaxation (or tension), of emotional repose and joy (or disquiet and discomfort). Later he is likely (even though he can think and speak) to act before he thinks or speaks and to dramatize in his play far more readily than he will conceptualize or experience in "pure imagination." It is my impression, therefore, that we do well to allow the child the benefit of passing the fourth test.

Wach insists that authentic religious experience must fulfill all four of his criteria; otherwise we may be dealing with what he terms "pseudo-religious" or "semireligious" experience. The former is a deliberate pretense that uses religious forms. In the case of the latter, the concern for the "ultimate" is missing despite the presence of the other three criteria. Whenever the intensity of "religious" feeling, commitment, and action have a purely finite focus, regardless of how sacrificial the devotion may be, Wach (and many theologians) would judge it to be "idolatrous" rather than "religious."

Here of course one must face the legitimate issue that the ubiquitous tendency to idolatry within all religions everywhere may well be present for the child. Not only will it constitute a dimension of some of his earliest stages of development, but it will also be a recurrent temptation emerging periodically throughout his life. Parents are obviously the most ready idols, after the self, and they will often be replaced by teachers, school chums and lovers. The fine line between seeing the ultimate through the finite and mistaking the finite for the ultimate is hard to maintain. Perhaps parents can contribute to the overcoming of idolatry of themselves by their frank admission of fallibility when the child begins to be able to discover and assimilate this hard fact of life.

The fact that religion is subject to corruption in no sense vitiates its re-

ligious character, but rather indicates that it is susceptible to some of the same temptations as are other basic experiences whose developmental sequence stems from the very beginnings of life.

THE EXPRESSION OF RELIGIOUS EXPERIENCE

Having submitted a case for the existence of intrinsic religion in childhood (over and above the responses of the child to any explicit religious orientation by the parent), we might examine next some of the ways in which children articulate their religious experiences.

For children, as for adults, religious themes have appeared in two major conceptual forms: myth and doctrine. The young child thinks and communicates religiously primarily by myth; through his spontaneous dream and fantasy life during the first five years he becomes expert in myth-making. Shortly thereafter, however, his temperament reacts radically, perhaps under the influences of education and our modern rationalistic pressures, and no doubt also in response to the need to repress the still-frightening myths of the family drama and the family romance. Nevertheless, the myth-mode will continue, but it will be less explicit in cultures and families where it is discouraged. (It should be noted, however, that by myth we are not implying that a story just plain is not so, but rather that it is a more or less artistic or poetic synthesis of the elements of a theme which is genuine and authentic for the person or the group that uses it. Hence in their fascination with fairy tales and in their tendency both to modify them upon a form which they can accept and to insist upon their unvarying repetition, they are expressing deep personal truth which cannot otherwise be communicated.) Yet myth is a mode of expressing the ineffable, making the "unspeakable" speakable, and of making the uncertain certain.

In his creating, sharing, and adopting many forms of ritual, the child indicates his access to actional modes of articulating his religious experience similar to those of adults. This is particularly true in the case of family ritual, often around meals. Here the syntheses of the family around the shared elements of commonly enjoyed nutrition and con-

versation are especially available as a channel for communication of religious meaning. (Strife and confusion at mealtimes may carry proportionately potent negative possibilities.)

The family as a community of continuity with the past and a community of memory has played a major role in the transmission of religious heritage and identity. In both the Easter and Passover services the re-enactment of deliverances in family rite imports a sense of participation in the ongoing life of the people of faith. In the Feast of Passover there is a dramatic dialogue of the re-enactment of deliverance between the oldest and youngest members of the family. The family as a religious unit deserves serious study, particularly in terms of the changing images of parents in the eyes of their children. Observers note that children not only imitate and adopt adult ritual, but also are inveterate inventors of "original" rites which express and declare their concerns about power, justice, love, and fate.

Another mode of articulation of religious experience that goes beyond action or doctrine is what Wach terms the "sociological" or "covenanting" mode. This aspect is variously expressed at different ages. During the first five years the "covenants" are obviously between parent and child with occasional exceptions in the case of pacts of nonaggression or of muted aggression vis-a-vis a younger sibling. However, again some time between six and sixteen, the emergence of the possibility of interpersonal expression of the child's spontaneous (and by now also acquired) religion with that of his peers and with adults as well means that in many ways it has the possibility of resonating or colliding with the religion of others. Furthermore, the specific modes of indoctrination and induction into the faith group of his family will by this time be well under way. But this means that the child is now leaving childhood.

Adolescence in modern Western civilization has ceased to be the young adulthood that perhaps it once was. Disappearing too are the rites of transition between prepuberty and postpuberty, the joint declaration by the young person and his community that he is now translated from his earlier existence as a child into an entirely new one as an adult. While our confirmation and Bar Mitzvah ceremonies and their preparations preserve a modicum of this meaning, a great deal is lost. The emergence of

self initiatory rites on the part of youth gives testimony to the deficiency in the adult-child mutuality which once made the puberty rite both sacred and somehow psychologically telling and irrevocable. How to bring to the problem of modern youth's search for identity and identity confirmation some new light and firm answer is yet unsolved. The alternatives seem to be identity diffusion (illness) and negative identities (crime). Each of these seems to be a form of substitute for identity confirmation, including its religious component.

These substitutes might be regarded both as symptoms of disorder and attempts at self-healing. They might be regarded as persistence and transmutation of the private childhood religion without benefit of creative interaction with that of adults. The persistence of a private religion is by no means rare, and to some extent we might be justified in assuming its presence as at least a mild internal protest against or supplement to the official religious affiliation of almost every person. However, if this private religion is deeply at odds with the professed faith and the character and personality of the individual, it is likely to express itself in the form of a latent or manifest neurosis.

One might paraphrase Freud, and consider the probability that many neuroses represent private religions that failed. This, it seems to me, is both the truer and the more acceptable of two alternate explanations which Freud propounded, the other being that religion is "nothing but" shared neurosis. Indeed, Freud himself, although preferring a scientific rather than a religious *Weltanschauung*, recognized that for many persons religion might be the only form of world view which would protect them from neurosis in the face of the competing claims of instinct and civilization. What Freud neglected were two possibilities: 1) That science cannot fulfill all men's needs, particularly in the areas of meaning and values; and 2) That it is precisely in these areas and precisely through its legitimate access to myth, symbol, and ritual that religion can meet these fundamental claims. To learn to take seriously the profound critique of neurotic, shallow, rigid, or inhibiting religious expressions which Freud has given us or made possible, is as much our responsibility as it is to recognize some limitations of his outlook vis-a-vis the positive possibilities for faith. It is for the sake of making the latter accessible to our children

and youth without concurrently destroying through negligent or oppressive religious training their own possibilities for authentic faith experience, that these words are addressed.

The way in which most of us come to know about God is through experience with people who, in the process of communicating something of themselves, share much of that which is deepest and most real for them, hence making available to the other the richness or poverty of their own religious life. Teaching the words of faith without their substance in experience is not enough. By faith I mean a capacity to trust in a divine being, the commitment to a system of values, and the participation in a way of life which makes all or significant aspects of life sacred. The experiences leading to trust cannot of course be limited to childhood. Yet it is the childhood preparation that often gives the deepest conviction of inner depth to later experience which resonates with or corrects in a meaningful way that which has gone before.

The spiritual value is present not only in the gifts of love, wisdom, and fellowship that we receive all through life, but also in the givens which we have from the beginning. Spiritual life as personal experience is based on a biological and genetic basis as well as on the interaction with the environment. It does not simply break through from the outside but in a sense it has been present all along. This may be what theologians have referred to as man's being made in the image of God. How has it been nourished and responded to? How stunted, distorted, and dulled? These are the questions for which answers need be sought. This approach needs to be tested, modified, and corrected. But if it has a germ of truth it may be that we adults will discover that we can be not only the teachers of religion to children, but the students of and grateful recipients of the experience of religion in children.

PART TWO

Problem Areas

COMMUNITY ORGANIZATION

Lester B. Granger

COMMUNITY ORGANIZATION can be viewed from a dual standpoint—that of the social work profession, and that of civic-minded community leadership. In either case, the process is aimed at the same objective—to improve through organized effort the conditions under which people live. Much of this effort is carried on by leadership groups and individuals, but to be fully effective it must involve the people, whether individuals, family groups or neighborhoods, who are most directly affected and who will most directly benefit from the changes which are being sought.

It is one of the universal characteristics of the human species that when people feel strongly enough that a particular factor in their community life is undesirable they will unite in efforts to do something about it. In the words of McMillen, the task of community organization is to "make capital out of this drive—to try to promote wider and more rapid recognition of detrimental elements in the environment and to guide the desire for reform by transforming emotional responses into disciplined progressive activity."

The difference between the professional and the nonprofessional standpoint is generally found in the conscious use of methods and skills perfected through training and experience which characterize the professional, and in the persistence with which the professional can be expected to pursue an agreed-upon social goal.

Lester B. Granger is Executive Director of the National Urban League.

The professional in community organization is the enabler, the indirect leader, the specialized consultant, and the creative participant. Not only are professional workers more apt than volunteers to be aware of the skills and methods which are a part of the community organization process, but they are apt to be regarded by some as having almost exclusive mastery of the process. So much is this true that to the average American citizen—even the active volunteer in civic affairs—the phrase "community organization for social change" is apt to have very little meaning. This is ironic in view of the fact that rapid social change, much of it the result of organized community effort, has been a prime characteristic of the American scene for nearly half a century.

What do we mean by social change? Obviously, the term can refer to any alteration in the conditions under which people live, and any alteration which influences their reaction to their social environment. The kind of social change which is the goal of consciously directed community organization effort is that which means improvement in the social and physical environment, the heightening of understanding and cooperation among segments of the population, and the lessening of tension and conflict. To achieve such social change there must be planning and action based upon past experience, current knowledge, and realistic hopes for the future. Without such planning, social change will be not only erratic and retrogressive, but dangerous as well. And without organized action to follow, planning is merely the stuff of which dreams are made.

Yet, inertia is as strong a characteristic of society as change, and it is this which often compels a slow pace in the achievement of new patterns despite the fact that they may be urgently needed and long overdue. It is one of the marks of effective community organization practice that it is able to overcome inertia, to build a climate and a readiness for new ideas, and thereby accelerate what otherwise might be an agonizingly long process.

Constructive social change is the result when, through the community organization process, people are brought together in concerted social planning and organized social action. That action may be aimed at a variety of selected objectives. It may seek change of the physical form of the city, elimination of glaring slum spots in favor of expressways, wider

streets, new housing, or increased park and playground areas. An objective may be provision of new schools in an under-served area, provision of badly needed youth services in a city plagued with a rising rate of juvenile delinquency, or perhaps a cleanup of City Hall, or the police force, or the hospital system. There may be serious breakdowns noted in public or voluntary welfare facilities. Or perhaps the flight to the suburbs is leaving the city dangerously bereft of those leadership elements which have the most to offer in training and experience. In these or other areas of interest the social objectives of community organization will depend partly upon leadership's evaluation of community conditions, partly upon the public's reaction to that evaluation, and partly upon the kind of community generally contemplated as desirable and achievable.

Our first community organizers were the colonists themselves. Primitive little outpost settlements of Massachusetts, New York, Virginia, and other early colonies exposed to the twin threats of starvation and Indian raids were quick to organize their best talents of brain, brawn, and courage in home building, hunting, extending their plant acreage, and creating simple but effective linkages between sparsely scattered settlements, both for defense against attack by hostile Indians and for raids in reprisal.

Without this sort of organization during the early years of the colonies there would have been no United States of America. There would have been only an East Coast approximation of the sprawling, loosely administered French and Spanish holdings to the south and west of the British colonies. This was community organization of a simple kind, adapted to the needs of a simply constructed society, and not essentially different from the efforts at self-organization which any community anywhere in the world undertakes in order to assure its own survival.

COMMUNITY ORGANIZATION TODAY

A great gulf separates those huddles of log cabins stretched along rutted or muddy wagon trails more than two hundred years ago from the present-day city of industrialized urban America. Not only is today's commu-

nity bigger than any of the early colonists could possibly have imagined; it is also complex beyond the wildest dreams of the eighteenth century. In fact, current metropolitan expansion trends have caused speculation as to the possibility of three or four gigantic metropolitan areas holding an overwhelming majority of our citizens by the end of this century. One could be a continuous residential-business-manufacturing community five or six hundred miles long, stretched from southern Maine down into Virginia. Another would hug the southeast and Gulf Coast of this country. Still another would blanket the Missouri, Ohio, and Mississippi River Valleys; and a fourth, more sparsely settled community would stretch down the West Coast, from Seattle to San Diego.

This may be the sheerest speculative nonsense, or it may be supported by sound deductive reasoning. In either case, it is still a fact that the American community has changed wonderfully in the past fifty years and will continue to change amazingly during the period ahead. And, all in all, it has been change for the better, even though there continue to be great inequities in the availability of essential community services in one section of the country, as compared with another. The experience of the United Community Defense Services (UCDS) makes it clear that such services are frequently lacking in communities of less than 100,000 persons, despite the fact that the residents of these communities have the same needs and the same problems as those of larger metropolitan areas. Yet the modern community, both large and small, is capable of providing more for its citizens and promises even more yet to come. But in return for fulfillment of its promises, it demands more of its residents.

This increasingly complex society which is present-day America has encouraged more and more specialization of skills and interests on the part of its citizens. The old approaches to once simple subjects are no longer effective. That citizen-leader, for instance, who in an early day would have consulted with his neighbors and fellow citizens on ways of handling a serious community problem now finds himself baffled by intricate ramifications of the problem when he tries to trace it through the convoluted political, industrial, and social structure of his modern city. He is apt to step back in confusion or irritation and leave the problem for "professionals" to handle. More and more, in consequence, social

work agencies are coming to assume the initiative in tackling those community organization problems concerned with health and welfare services. Other specialist groups now assume responsibility for various other types of community planning and inquiry. Thus, organizations which have at their disposal trained, full-time staff leadership have gradually taken over the conduct of community planning as independent volunteer leadership has tended to abdicate.

Development

Community organization in the past decade has come of age. It has sharpened its tools and improved its skills. It has recognized the significance of the power structure concept and found ways to apply it in practice. It has begun to relate to physical planning and to share its skills and insights with the professionals in that field.

American social welfare, traditionally oriented to the needs of the individual and the small group, has awakened to the realization that certain kinds of needs and problems will respond only to the broad-gauge approach of community organization. Only recently identified as a process deserving special study, community organization began with a focus on coordination and later concerned itself with achieving communitywide support for services through joint financial efforts. During the last few years, however, the focus has been on planning for unmet needs, and it is in this area that it can make its maximum contribution, both to the American community and to other countries around the world, particularly the underdeveloped nations. In the Philippines, India, and in certain emerging nations of Africa, the community development worker can be seen conferring with the village elders on improvements in rural life, which are being achieved by what is essentially the community organization process. These efforts pay dividends in the form of increased family income, reduced malarial rates, the improvement of the breed of livestock, or the provision of schools and roads where none were found before.

The application of community organization has helped to shape the growth of community chests, united funds, and social planning agencies in 2,000 cities across America. It has influenced the growth and development of 100 national service agencies. Formal courses in schools of so-

cial work have been instituted to prepare graduates for staff and community leadership in this field.

This has been good for the development of social welfare programs in this country. Indeed, it has been essential, for without trained, full-time specialists social work could never have managed to stay even remotely abreast of social change, which has affected everything that every social agency seeks to do. However, to the extent that the community organization process has become "institutionalized"—to the extent that citizen-leaders are thereby tempted to consider the organizing tasks as not manageable by an "amateur," but rather the prime responsibility of "pros" —to such an extent does the professionalization of community organization inhibit rather than advance the well-rounded, solid development of the American community.

It should be re-emphasized: Community organization is the means by which American leadership is able to pool the resources of citizens and neighbors and marshal them into effective, constructive action for protecting and improving urban and rural life in the United States. In such efforts, the leadership and applied skill of persons professionally trained for the purpose are priceless adjuncts. However, they cannot compensate for a loss of initiative and venturesomeness on the part of groups of citizens working together under their own steam—though in consultation with professionals—to effect social change simply because of their love of community.

Many agencies whose prime responsibility is the planning and coordination of health and welfare services, including services to youth, have begun to be concerned during the past decade about the hazard of professional domination, not because of any widespread drive for power on the part of professionals themselves, but more frequently because of abdication by the volunteer. There is difficulty in obtaining and retaining competent influential and interested lay leadership. Often the community planning council must rely on a third level of interest, which is to say the interested citizen-volunteer must give primary attention to his own vocation. Next in line comes the particular agency, usually a direct service agency, which has captured his interest. When he is named delegate to represent that agency in the planning council, the council itself

gets only the remnants of his time and attention. This has meant that many councils have placed primary lay leadership responsibility in the hands of "members-at-large," but here the danger is that such citizens may not be related closely enough to the field to have a mature understanding of the problems being dealt with.

Three Types of Objectives

Generally speaking, three types of social objectives are sought through community organization: 1) provision, improvement, or better distribution of welfare services and facilities; 2) passage of legislation to correct social and economic injustices or to strengthen democratic procedures; and 3) development of cooperative relationships between groups of people and equalization of opportunities for social and economic growth. This definitive interpretation, it must be stipulated, is not accepted by all interested in the subject; some would define community organization as largely limited to the first category—improvement and coordination of social services; some would define legislative activity as "social action." Others would define efforts to equalize opportunities and increase intergroup cooperation as educational activity, or would term it "intergroup relations" or "human relations."

Such distinctions, however, are a matter of semantics, not method. The same basic methods and motivations that determine success or failure in one category will operate similarly in another. And the same steps are generally taken in the same sequence as the community organization process moves from study of a situation and selection of objectives to their achievement. The method and motivation of community organization are based upon social conviction and purpose, knowledge and use of community resources, and generalship in their application for the purpose of constructive social change.

Components of the Process

The steps in a full-fledged community organization enterprise follow more or less a classic pattern. Discussion of a social problem points the way toward tentative aims. These discussions must include the individuals most directly affected in order to make certain there is a subjective,

as well as an objective, understanding of the problem under consideration, and to lay the basis for subsequent active participation in whatever remedial efforts are mutually agreed upon.

Further study on the basis of organized factfinding, or deeper research, clarifies understanding of the situation and firms up the selected goals.

Public interpretation of the facts builds up a body of supportive public opinion and facilitates leadership recruitment. Such leadership gives further impetus to the drive for public support.

Analysis of the deeper phases of the situation proceeds in an atmosphere of public approval of the purposes sought.

Conferences, discussions, and negotiations with those individuals and groups in a position to advance social change are sought.

Prior demonstration of the validity of the objectives sought and of the quality of public support developed will, of course, help to create a favorable atmosphere for these discussions. In the same way a concluding report to the public, or a report of progress (or lack of progress) serves to identify for the public's benefit its continuing stake of interest.

THE MIGRANT FARM LABOR PROBLEM

All of the component steps in the community organization process may be identified in the study of any one of several problem fields. The one selected is one which has engaged a wide public interest over a considerable period of years, and yet the social change which is required for its solution has not yet been achieved. This is the amalgam of problems experienced jointly by migrant farm workers and the communities in or near which they work. These perpetually migrant farm families are the backbone of a large part of our national farm production.

The rapid spread of mechanization in agriculture during the past quarter-century has caused a concomitant spread of large-scale farming —industrial farming. This has increased the need for large numbers of seasonal farm workers who follow the crops in steady succession from Florida and the Gulf Coast all the way north to the Canadian border. There are currently estimated to be about 1 million of these workers, but

to that number must be added the families of many of them. In 1951, for instance, there were estimated to be about 400,000 migrant children between the ages of 10 and 15.

These workers are recruited principally from the Negro farm population of the South and the Spanish-American population of the Southwest. Added to these are 100,000 Mexicans who cross the border as government-approved contract labor and possibly four times their number who enter this country year after year as "wetbacks," illegal entries who are presumed to ford the Rio Grande by night. The ranks of migrant farm labor have been further swelled in recent years by Puerto Ricans and a small number of contract workers from the West Indies.

Not merely wretched pay (by American standards) earned by adult workers, but also the even more wretched conditions affecting their children have caused widespread grave concern over the years. Unschooled in large measure, left untended while their parents are in the fields, or employed themselves in the fields at a too early age in defiance of child labor laws in a few states, but in conformity with too loose laws in others, these children of migrant farm workers have for many years constituted a social problem attaining the proportion of a national scandal.

Here is a problem situation which would appear to be responsive to a full-scale application of the community organization process, and not likely to be solved without it. Factors involved include the need for improved and better coordinated health and welfare services, passage of corrective legislation, and advancement of understanding and cooperation between the problem-plagued communities and the problem-crushed workers concerned. It is a problem that contains the ingredients of insufficient legislation, lax administration, open and covert exploitation by many employers and public officials, ignorance, lethargy, or docile conformity by a majority of the workers, corresponding lethargy, ignorance, or confusion and irritation of the public in communities directly affected —and an aimless, ineffective interest by the national public as a whole. Inject into this situation the important factors of racial differences and language difficulties and the widespread attitudes of prejudice which relate to both of them, and the resultant compound appears, at first examination, hopeless of solution.

Actually, this is anything but hopeless, given the skillful, persistent application of community organization process. Already there has been a vast amount of effort in connection with the problem. What has been lacking is coordination of that effort into a national master plan and national leadership agreement on short-range and long-range objectives.

Sufficient exploratory work, the factfinding phase of community organization, has already been done. A special commission appointed by President Truman presented a report on migratory labor in American agriculture in 1951. It found housing for migrant workers practically unregulated in most states, the main concern being "reasonable protection against the weather." Health and welfare conditions were abominable, unhygienic living conditions being reflected in a rate of disabling illnesses 74 percent higher among migrant families than among resident families. Even in comparison with the poorer residents, the migrant illness rates were 50 percent higher; nor do morbidity statistics tell the full story, as, for instance, in the case of malnutrition among children. Truck travel, the use of hazardous tools and equipment by inadequately trained and poorly supervised workers, and the increasing use of noxious chemicals all contribute to give agriculture generally one of the nation's highest accident rates. This is especially the case on farms using migrant labor and usually having no vestige of safety training.

As for the use of child labor in the fields, only six states have laws covering children both in and out of school, while six more cover the employment of school-age children only during school periods. As might be expected from their educational transiency, migrant children of the East showed school retardation from two to five years.

Factual data of this sort when applied to the problem provide the raw material for the discussion, public interpretation, and leadership recruitment phases of the community organization process.

One element ordinarily considered essential to any successful community organization process is the involvement and active participation of the individuals and groups who are most intimately affected by the problem situation, who suffer from its effects, and who will benefit most immediately and most directly by change for the better. One reason why the migrant farm labor problem has so stubbornly resisted solution is the

difficulty in achieving this kind of involvement and participation on the part of farm migrants themselves. Not only are they hard to reach, they are generally uneducated, inarticulate, and unorganized politically and socially. As a group they are almost completely at the mercy of their social environment.

Nevertheless, corrective steps have been initiated in a large number of local communities and, in a few instances, tentatively on a national scale. Nationally, sustained, professionally directed attention has been given by the National Council of the Churches of Christ in the U.S.A., the National Catholic Welfare Conference, and the National Child Labor Committee. The Federal Interdepartmental Committee on Children and Youth, as well as the President's Commission on Migratory Labor, has kept the subject before the attention of governmental agencies and provided some guidance to citizen groups. In a growing number of cities, towns, and counties in the path of the migrant labor movement, public and voluntary committees are taking hold of certain aspects of the problem.

In some instances (Fresno and Denver, among the larger cities) special schools or special courses have been set aside for the two to three months of school the migrant children can receive in passing. Smaller cities, such as Kings Ferry and Auburn, New York, and Hoopestown, Illinois, have been cited for "good neighbor" action on the part of voluntary committees which have sought to share with migrants, however briefly, some exposure to a stable and friendly environment. In other communities, mobile health clinics have been brought into service, day-care centers have been established, and traveling film and book libraries have been made available to migrant children. These examples, individually and collectively, suggest the kinds of results which can be achieved by the effective utilization of the community organization process at the local level.

Nevertheless, and in spite of such stirrings of social concern over the size and persistency of the migrant labor problem, the national situation is generally about where it was when the President's Commission made its report nine years ago. Matters have not moved because certain essential elements of a full-scale community organization effort are lacking:

1. There has been no comprehensive, sustained, voluntary, widely-supported effort to interpret the situation to the American public.

2. There has been no federation of interest among the major parties of interest—farm employers, organized labor, representative religious and civic organizations, officials of city, state, and federal agencies most directly involved, and the migrant farm workers themselves.

3. There has been little advertisement of successes registered by local communities to serve as counteraction to the defeatist attitude generally displayed by migrant-affected communities.

In short, there has been no overall coordinated community organization approach at the national level. Such an approach to a social problem of this magnitude and complexity would call, first of all, for increasing, regularizing, and coordinating the conferences and discussions on the subject which are now being carried on in a largely sporadic fashion. It would call for the organization of a strong body of nationally known leaders who would be able to take the 1951 findings of the President's Commission as their continuing responsibility, pressing for such legislation as is indicated, calling the attention of the existing national agencies to methods of service they can render, each in his own way, and raising funds where they are needed for supplementary purposes or for new studies and demonstrations. In these and related ways, body and impetus could be given to an expression of public interest that, so far, has been ineffective because it has been unguided.

This would be community organization for social change of a type and quality befitting the professional skills and material resources this nation now possesses. Now that our understanding of the community organization process has advanced as it has over the past decade, and we are beginning to appreciate its full potential, we must assume the responsibility which this knowledge carries with it, the responsibility to bring health and welfare programs and resources into a much closer approximation of human need than has thus far been achieved in our national history. We must learn to apply more effectively what we already know to the complex social problems which face us now and in the years immediately ahead.

JUVENILE DELINQUENCY

Norman V. Lourie

JUVENILE DELINQUENCY continues to attract wide attention and arouse deep concern. There are many theories about its nature and cause. A limited definition of the juvenile delinquent refers to the child who comes in contact with an official law-enforcement agency because of an alleged act of delinquency or misconduct. Many other children commit similar acts who are not apprehended or whose misdeeds are not unlawful according to local statutes. Compared with most other classes of offense or status covered by modern law, juvenile delinquency is peculiarly difficult to define in terms of its behavioral connotations.

There is no general agreement as to the etiology or single treatment for delinquency. It is becoming generally accepted, however, that delinquency is not a distinguishable syndrome but is a rather loose evaluative term which covers a wide conglomeration of interpersonal and environmental phenomena.

Those who believe delinquency to be primarily psychological feel that while it may arise independently of social forces in any given culture, its expression is modified and undergoes change in accordance with cultural standards and values. The dynamics of the underlying, unconscious needs are seen as being the same in any society; the deviate is one who has difficulty in sublimating his wishes to the group. This theory holds that most cultures have contradictions in their values, as is illustrated in the

Norman V. Lourie is Deputy Secretary, Pennsylvania State Department of Public Welfare.

difficulties of teaching the Golden Rule in the face of the need to teach a child how to get along in an intensely competitive economic environment. Researchers continue to conclude that while a simple society produces children who know what is expected of them, an unstable and complicated society produces children who are not sure of themselves. Where we cannot offer children a firm understanding of who they are or assure them of what is true, desirable, or moral, or whether love or hate should prevail, we can hardly expect stability or ordered behavior from them.

Experts seem to agree that major changes are needed in our laws, services, and treatment practices to close a gap between modern knowledge and practice. Wide public education is called for if the public is to support the changes needed and if children are really to be treated and rehabilitated. Despite the great public clamor about juvenile delinquency the services are underfinanced and undermanned, and continue largely to be measures for correction rather than measures for child welfare and mental health.

This is not a universally accepted concept. Writing for the United Nations, Paul Tappan says: "By the indifference and default of others, children's care through courts as well as through social agencies generally has come into the hands of a group that is oriented rather completely to the philosophies of voluntary social work, with emphasis upon individualized diagnosis and therapy for emotionally unadjusted clients" (1).

The point of view of those who regard cultural elements as the major causes is best stated by Kvaraceous and Miller as follows: "The major problem of delinquency . . . is not to be found in the middle class . . . Delinquency prevention and control, viewed from any angle, whether prediction, study, diagnosis, or treatment, remains largely a problem of a lower class delinquent, the lower class family, and a lower class community" (2). The core of this hypothesis, which arises out of research described by the authors, reveals that what constitutes "norm-violating" behavior in one group or locality may be accepted in another, and that the modalities of norm-violating behavior exist within a broad spectrum of delinquency. The differing social and cultural conditions in the middle class and lower class milieus create special problems for the youngsters of

each class; and the conclusion is set forth that delinquency as norm-violating behavior usually represents adapted behavior for the individual delinquent; that the individual delinquent act may often represent the only resolution a youngster can find to a direct personal social problem. This is consistent with the work of Lander, Merton, Durkheim, and others.

Since the turn of the century, concern over juvenile delinquency has resulted in advances in child welfare and child psychiatric work. There has been an increase in the number of child guidance clinics, child psychologists, child welfare workers, psychiatric social workers, and other personnel who function mainly in diagnostic and therapeutic roles. However, Freudian orientation has not dominated the scene; attention has been given to the genesis of delinquency as well as to its treatment. Facilities and services of a nonpsychological character have been developed, directed recently in large measure toward research in prevention.

SOME FACTS ABOUT JUVENILE OFFENSES

More boys than girls are known to courts (the ratio is 5 to 1). The age of the children when they are referred to court is usually between fourteen and fifteen years. School retardation, chronic truancy, and attitudes of hostility, defiance, and suspicion are often present. Frequently the delinquents come from homes broken by death, divorce, or desertion or from homes which lack stability and standards of child care. Emotional and economic deviation are more frequent than not; yet many delinquents do come from families with economic, social, and emotional stability.

Boys most often commit acts of stealing or malicious mischief, while girls often present problems of ungovernable behavior, running away, or sexual offense. Most cases have histories of problem behavior.

The Uniform Crime Reports of the Federal Bureau of Investigation for 1957 showed that 21 percent of all persons under eighteen who were arrested were held for larceny of articles with a value of $50 or less; 27

percent violated state or local laws, mostly pertaining to running away, truancy, curfew violations, and others; 1 percent were arrested for robbery; 1 percent for aggravated assault; and less than one-tenth of 1 percent for criminal homicide. Eleven percent were charged with burglary and 8 percent with automobile theft (3).

Statistics continue to be inadequate but provide relative measures of the incidence of delinquency. The FBI and the U.S. Children's Bureau gather statistics nationally. They depend on voluntary reports; and while many agencies respond they do not provide comprehensive or representative samples. The Children's Bureau reports juvenile court cases without listing the reasons for the arrests—which range from traffic violations and misdemeanors to homicide and arson.

Cases reported to the Children's Bureau by juvenile courts began to increase in 1948 and have continued to rise for nine consecutive years. Between 1948 and 1957 these cases doubled. In 1957, more than 600,000 cases of delinquency were referred to juvenile courts. An estimated one-half million different children, or about 2.3 percent of all children in the ten- to seventeen-year age group in the United States, were involved in this one year.

A better notion of the size of the problem can be had by estimating the percentage of all children who are involved in at least one court case during their adolescence. Including repeaters, who are involved in about one-third of all delinquency cases, the percentage is roughly estimated to be 12 percent (assuming a continuation of the 1957 rate). For boys alone it is much higher—about 20 percent. Boys contribute about five times more to delinquency statistics than do girls, while the distribution of girls and boys in the population is about equal. The U.S. Children's Bureau points out that these data include traffic violations (30 percent of all cases in 1957). Other studies also reveal that the size of the problem is greater than appears from one year's figures because, for one reason, the police see many who never appear in court.

The FBI reported that police arrests increased 10 percent in 1957 over the previous year. Juvenile court cases increased 10 percent. In 1956 court cases increased 21 percent over the previous year. Police arrests increased

17 percent. The increases of police arrests were greater in the smaller and rural areas than in the urban. Between 1956 and 1957 the increase in arrests of children under eighteen in rural areas and small cities was 16 percent over the previous year, while it was only 8 percent in cities of over 25,000 population.

The soundest analyses indicate that despite the controversy as to whether the rise in delinquency is real or not because of various unmeasurable factors, including the more efficient operation of our facilities and the increase in child population, the increase appears to be not only real but potentially staggering. Fuller reporting and stricter law enforcement are not the only explanation of higher delinquency statistics, according to authorities.

The U.S. Bureau of the Census predicts that we will have from the 1957 base a 35 percent rise in the ten- through seventeen-year age group by 1965, and 48 percent more in 1970. With an estimated 30 million children in the United States by 1965, if the juvenile court cases continue to increase as they have since 1948, the juvenile courts will be handling about a million cases a year. Even if the rate of juvenile court delinquency cases remains fixed at the 1957 level, juvenile courts will be handling about 800,000 cases in 1965. And by then, there will also be, if past experience is a guide, a much greater number of police cases which never reach the courts (3).

There is also a very large group of delinquents who are seen by community agencies and not referred to the police or the courts. Some studies of the size and composition of this group are available and more are needed if we are to determine how our culture affects youth and how we must change it if we are to do a more effective job of preventing juvenile delinquency.

The U.S. Senate Subcommittee to Investigate Juvenile Delinquency has estimated the cost of property stolen by juveniles to be about $115 million per year. Public services for delinquents, including the police, courts, detention facilities, and institutional care, are estimated to cost over $200 million per year. The FBI estimates the current average cost of all crime, including adult crime, to be around $20 billion per year.

PREVENTION

The U.S. Children's Bureau has continued its intensive studies of prevention, begun several years ago (4). In the March, 1959, issue of the Annals a spokesman for the Bureau, Helen Witmer, indicated that new programs and methods give promise of more favorable findings (5). She points out that the most striking change is in the level of sophistication. Psychological and sociological knowledge have been applied to some of the newer projects and sounder evaluation methods have been used. Miss Witmer says in her Foreword to the Annals symposium: "Perhaps the most important contribution of this series of articles lies in the picture it provides of the kinds of youngsters that are likely to become chronically delinquent and of the kinds of homes and neighborhoods they live in. . . . The articles deal with small programs. . . . Few of them report scientifically established results. Nevertheless, in their conception of what needs to be done and in their suggestions for some ways of doing it, they hold the hope that the problem of delinquency can be reduced if communities are willing to put the effort required into the work."

While the articles referred to report and evaluate a series of efforts not too unlike others seen before, two of them are worthy of special mention. "Co-ordination of Services as a Means of Delinquency Prevention," by Gisela Konopka, describes a cooperative effort on the part of law enforcement, health, and welfare agencies and of public schools working together in an area of high delinquency. The impact, the author says, is in three areas: "A genuine rethinking of social agency practices . . . a clearer realization of what kinds of staff are needed to work with our most neglected, hurt, least verbal citizens who are prone to delinquency . . . and a deepening of the understanding that juvenile delinquency is a total community problem of child rearing and therefore calls for an attack on the whole community culture and cannot be solved by segmented institutions or individuals."

The article, "A Research-Based Proposal for a Community Program of Delinquency Prevention," by Eva Rosenfeld, is also significant because it describes the elements of a community program which might reduce

delinquency and indicates not only the specific service elements which should go into the program, but lists for each the research values and hypothesis. In a field which has so much amorphous quality there is presented a design which, if followed consistently in a number of communities and over a period of time, might be productive of some solid, tested facts.

In 1955 Lander made a significant and provocative contribution in his report on 8,464 cases of juvenile delinquency in Baltimore (6). It is related to the works of Durkheim, Merton, and Parsons. This work, using concepts of normlessness (anomy) and social disorganization, has potential for more scientific understanding of delinquent behavior and its causes. A good deal of the more recent approach to understanding the cultural normlessness of juvenile delinquents undoubtedly had its roots in this type of thinking.

A most significant approach to the problem of delinquency in its broader sense has been the work of Community Research Associates (CRA), a nonprofit research body. This group pinpointed problems through studies of families who had come to be known as "multiproblem families" and the "hard-core" or "hard-to-reach," and found that these families represent the major health and welfare challenges in every community and that service to them and their members has been quite ineffective. Further, these studies show that many communities have been "picking up the pieces" after crises like delinquency, illegitimacy, and neglect have arisen, rather than investing at the source of costly human breakdown with preventive and rehabilitative work.

The CRA studies have revealed that the entire structure of worthwhile, desperately needed welfare services is impaired by "archaic" techniques which make many of the present welfare programs little more than "mopping up" operations. In public agencies which support so many of the problem families whose offspring turn into juvenile delinquents, very little of scarce skilled personnel time is given to direct help. Caseloads are too large, and as a result agencies have not been giving needed service.

The key study carried out by CRA in 1948 in St. Paul revealed that 6 percent of the community's families were using more than half

of the health and welfare budget. Duplication was rampant, with some families being served simultaneously by 10 or more agencies often working at cross purposes with the others. Some families had been receiving help for as long as twenty years, and their basic problems had been regenerated in their offspring. This study resulted in a family-centered project which brought agencies together in a coordinated approach to a group of these families, with amazing success. Of the first 50 families to get treatment in the project, 15 made marked progress, 14 progressed moderately, 15 made slight progress, and only 4 did not change at all.

A later study of more families showed that 30 percent of them had shown no movement backwards, 26 percent had registered moderate progress, and 41 percent had shown considerable progress during the period of treatment. In the opinion of the personnel working on the project, if more trained staff and means were available to work with all of the families in the "6 percent" group the situation could be changed to one in which about 2 percent would require no more than 20 percent of the service. CRA has conducted similar projects with different emphases in other parts of the country, and at present is working with several public welfare departments to help them reorganize their work methods (7).

JUVENILE AND FAMILY COURTS

Juvenile courts in the United States had their origin largely in English common law and English judicial background. The formality of the common law had produced the chancery, offering a special "prerogative of grace to those who might otherwise suffer hardship in the common law courts." Children were among these. The crown began to act as *parens patriae* for infants. Children were wards of the state and therefore it was felt that they should get special protection.

The American juvenile courts adopted this philosophy, raising the age standards in doing so. It accepted from the chancery court the elements involving the protection of the child, the administrative measures of control, and assistance and informality of procedure. To these have been

added the concepts and techniques of modern casework and ideologies of the child welfare movement regarding the rights of children and what is needed to meet their needs. Social casework has affected the operation of juvenile courts more than the historical elements.

The first juvenile court in the United States was established in Illinois in 1899. In 1938 a federal juvenile court act was passed, providing special procedures for handling juveniles committing federal offenses.

The juvenile court is said to be the most outstanding improvement in the administration of criminal justice since the Magna Carta in 1215. Every state now has some form of court with jurisdiction over juveniles. Not all of these are specialized juvenile courts; in many cities, and most often outside of cities, the circuit court, court of common pleas, justice of the peace court, probate court, or other court is given jurisdiction.

Most courts provide private hearings separate from adults and allow the judge freedom with respect to technical procedural rules. In recent years there has been considerable debate about the legal rights of children in these courts since the offenses in a petition for delinquency need not be established beyond a reasonable doubt. The arguments that civil rights of children are violated by discouraging the presence of legal counsel and by avoiding legal evidence are countered by the theory that the task of this special court is to rehabilitate rather than merely to adjudicate and punish.

The age of original jurisdiction of the children's courts is eighteen years and under in 29 states and in parts of 2 others (and the same for girls in an additional 2 states); sixteen years in 5 states and in parts of 2 others; seventeen years in 7 states (and the same for boys in 2 others), and 21 in 3 states. Further complicating is the fact that in 21 states the criminal courts have control over juveniles who commit certain crimes or offenses which in some states carry no specified age of exception. In nearly half of the states the criminal court either has jurisdiction over juveniles who commit certain crimes with power to transfer to juvenile court (12 states) or concurrent jurisdiction with the juvenile court (11 states). This policy indicates that the public desires to protect itself in some instances, along with its desire to deal leniently with children (1).

The general trend has been to raise the age limits of juvenile court

jurisdiction. Under the leadership of the American Law Institute—which in 1940 published the Youth Court Act, a companion bill to the Youth Authority Act—there has been a movement expressing the view that young adult offenders are a group distinct from children because of the seriousness of their problems and treatment needs. This has not been followed in detail in many states. The Standard Juvenile Court Act has been revised and the revision published (8).

In 1959 there was published the Standard Family Court Act, a document resulting from several years' work by the Committee on the Standard Family Court Act of the National Probation and Parole Association in cooperation with the National Council of Juvenile Court Judges and the U.S. Children's Bureau. This is the first guide ever to be made available for the establishment and operation of family courts. Interest in such courts has been growing. The first family court was established in 1914 in Cincinnati. Among such courts in existence today are those in eight counties in Ohio, in six counties in North Carolina and in Portland, Ore., Des Moines, Omaha, and St. Louis. It is expected that the new Standard Family Court Act will stimulate considerable interest in other localities.

DETENTION

About half of the children brought to juvenile courts are held in some type of detention before hearing. In more than three-quarters of the juvenile court jurisdictions in America in 1956, children were detained in jail or a jail-like facility such as a court house or basement cell. Too many children were held in detention.

Modern detention programs which, in effect, are diagnostic facilities have developed in larger cities (for example Youth House in New York City and Youth Study Center in Philadelphia). There has been some establishment of regional facilities for which several counties join forces where one alone could not finance or fully use a service.

Cities in the same state and close to each other report widely different estimates about the proportion who should be detained. This leads to

the conclusion that detention of children may often be unnecessary and that police and probation officers, if better trained, might detain fewer children.

INSTITUTIONAL TREATMENT

Specialized institutional facilities for juveniles can be traced back to 1704 in Rome, where a center "for the correction and instruction of profligate youth" was established. Similar institutions were established in Germany and other countries during the first half of the nineteenth century.

A school for the children of adult criminals was established in London in 1788, and during the early nineteenth century schools were founded for neglected children. The Kingswood Reformatory was established in 1852 for "unruly children" who infested the streets of the new industrial towns of England. Following an investigation by the Society for the Prevention of Pauperism in New York City, the House of Refuge was established in 1825 as a special institution for juveniles. Several cities followed this step, and institutions for the care of delinquents were established.

Massachusetts established the first state institution for delinquent children in 1847. By 1900 there were 65 institutions for delinquents in the United States, including those under local public and private auspices. A Children's Bureau directory published in 1955 listed 183 public training schools in the United States. There were also estimated to be 133 private training schools. Some $55 million was spent between July, 1952, and June, 1958, by the state training schools.

The programs vary in the state institutions. Few do a treatment job. The Children's Bureau has described a well-rounded program of treatment as follows: "Making the relationship between the total environment and the child a crucial element of treatment does not discount the importance of special clinical services and program activities within the training school. On the contrary, it allows each aspect of institutional living to be viewed and used as a medium of treatment. Given the cli-

mate of treatment the acquisition of new attitudes and skills, medical and psychological services, educational and vocational curricula, cottage life and religious programs will change the child's concept of himself and the world he lives in. These special services or activities provide necessary preparation for subsequent adjustment to community living. But they mean little in the absence of that kind of environment which develops within the child the feeling that adults are there to help, understand, and to persuade—and not to punish. It is only in such a climate that growth and learning can take place" (9).

Private training schools have been established in most states, operated either by sectarian or nonsectarian groups. They are relatively limited in their accommodations and generally set a more rigid age limit and more restrictions on the types of delinquents whom they admit than do the publicly operated institutions. Most states either license or inspect these institutions yearly. The federal government uses some private institutions for the care of its juvenile prisoners. Some states pay the entire cost of operation, and in other instances the state and county share the cost or share it with a private group; there is no fixed pattern. Sometimes parents share some of the cost of care. In general, the private institutions are more treatment-oriented than the public ones but this is not always so.

Most state institutions are for either boys or girls, but in each of 11 states and 6 local jurisdictions there is 1 coeducational public institution. The Children's Bureau estimates that 45,000 children were placed in state training schools from October, 1952, to September, 1958, and that 72 percent of these were boys. Approximately 40 percent of the schools had a capacity of over 200 children each. The average length of stay was 10.8 months for boys and 15.5 months for girls. The average annual per capita cost was $1,985, with a range from $439 to $4,899.

Interesting recent developments include the introduction of specialized facilities in training schools to the end that they may function more as treatment centers. Some state institutions have followed the lead of the pioneering private institutions in making such changes. Considerable difference of opinion exists as to whether the training school should be a place for total psychological-milieu treatment, or a reeducative device

in which educational and corrective techniques prevail. Combinations of both ideas seem to be the most prevalent.

The development of forestry camps and small public institutions, such as the New Jersey Highfields institution, are new departures. The latter brought together a small group in a work program, with group discussion therapy as a treatment device. The project was characterized by short-term stay, staff participation in the work, planned research, simplicity of living conditions and daily life, and low cost, and was regarded as a successful experiment (10).

PROBATION

Probation services are the social services available to the juvenile courts. Probation department functions should, and in some communities do, include preliminary investigations and social study for presentation to the judge to help him arrive at a disposition decision, arrangements for detention or other temporary care pending final court disposition, and supervision of children placed on probation or under the supervision of the court. About 60 percent of all children who appear before the courts are placed on probation.

Practically all juvenile and domestic relations laws authorize the appointment of probation officers, generally by the courts themselves. Variation exists in states and communities in the use of probation officers for juveniles appearing in the courts. In some states only a few large cities or counties have a full-time paid probation officer. More than half the counties in the United States have no probation service for children.

Of the probation officers throughout the country in 1954 only 1 out of 10 had completed social work training and only 6 out of 10 had a college degree. Variations exist in salary standards and conditions. The National Probation and Parole Association has developed standards for probation and parole officers which in the main reflect the conviction that professional social work training is desirable, and has recommended the casework approach in the practice of probation.

The quality and nature of the probation supervision of children varies

greatly, depending on the qualifications and professional supervision of probation staff, the attitude of judges toward probation service, and the size of the caseloads. The National Probation and Parole Association is currently engaged in a series of studies which will bring national probation information up to date.

NONINSTITUTIONAL TREATMENTS

Some communities have developed institutions which offer clinical observation of children and report to the court. Child guidance clinics began originally because of public concern with juvenile delinquency. The first such clinic was started in connection with the juvenile court of Cook County, Illinois. The emphasis in child guidance has been away from the problem of delinquency over the years. Many clinics now do not deal with delinquency as such, and a number of courts as well as public departments have developed their own facilities.

There are a number of types of noninstitutional actions possible. Among these are: a court warning or admonition; placement in a foster home under the supervision of the court or a welfare agency; adoption, when feasible; increased supervision by school authorities; house arrest, which is rarely used; supervision by public child welfare casework agencies, usually in small communities where there are no separate probation services; supervision by nongovernmental child welfare agencies, such as societies for the prevention of delinquency in children. Most private social agencies have been reluctant to accept delinquent children after they have been to court. Supervision by police officers has been utilized in a number of places, particularly where there have been specialized police units. Restitution has been specifically authorized by statutes in some states, and federal law provides that a child may be required to make restitution. Fines ranging from $5 to $500 are provided by statutes in a few states. (The federal courts do not impose fines on juveniles.) Parents may be fined or punished for contributing to the delinquency of children, and in a number of states may be held responsible for damage done by their children.

RECENT DEVELOPMENTS

The 85th Congress considered legislation to deal with juvenile delinquency but despite considerable documentation, hearings, and Congressional studies, did not act on it. The 86th Congress considered a series of similar bills. The most popular would have set up "juvenile delinquency control projects" authorizing grants to public and private organizations and agencies, which would be utilized toward "discovering, developing, evaluating, or demonstrating techniques and practices for the prevention, diminution, and control of juvenile delinquency." Special training provisions were included in some bills. The testimony of many of the witnesses revealed that they believed in a broader approach such as was incorporated in the original delinquent children's bill of 1956. Compromises were made to accommodate points of view and arrive at a common denominator. The House and Senate Appropriations Committees of 1959 directed the National Institute of Mental Health and the U.S. Children's Bureau to do a thorough study of what is needed in the field of juvenile delinquency and make fiscal and legislative proposals to Congress in 1960.

As one reads Congressional testimony and examines federal appropriations there seems to be considerable overlap in the activities of the several agencies in the Department of Health, Education, and Welfare with respect to work in the field of delinquency. This is equally true in the mental health, child welfare, and correctional fields.

The National Council of Juvenile Court Judges has organized a juvenile court judges foundation for study and research in the field of juvenile delinquency and juvenile courts. Yearly training institutes are held at the Pittsburgh Juvenile Court, and several hundred judges have already come to receive special training.

Major advances at the federal level have been made in amendments to the Social Security Act. In 1956 Congress amended the act to give emphasis to social services in public assistance programs—services that lead to the strengthening of family life and that stimulate city and community efforts to help families and individual people with their social problems.

In 1957 the act was amended to extend child welfare services administered by the Children's Bureau to children in urban as well as in rural areas. As these help strengthen family life they will have an impact on services to children who are in danger of becoming delinquent. Emphasis on the social services in the public assistance program which will stimulate the states to improve their work with multi-problem families should help immeasurably in the solution of the delinquency problem over the years.

The Federal Office of Education has contracted with universities and colleges for research and studies on various aspects of juvenile delinquency in relation to education.

The National Defense Education Act, passed by the 85th Congress, sets up a nation-wide system of testing, counseling, and guidance which should have some effect on delinquency rates. The Administration proposal to the 86th Congress to help communities build new classrooms which would relieve overcrowding and present split-shift school hours is important.

The Public Health Service through its National Institute of Mental Health has been doing some important work in juvenile delinquency by developing a better basic understanding of the mechanisms of psychological development of human behavior. Throughout the country, $54 million was expended in 1958 for community mental health programs and 7.4 percent of this was federal funds. These clinics do some work with delinquent children. The training and research programs in the fields of mental health also have an effect on juvenile delinquency.

The Citizen Action Program of the National Probation and Parole Association, launched in 1955 by a five-year, $600,000 Ford Foundation grant, has had good effect in the eight states which established such programs. Each state council works with judges, bar associations, and correctional administrators to: examine and evaluate specific ways in which the state deals with the offender from first contact to disposition and treatment; recommend innovations and improvements, assigning each recommendation a priority according to its urgency; inform the public in every way it can, so that deficiencies are considered openly,

widely, realistically; and act to get public and private individuals and groups to work for the recommended improvements.

In Texas a citizens' committee was instrumental in the establishment of a paid parole system and continues to press for funds to expand the system to meet the needs of the state. In 1958 it began a study of the juvenile problem in Texas, a state almost devoid of county services for children in trouble with the law. In Oklahoma a citizens' committee was both shocked and embarrassed at the antiquated methods and facilities of its correctional system and has directed its efforts to legislative reforms, with the creation of a department of correction as a priority. In the various states the activity of an intelligent informed citizenry has been most helpful in the creation of an awareness of the problems that exist and the means or lack of means for meeting the problem.

The Interstate Compact on Juveniles developed by the Council of State Governments was adopted by 24 states by 1958 and 2 additional states were waiting for action by their governors. The chief use of the Compact has been for the out-of-state supervision of juvenile delinquents on probation or parole.

Very little use has been made of the Compact in returning nondelinquent juveniles or delinquent juveniles who run across state lines. The chief benefit of the Compact to date has been the acceptance by member states of the judgment that the out-of-state supervision of a child should be based on the validity of the treatment plan rather than upon residence requirements or the inclination of a particular community. The Compact administrators guide the actions of community agencies concerned with children crossing state lines.

The United Nations publishes reports dealing with juvenile delinquency in many countries. One, the Comparative Survey of Juvenile Delinquency in North America, was published in 1958.

The American Public Welfare Association (APWA), in testimony before the Subcommittee on Special Education of the House Committee on Education and Labor, said that more specific provision should be made for federal financial assistance to states for stimulating and supporting programs for the prevention of and control of juvenile delinquency.

The state welfare departments are declared by the APWA to be the agencies of state government in the most strategic position to provide the primary action within the state and to give the overall unified administrative direction essential to a fully effective program. The reasons given for this are: prevention and treatment of delinquency require a wide range of services; public welfare has an existing structure in every locality in the nation; public welfare agencies are already in touch with a large segment of the population that is highly exposed to conditions which make for juvenile delinquency; and the welfare departments are already deeply involved in community organizations in developing needed services for families and children.

The National Association of Social Workers at its Delegates Assembly in 1958 approved policy statements and published them as Goals of Public Social Policy. Included in these is a statement on juvenile delinquency which calls on communities and public welfare departments to provide: coordination by assuming a leadership in planning; experimentation in types of preventive service by encouraging social and health agencies to intensify their programs; treatment of those delinquents who remain in their own homes and of those who require a substitute arrangement, with emphasis on individual needs; law enforcement by encouraging and promoting good practices such as providing sufficient numbers of trained youth officers and policewomen who can help young people keep within the limits of the law; and conduct of juvenile and domestic relations courts in a way that will exemplify a concept of individual treatment and rehabilitation within the law. Such courts should be headed by qualified judges and should have social workers, physicians, psychiatrists, and proper detention and diagnostic facilities.

The Juvenile Delinquency Division of the U.S. Children's Bureau, Department of Health, Education, and Welfare, listed the following as important demonstration needs: intensive institutional treatment programs for psychopathic juvenile delinquents including the sexual deviant; effective clinical treatment programs for adolescent, recalcitrant girls; training of specialized personnel in law enforcement, probation, and juvenile court work; residential treatment centers for young, emotionally disturbed offenders involved in serious offenses such as arson, assault,

and habitual, ungovernable behavior in the community; and group foster homes and residential centers for returnees to institutions for the rehabilitation of delinquents (11). This Division, although inadequately financed, has developed an effective consultation service to states and has done a good deal to develop national standards and help set national direction.

The National Education Association conducted an extensive project in 1958 to 1959 culminating in a two-day conference where several basic and provocative documents on etiology and practice were reviewed (2).

Consistent with the trend to get at the cultural roots of problems, the 1960 White House Conference on Children and Youth adopted the theme: "Opportunities for Children and Youth to Realize Their Full Potential for a Creative Life in Freedom and Dignity." The 1950 Conference stimulated considerable new development in the field. Two new university-community efforts to conduct research, demonstration, and training programs in the area of youthful behavior are supported by the Ford Foundation. In the Youth Development Center at Syracuse University, New York, and Youth Studies Center at University of Southern California, faculty and citizen interest are combined in search of answers to prevention.

CONCLUSION

Several facts stand out in an analysis of local and state activity:

1. Local communities alone cannot finance prevention and treatment programs but require state financial assistance.

2. Programs for delinquent children are more and more being combined operationally with other programs for children, since basic needs of children requiring social and psychological services are seen as similar.

3. There is growing acceptance of a central diagnostic classification and placement function under administrative rather than judicial auspices. Central commitment by juvenile courts to state agencies is increasing.

4. Local preventive programs are emphasizing bringing professional services to the child and family rather than waiting for the breakdown

and subsequent application of police or court action. Social agencies and schools have increased their efforts, child welfare agencies are retooling their services to help delinquents in addition to dependent and neglected children, and dependency institutions are converting their programs to serve this group.

5. Citizen activity to prevent juvenile delinquency serves to strengthen all basic local services for children.

More accurate data and research techniques are required in order to provide sound public information and to stimulate citizens and agencies in developing programs which will extend and improve services to delinquent children. Evaluations of programs for prevention, control, and treatment cannot-be made without full knowledge of the nature and types, as well as the volume, of delinquency.

It continues to be clear that there are no firm answers to the problem of juvenile delinquency. These are being sought in the ills of family life, the increasing divorce rate, and larger numbers of the mentally ill. More search is being made in the adult-created culture. The general public continues to put the blame to some degree on what many describe as the innocent victim, the juvenile delinquent.

PORNOGRAPHY AND YOUTH

Herbert B. Warburton

FORMER PRESIDENT HOOVER recently called the "increasing moral slump" one of the six great crises facing the nation. He pointed to the soaring crime rate and public corruption as proof of this charge. Thus, once again, the charge which has been of concern to many individuals and organizations since the end of World War II was placed before the public.

No means exists for measuring the level of the nation's moral standard today as compared with ten or twenty years ago. However, measurement can be made of certain factors and conditions which generally are recognized as composing—for want of a better term—the "moral attitude," and their levels in various years can be compared. The rate of commission of known major crimes is one of these, and statistics upon this subject, collected and collated by the Federal Bureau of Investigation, are published from time to time.

President Hoover cited the increase in the rate of major known crimes in the 1946 to 1958 period as proof of his conclusion. He noted that this increase was three times as great as the rate of increase of the population. Significantly, he noted that the rate of commission of known crimes had increased 9 percent in the single year, 1958. Over 2,340,000 persons were arrested in that year for committing major known crimes. Statistics for 1959 are not yet available.

Herbert B. Warburton was formerly General Counsel, U.S. Post Office Department.

The alarming fact in these statistics, is that in 1958 over 12 percent of these 2,340,000 persons were under eighteen.

The juvenile delinquency rate has been rising for the past ten years. Commentators give various reasons for the high incidence of juvenile delinquency. Some say that the family attitude has changed, so that parental control and the influence of family discipline over the child have lessened. The substitution of the TV tray for the dining room table has been cited as a factor. Others blame inadequate educational resources that make it that much more difficult for teachers to exercise traditionally adequate influence and discipline.

Sociological factors have been blamed, such as the influx of Puerto Ricans into Harlem and related New York City areas coupled with the inability of our society to assimilate these citizens into the "Mainland" way-of-life—socially, culturally, and economically. It is maintained by others that our whole society is experiencing a condition of unrest, brought on by uncertain world conditions, and that our children react to this uncertainty by rebelling. The rebellion is against traditional or "accepted" routines and disciplines, and is manifested by the practicing of ultra-sophisticated or "exciting" activities. The rationale is stated to be that the previous generation has failed and has left nothing for the future.

The influence of pornography and obscenity upon our young people is also cited as a reason for the increase in the juvenile delinquency rate. In the minds of some observers, pornography and obscenity are coupled with television, radio, newspaper, and comic-book violence.

WHAT ARE PORNOGRAPHY AND OBSCENITY?

The dictionary defines pornography as "obscene or licentious writing or painting." It defines obscene as "offensive to chastity of mind or to modesty; expressing or presenting to the mind or view something that delicacy, purity, and decency forbid to be exposed; lewd, indecent."

Difficulty is encountered when the effort is made to determine if an apparently objectionable piece of material is obscene. The current legal

definition of obscene material is that it is "material which deals with sex in a manner appealing to the prurient interest."

Both the dictionary definition and the current legal definition of "obscene" possess the inherent defect of not conveying to every person the same concept. This is so for two main reasons. First, the viewer's reaction to obscene material is subjective. That which is obscene to one person may not be obscene to another. Second, the meaning of such words and phrases as "offensive to chastity of mind or to modesty," "lewd," "indecent," "appealing to the prurient interest," and the like, is not precise. In other words, they do not establish an objective standard which does not involve individual judgment.

It must first be understood, however, that there is one area within the whole subject which is so offensive that its material is recognized almost universally as being obscene and therefore legally actionable. This so-called "hardcore pornography" generally depicts, graphically or by words, the actual commission of sexual acts of either a natural or an unnatural kind. Since this type of material is easily identified and usually does not create any difficulty of definition, practically or legally, it will not be further discussed in any substantial detail.

Some examples may help to illustrate the uncertainty which prevails when a decision must be made as to whether material which is not "hardcore pornography" is or is not obscene.

Is a photograph which depicts a semi-nude or nude female model obscene? Many people feel that it is. Undoubtedly, an equal number feel that it is not. The expression of the courts is that mere nudity is not obscene; this means that such a photograph does not treat of sex in a manner appealing to the prurient interest.

But suppose that a so-called "men's magazine"—of which the volume is constantly increasing—devotes a substantial part of an issue, as is usual, to the reproduction of photographs, singly or in series, of semi-nude and nude models? Does this massing of such photos constitute obscenity? Apparently the court's attitude is in the negative.

Are "stag" movies which portray semi-nude or nude female models obscene? Again, the current answer appears to be in the negative. If

they are not, do they become obscene if the model performs a "strip tease"? Again the court's attitude appears to be against finding such material obscene.

These examples illustrate what is usually denoted as the "borderline" area of obscenity. It is with respect to this material that the greatest difficulty is encountered in determining whether it is or is not obscene. Certainly, it may be said that many persons object violently to this type of material being publicly available to anyone, and especially to juveniles, as it is via "men's magazines," nudist publications, "art" photos, and "stag" movies.

Aside from legal aspects there is the factor of the producer's motive. Frequently, his obvious and sole motive is to capitalize on curiosity concerning sex. This commercialization becomes highly specialized. Some producers, for example, cater only to those who have homosexual tendencies, or to those who are sadistically inclined. It is safe to say that there is material to appeal to every known sexual aberration, all of it available to the juvenile.

One further point is pertinent to this subject. A distinction should be made between material that is obscene (as difficult as the making of this identification currently appears to be) and material which is not obscene, but is crude, coarse, or vulgar, a degree of objectionableness which is considerably less than true obscenity presents. Failure to make this distinction imposes the danger that efforts to obstruct this type of material cannot be sustained in court, and such failures weaken efforts to obstruct or eliminate the dissemination of true obscenity.

The issue of obscenity is now in plain public view. In recent months considerable controversy has occurred, stemming primarily from the Post Office Department's effort to deny passage through the mails of the unexpurgated Grove Press edition of *Lady Chatterley's Lover,* in early 1959.

The issue which is involved is a constitutional one, namely, whether "obscenity is utterance within the area of protected speech and press" (1).

The difficulty, then, is in determining whether particular material is obscene. If it is not, it is entitled to the constitutional protection; if it is obscene, the protection is not available.

A brief examination of the law's treatment of this subject is both interesting and enlightening, particularly in view of the situation which appears to exist today, namely, that the courts, at least on the federal level, tend toward a liberal interpretation of the meaning of "obscene."

THE LEGAL BACKGROUND OF OBSCENITY

Prior to the nineteenth century, little specific legal effort was made to control obscenity. Apparently, it was grouped with such offenses against the public order as cursing and blasphemy.

In the United States the first federal statute was passed in 1842, although a few states had previously taken cognizance of the subject (2). The 1842 statute, aimed at confiscating pictorial material which was imported, contained no expressed definition as to what made particular material obscene. The decision was left to the judge and the jury. (This situation continued until 1957.) Thereafter, little federal attention was paid to the matter until 1865.

In England, Parliament enacted Lord Campbell's *Obscene Publications Act* in 1857 (3), which was directed against the circulation of any material deemed obscene. It furnished no definition of what constituted obscenity. In 1868, the Court of Queen's Bench decided the case of *Regina v. Hicklin* (4). This case represents the first real effort, legislative or judicial, to establish a standard against which alleged obscene material could be measured. Lord Cockburn enunciated a "test"—not a definition—as to what constituted obscenity. The question was whether the "tendency of the matter is to deprave and corrupt those whose minds are open to immoral influences and into whose hands a publication of this sort may fall." The criterion was, in effect, that the obscene character of suspected material was to be judged according to the effect it could have on the most susceptible members of society. This meant, in other words, that a book, for example, which might be judged innocuous in its effect on adults, could be judged obscene if it was believed that it could corrupt a child. But, in 1865, three years before the Hicklin decision, the United States had enacted, through a postal statute, a law on

obscenity which authorized the criminal prosecution of persons who furnished obscene material to Union soldiers (5).

In 1873, Anthony Comstock secured passage of the law which still bears his name—an all-inclusive antiobscenity measure which purported to regulate the importation, the distribution in the territories, and the transmittal through the mails, of obscene material (6). Portions of that act are the basis for the current criminal postal statute (7).

The "Comstock Law" followed the pattern of previous statutes in failing either to define or provide a test for obscenity. Its basic terminology, with respect to identifying the material which it was intended to cover, consists of repetitive adjectives of general import; i.e., "Every obscene, lewd, lascivious, or filthy book, pamphlet, picture, paper, letter, writing, print, or other publication of an indecent character."

Congress' failure to define obscenity in this statute left the courts to their own devices. The Hicklin test was applied indiscriminately for the purpose of judging the obscene nature of suspected material.

This was the situation until 1934, although Congress, in 1929, considered eliminating a provision in the Tariff Act which permitted the confiscation of obscene books which individuals attempted to import. While the ban was not completely lifted, Congress granted the Secretary of the Treasury latitude allowing him to authorize the importation of obscene classics and books of recognized and established literary or scientific merit, provided the importation was for noncommercial purposes (8).

In 1934, the *Ulysses* case was decided (9). This case was the first step toward the abolition of the Hicklin test which, in effect, found obscene "anything which (might) tend to corrupt, sexually, the corruptible" (10).

Ulysses involved the Bureau of Customs' efforts to deny the importation of Joyce's book. In effect, the case resulted in the establishment of a test for determining that material was obscene by measuring its total effect on the viewer, as a normal adult. Paul and Schwartz express this test as, "Will the work, judged as a whole and with regard to its artistic or educational purpose and merit, stimulate the 'lewd' thoughts or 'sexual feelings' in the normal adult reader?" (11).

Related to this test was the question of the community standard, which

Judge Learned Hand first injected into the question of obscenity in 1913 (12). In the Kennerley case, he said that the word obscene "indicates the present critical point between shame and candor at which the community may have arrived here and now."

The year 1957 marked a turning point in the legal history of obscenity. The U.S. Supreme Court ruled in a series of four cases, three of which involved the application of state criminal obscenity statutes and one of which involved a criminal prosecution under the federal postal statute—the so-called "Comstock Law."

The Court ruled first upon the Michigan obscenity statute in *Butler v. Michigan.* The statute incorporated, as its test for determining obscenity, almost the identical language which Lord Cockburn had advanced in the Hicklin case (13). The Court, by its invalidation of the statute, destroyed the concept that the obscenity of material depended upon its effect on the most susceptible viewer.

Thereafter, the Court heard argument on three further cases: *Alberts v. California* (14), *Kingsley Books, Inc. v. Brown* (15), and *Roth v. United States* (16). These statutes did not define what the term "obscenity" meant. The Supreme Court was divided in each of these cases. However, it sustained the validity of the one federal and two state statutes involved.

In the Roth case, the Court, through Justice Brennan, announced its definition of obscene material: "material which deals with sex in a manner appealing to prurient interest." The Court also stipulated the current test for judging obscenity to be "whether to the average person, applying contemporary community standards, the dominant theme of the material taken as a whole appeals to the prurient interest."

The importance of this case, in one respect, is that it expressed for the first time at that level both this definition and this test for obscenity. Its importance, in a second respect, is that the Court held firmly that "obscenity is not within the area of constitutionally protected speech or press." On this score it said:

All ideas having even the slightest redeeming social importance—unorthodox ideas, controversial ideas, even ideas hateful to the prevailing climate of opinion —have the full protection of the guaranties, unless excludable because they en-

croach upon the limited area of more important interests. But implicit in the history of the First Amendment is the rejection of obscenity as utterly without redeeming social importance.

This position engendered substantial controversy both within and without the Court. The controversy involved several points, all of which are important in relation to the treatment which *may* be accorded to obscene material in the future. Thus, it was contended, and the contention was overruled, that the definition and test are vague. Also, it was alleged that there is no federal power to regulate speech or its contents in order to protect morality within the intent of the First, Ninth, and Tenth amendments. A majority of the Court met this contention by reiterating that obscenity is not expression protected by the First Amendment. One justice could not support the position that written material which tends to stir sexual impulses can be found by this fact alone to be without redeeming social importance. Another justice concluded that there is no federal power to protect morality by regulating sexual expression, although such power may be exercised by the states subject to the regulation's being reasonable.

The only conclusion which can be safely drawn as to the effect which the Roth decision had on the position of obscenity is that, while it promulgated both a "current" definition of obscenity and a "current" test for determining what constitutes obscenity, it increased the uncertainty surrounding the subject. Furthermore, in today's context it indicated that the four minority members of the Court held serious doubts as to which sovereign—federal or state, if either—had power to regulate written sex expression to protect morality, and how such power, if it existed, should be exercised.

The fact of this added uncertainty was testified to in 1959, when the Court, *per curiam,* rejected the contention that two nudist publications, *Sunshine and Health,* and *Sun,* and a homosexual publication, *One,* were obscene. The apparent rationale is that such publications are constitutionally protected so long as they advocate a *bona fide* philosophy of life (17).

One remaining point in the Roth case is of the greatest importance to any group considering the effect which obscenity may have on juveniles.

That point is whether exposure to obscene material motivates misbehavior.

When the Circuit Court of Appeals considered the Roth matter (18), Judge Jerome Frank strongly dissented from the Court's affirmation of the defendant's conviction in District Court. He dissented because he concluded, after examining the very little bit of scientific evidence available, that no relationship between exposure to obscene material (and the lustful thought such exposure might generate) and motivation to misbehavior could be demonstrated. The Supreme Court found this contention irrelevant. In effect, it said that, since obscenity is utterly without redeeming social importance, it was immaterial whether it did or did not create a clear and present danger (of inciting misbehavior).

THE EFFECT OF OBSCENITY ON YOUTH

It is undeniable that recent years have seen a swelling volume of material which is objectionable to an exceedingly large group of citizens, even though it may be questionable whether any or all of it would be considered obscene under the current uncertain legal situation. This material consists of magazines, films, filmstrips and slides, novelty pieces, sets of photographs, and various other items whose number apparently is limited only by man's ingenuity. In the main, this material is easily available to any and all members of the public who desire to respond to advertisements carried in the more flamboyant publications. It is, further, a standard practice for the purveyors to secure and utilize mailing lists, school graduation annuals, and like sources to secure the names and addresses from which their own mailing lists can be made. Examination of the advertising columns of certain magazines also demonstrates that purveyors will aim advertisements for toys of various types at children and on another page advertise the sale of photographs of semi-nude and nude females; the connection is obvious.

The postal service has demonstrated, as an illustration of both the technique and the scope of this type of operation, that known purveyors

have deposited on a single day mailings of circulars advertising various types of these items in amounts exceeding 100,000 pieces. The addressees ranged throughout the population, and no effort was made to screen juveniles out of such mailings. The number of complaints to the postal service from parents and other persons against this traffic now stands at about 75,000 for the fiscal year 1959–60.

Basically, this type of operation is in the shoe-string category, and the opportunity for reward is staggering. One notorious operator testified that she invested a few thousand dollars to make sales of over a million dollars a year. Another operator, who specialized in photographic merchandise featuring sadistic subject matter, testified a few years ago that he grossed over $1.5 million annually.

Paul and Schwartz have stated very concisely the present puzzling status of the matter. They say:

The . . . description of recent federal experience (i.e., the difficulty of the Post Office Department in being able to meet every mailing of objectionable material) probably reflects, too, a good many of the problems confronting state and local law enforcement, for much of the "obscenity" which may flow into a community may flow in via channels which are beyond local policing. And all this suggests that our obscenity laws pose something of a dilemma. On the one hand restrictions have been and are being put upon interests protected by our "first freedom," particularly the freedom of adults to decide for themselves what they are to read. On the other hand businessmen, for money making purposes, are exploiting commercially various species of "speech" which, when disseminated on a mass scale to audiences recklessly solicited via methods deliberately calculated to whet one's appetite for salacity, may work social harms to be avoided—although the precise effect which "bad" sex expression works on persons exposed to it is unknown (19).

It must be baldly stated that there appears to have been no basic sociological or psychiatric research done upon the question of whether exposure to obscene, or otherwise objectionable, material leads to misbehavior.

Some psychiatrists hold the opinion that exposure to this type of material is certainly capable of influencing juveniles adversely, if not to the point of causing the commission of overt acts, at least to the point of fostering undesirable sexual tendencies. On the other hand, equally

competent psychiatrists maintain that exposure to such material may result in the juvenile's, or even the susceptible adult's, practicing masturbation, for example, with the further opinion that such result is socially beneficial because it provides a release and deters overt social misbehavior.

However, law enforcement authorities, including the Postal Inspection Service and the Federal Bureau of Investigation, are convinced of the validity of the premise that exposure can motivate overt sexual behavior. This conviction is based upon the number of instances in which apprehended violators of the law have been found with this type of material in their possession and have admitted that it influenced them to commit criminal acts of one sort or another.

Conceding the lack of research on the subject, it seems just as valid to conclude that this type of material can stimulate the commission of undesirable or antisocial acts and can have an adverse effect, particularly on the juvenile viewer, as it is to contend that, since we have no proof of harm, none has been done.

It is certain that there is no disagreement upon one fact. The purveyors of this type of material have only one objective—to commercialize upon sexual curiosity. The size of the business, estimated by some sources as $500 million a year, would indicate that they do so successfully. Their business methods, and particularly their lack of discrimination as to who their victims are, would also indicate that they have no concern about whether their merchandise can cause personal or social damage.

YOUTH AND THE AUTOMOBILE

Ross A. McFarland and Roland C. Moore

IT IS CERTAINLY OBVIOUS that the wide use of motor vehicles is one of the outstanding characteristics of modern life. In the United States, during the past fifty years, the automobile has developed from a rare and expensive luxury to a common necessity. Today the family car is so much an essential to our way of life that it is included in cost-of-living indices. A large proportion of jobholders are dependent on highway transportation for getting to work, either by bus or private car. For the movement of goods, trucks are a prime necessity. Our civilization is, indeed, based on the mobility provided by motor vehicles.

As one writer has said, "Most of us know or suspect how heavily our post war prosperity rests on the twin supports of new cars and new suburbs; in fact, the latter depends primarily on the former. The leisure life of these suburbs is nonlivable without the car, and the two-car garage is spreading even in the 'tract' houses of the mass-produced suburbs, freeing the wives for sociability, shopping, and chauffeuring children. In this connection, one should think not only of the new suburbs ringing the old cities but also of those parts of the country, such as California, which may be regarded as suburban to the urban East. The car not only enhances the freedom of people to move west and southwest (and to Florida) but helps shape the image of the good life

Ross A. McFarland is Professor of Environmental Health and Safety, School of Public Health, Harvard University and Director, Guggenheim Center for Aviation Health and Safety. Roland C. Moore is Associate in Industrial Psychology, School of Public Health, Harvard University.

which these suburban states symbolize, a life in which at work or play one always has one's car beside one as a potential escape mechanism" (1).

A few examples of the extent to which the use of automobiles and vehicular traffic has increased in modern times will help to delineate the magnitude of some of the problems which have accompanied this "progress." In 1958, automobiles, taxis, and trucks, operated by 82 million licensed drivers traveled some 665 billion miles on the highways in the United States. Drivers and passengers in automobiles and taxis alone accounted for more than a million millions of passenger miles of travel in that year. About one-fifth of this total was accomplished on turnpikes and toll highways alone (2). Or, to use another index, in 1950 there were approximately 40 million privately owned automobiles registered in the United States. At present, there are about 70 million; by 1970 this figure is expected to reach 90 million.

It is obvious that youths or young adults have both participated in and have been influenced by the use of the automobile in American culture. The attempt will be made here to review the role of the automobile in the cultural and behavioral patterns of young persons. Attention will be given especially to the problems of safety and we will outline and evaluate attempts to solve these problems.

NUMBER OF YOUTHFUL DRIVERS

One of the difficulties in arriving at an exact number of youthful drivers arises from the fact that different states set different minimum age requirements for legal operation of a motor car. Persons who have not passed their sixteenth birthday are regarded as too young to drive in 37 states, but in 2 states one needs to be only fourteen years old. Nine states permit driving at fifteen. On the other hand, one must be seventeen, eighteen, or twenty respectively to secure a license in 3 states (3).

Certain states also enforce various restrictions on young drivers. In Connecticut, for example, drivers under eighteen may not drive at night unless accompanied by an older licensed operator. In some states, only driving to or from school is permitted, certain insurance requirements must

be met, or driving is permitted only during certain hours or in certain areas (4).

The National Safety Council has estimated the age distribution of the driving population on a countrywide basis for the year 1958. This distribution is shown in Table 1 (2).

TABLE I. AGE DISTRIBUTION OF LICENSED DRIVERS IN THE U.S.

| | Licensed Drivers | |
| | Number | |
Age Group	(millions)	Percent
Total	82.0	100.0
Under 20	5.9	7.2
20–24	9.2	11.2
25–29	10.4	12.7
30–34	10.3	12.5
35–39	9.5	11.6
40–44	8.4	10.3
45–49	7.5	9.1
50–54	6.4	7.8
55–59	5.1	6.2
60–64	3.9	4.7
65–69	2.5	3.1
70–74	1.7	2.1
75 and above	1.2	1.5

From Table 1 it is apparent that about 18.5 percent of the licensed drivers in the U.S. are in the teenage or young adult (under twenty-four) age range. The figures do not, however, indicate the relative numbers of boys and girls and young men and women in these totals. It has been estimated that in the total driving population, males outnumber females by about 2.4 to 1. With regard to youthful drivers, however, the data are incomplete. Information from 2 states in recent years (Michigan, 1958, and Connecticut, 1955) indicates that licensed male drivers at sixteen are about three times as numerous as their female contemporaries (5, 6). By nineteen and twenty, females in increasing numbers obtain their licenses, so that the ratio between males and females at this age is about 1.6 to 1. If these figures are related to census data it would appear that by age nineteen, and on a national basis, about 4 or 5 out of every

6 boys and 2 or 3 girls out of 6 are licensed drivers. These ratios would, of course, vary somewhat from locality to locality.

With regard to the amount and kind of driving performed by young persons, there is very little factual information available. In general, it is known that the total mileage for young male drivers is several times greater than for their female counterparts. Furthermore, young males do more night driving than girls; also, especially in the late teen and early adult years, they do more of their driving at night as compared to older drivers. The implications of these observations for safety relate to the finding that accident rates at night are three times as bad as in the daytime.

One estimate on the amount of driving done by youth may be read from Table 2, which was prepared by the American Automobile Association.

TABLE 2. ESTIMATE OF AMOUNT OF DRIVING DONE

Age of Driver	Total Mileage (in percent)
15–17	1
18–20	4
21–24	10
25–44	58
45–64	24
65 and over	3

There seems to be a common belief that young drivers operate their cars at higher average speeds than do older drivers, but very little factual data are available. One study, covering vehicles operating in daylight on a rural highway, cites the highest average speeds for drivers under thirty, but does not break down the age classes within this group (7). Another study, in Iowa, was based on samplings of drivers on the road throughout the 24 hours of the day and night. It was observed that during daytime hours, youths under twenty comprised 6 percent of the drivers on the road, while from dark to midnight they comprised 14.8 percent and in the hours after midnight, 20.4 percent. In general, it was observed that higher average speeds were associated with the younger drivers, but density of traffic and age of car were also factors which were related to

speed. There was some indication in the data that about 10 percent of the drivers in their late teens and early twenties who drive late at night tend to operate at excessive speeds (8).

BEHAVIORAL AND CULTURAL IMPLICATIONS

Automobiles, besides providing transportation and mobility, often seem to serve additional individual needs or motivations of their owners or operators. The automobile, as a symbol of economic and social worth, has long provided its manufacturers a promotional approach based on the inner needs of prospective purchasers. A vicarious sense of power in the operation of a motor vehicle has also been cited as an important satisfaction in the lives of many who are denied outlet for such yearnings in other aspects of their lives.

For the adolescent and young adult the symbolic value of the automobile, beyond its basic functional use, may be of particular importance. To many it may represent freedom and escape from parental control and supervision. Also automobiles have become a factor of great importance in adolescent culture. For example, in many cities it is an accepted pattern that in order to date a girl, a boy must be able to provide a car for transportation; she may not go in a cab or allow herself and her date to be driven by parents (1). To many boys the car itself becomes a dominant motivating force. Having acquired a car for transportation, socialization, and dating, a boy becomes so involved in its care and upkeep he has little time or interest left for other activities (9).

One psychiatrist has expressed the view that driving an automobile is one aspect of contemporary life which makes it possible for persons to express hostility, discourtesy, and emotional conflict without too much fear of reprisal, and often with complete anonymity. In poor driving he sees a factor of revolt, expressed in a variety of adjustments used by the young driver (as well as others) to relieve him of ordinary restraints and to deny authority. Thus an aggressive person may show his revolt by such behavior as cutting in, stealing the right of way, or horn blasting. A youth who is oversensitive to the actions of others may react with "get even"

behavior, finding an excuse for racing and speeding, or employing obstructionist tactics towards other drivers. Or, in an attempt to prove his mastery of the situation and his maturity, the uncertain and insecure youth may race, stop with a screech, and overcompensate with show-off kinds of driving (10). Other writers have pointed out that the youthful driver may often use the automobile to "act out" the tensions and latent aggressions which arise from the increasing amount of social control which the teenager faces in many areas of his life (11). Thus, the desire for status, for escaping special situations, for isolation, for working off tensions, and the like, all may affect the individual's behavior as a driver.

The "Hot-Rodder"

A detailed analysis of young drivers has been made with regard to the so-called "hot-rodder." This study, carried out by psychiatrists, summarized the distinguishing features of 30 young "hot-rod" drivers (12). Additional studies of larger groups might alter some of the following generalizations, drawn from this study:

Physical characteristics: the majority are physically advanced and strong.

Background: their early history shows evidence of emotional deprivation with an ambivalent relationship to the mother. Most of the boys come from middle-class homes.

Interests: they show an interest in automobiles at an early age. At fourteen years old they want to drive a car. They do not participate in competitive sports, and are uninterested in reading. They have a low verbal ability compared to their mechanical ability.

Personality dynamics: they have aggressive temperaments which were probably manifested quite early in life. Rorschach responses and dream material indicate that they have oral-sadistic fantasies (a lion is going to eat me). There is also evidence of severe compulsive early training. They usually manifest two alternative moods—a mood of boredom and a stimulated mood that is attained on wild rides. Neither of these moods, however, is extreme enough to be classified as either depression or hypomania.

Perception of the automobile: the cases reveal that the automobile can

become part of the body image with the ego expanding to include the car. This gives the driver a feeling of megalomaniacal power and invulnerability. The present increasing tendency to give the car a non-feminine name is an indication of their expanded body image.

Accident experience: these drivers tend to be involved in few accidents. Although a self-destructive element can be seen in their behavior, the vitality, urge to live, and skill of the drivers pulls them through. The "near miss" is the important thrilling event.

Problems of School Adjustment, Social Adjustment, and Delinquency

Many educators have expressed concern over the competition which the automobile presents to an academic program, and hence to the schools' basic purpose of education. The view is commonly held that, among boys especially, the desire to get a driver's license and to own a car is probably the most powerful anti-intellectual force that our schools meet.

One study carried out in a California high school was concerned with this question, and the findings offer some support to the above views. In this study, those boys frequently driving to school were compared with those not driving to school in regard to several indices of school adjustment. While the findings are not considered solely a function of the automobile, the suggestive items are as follows: 1) dropout rate was about four times higher in the frequent-driving group than in the nondriving group; 2) absenteeism was approximately twice as great in the driving group; 3) grade point average, on the whole, was about one-half letter grade higher for the nondrivers, and 4) fewer courses were failed by the nondrivers (13).

Factual information relating to the role of the automobile in social adjustment of adolescents in other areas and in relation to delinquency is very scarce. Some examples of the opinions about this relationship are outlined below.

Various juvenile and adult courts, as well as enforcement officers, have pointed out that a large majority of those who are fifteen to eighteen years of age come to their attention either directly or indirectly as the result of the ownership or use of the motor vehicle. For example, offenses

peculiar to the operation of an automobile, such as stealing gas to keep the car on the road, are said to be very common (4).

One probation officer has outlined the social problems that arise out of adolescent driving: "For many, the clubhouse on wheels is a medium for holding a party, to get out from under the control of parents, for having dangerous 'drag' races, conducting gang meetings, committing a crime, or assaulting a girl. The list of problems resulting from driving is a long one: loss of control and supervision by a parent, increased temptations in the area of morals and liquor, giving up of school to work in order to operate and maintain that idol, the car, hoodlumism and bumming, crime, pseudo-sophistication and materialistic attitudes, and a false sense of values" (4).

ACCIDENTS AND MOTOR VEHICLE VIOLATIONS

One of the most serious problems in regard to youth and the automobile is the disproportionately high loss of life and the great number of injuries from motor vehicle accidents in this age group. Of 38,702 motor vehicle deaths in 1957, nearly one-fourth (8,667) were young persons between fifteen and twenty-four years of age (14). In addition, approximately 27,000 members of this age group received permanent impairments of one kind or another, and about 300,000 received injuries which were temporarily disabling.

Traffic deaths in this age group are of special importance since they cut short the most productive years of life. A better realization of the significance of traffic deaths, than is possible from their mere enumeration, may be gained from an estimate of the years of life which these individuals otherwise might have had. Using the life expectancy figures for persons at different ages, worked out by the U.S. Office of Vital Statistics in relation to the data for 1957 cited above, it can be estimated that a total of approximately 1,440,000 "life years" were lost in these fatal accidents during only one year. Deaths in the teenage-young adult group (fifteen to twenty-four) alone accounted for 500,000 of those "life years" lost, and if the victims younger than fifteen are included, the total for persons under twenty-five years of age reaches 800,000 "life years."

Accident Rates by Age of Driver

The evidence of the past few years indicates not only that youth is heavily involved in death and injury from motor vehicle accidents, but also that youthful drivers, as a group, are more frequently involved in accidents and show higher accident rates than would be expected on the basis of their numbers in the driving population. The results of two recent studies in Connecticut and Massachusetts, are shown in Figure 1. These data indicate that the highest rates are for the youngest drivers, those of age sixteen, which in these 2 states is the minimum age for licens-

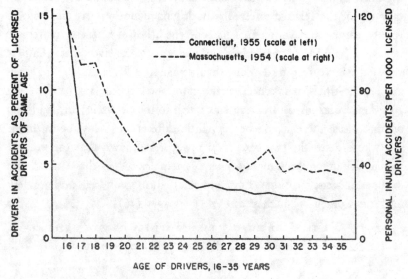

DRIVERS IN ACCIDENTS, AS PERCENT OF LICENSED DRIVERS OF SAME AGE

PERSONAL INJURY ACCIDENTS PER 1000 LICENSED DRIVERS

——— Connecticut, 1955 (scale at left)
– – – Massachusetts, 1954 (scale at right)

AGE OF DRIVERS, 16-35 YEARS

1. ACCIDENTS AMONG DRIVERS AGED 16 TO 35 IN CONNECTICUT AND MASSACHUSETTS.

ing. The rate decreases with succeeding years of age, rapidly at first, and then more slowly, so that at about age twenty-five to thirty the rate becomes lower than would be expected if age were of no significance. Another analysis of the Connecticut data shows a similar curve in relation to age of driver, when "found at fault" in accidents is the factor studied (15). There is also some evidence that in states where the youngest operators may drive only under restrictions, the highest accident rates are reached at about eighteen years.

The question whether there is a difference between youthful males and females in regard to motor vehicle accident rates is very difficult to answer because of differences in amounts and kinds of driving. Perhaps the most direct information comes from the Connecticut study mentioned earlier and summarized in Table 3 (6).

From this table, based only on the number of drivers and without reference to how much they drive, i.e., exposure to the possibility of accidents, it is clear that female drivers, in Connecticut at least, are far less frequently involved in accidents than males. The implications of such information are valuable to insurance companies in identifying high-risk groups and for criteria for adjusting premiums. As far as the question of the relative safety of the driving done by girls and boys or young women and young men is concerned, however, these figures are not very helpful, because they do not reflect the fact that youthful males drive a great deal more than females. If boys and young men drive three times as much as members of the opposite sex of the same age, they are exposed three times as much to the possibility of accidents; on that basis, there would be very little difference, if any, between the safety records of the two sexes. Moreover, it is known that the peak of annual driving mileage occurs later for females, when they are driving to supermarkets, to bridge clubs, and chauffeuring children, and accident rates for women are highest at these later ages (16).

TABLE 3. SIXTEEN- TO TWENTY-YEAR-OLD DRIVERS IN MOTOR VEHICLE ACCIDENTS OR ARRESTS, CONNECTICUT, JULY 1955 TO JUNE 1956

	Total Licensed		Percent of Age Group in Accidents		Percent of Age Group Arrested for Motor Vehicle Violations	
Age	Male	Female	Male	Female	Male	Female
16	2,306	853	38.2	17.5	31.1	4.0
17	8,716	3,832	14.1	5.2	28.9	2.5
18	12,106	6,239	10.1	3.4	24.1	2.5
19	12,133	6,925	9.4	3.3	23.8	2.1
20	12,575	7,486	9.2	2.9	21.8	2.4

The significance of the differences in violation records of teenage boy and girl drivers in the table may be questioned, and there are not enough

facts available for an answer. On the surface, the Connecticut data suggest that girl drivers conform to safety and motor vehicle regulations to a considerably greater extent than do the boys. One should keep in mind, however, that driving by girls may be more closely supervised by parents, that our culture tends to result in less nonconformity on the part of females, and nightdriving in this age group is largely a male prerogative.

Driving Errors Leading to Accidents by Age of Driver

Special research groups and state motor vehicle agencies have demonstrated relationships suggesting that a disproportionate number of teenage drivers are involved in certain particular aspects of accident patterns. Statistics compiled by the Ohio Department of Highway Safety show that teenagers were involved in 22 percent of all night accidents, as against 17 percent of day accidents. They were involved in 25 percent of the accidents occurring between 6 p.m. and midnight (17).

Reports of the frequency of single car accidents have indicated that these accidents are primarily problems of drivers under twenty-five years of age. The Annual Statistical Report of the California Highway Patrol for 1956, based on 150,000 drivers involved in approximately 88,000 accidents, demonstrated that for all ages combined, 3 out of 4 accidents involved other vehicles, with noncollisions, pedestrian, and fixed-object collisions next, in that order. An analysis of the accidents of drivers younger than twenty-five years old revealed that they had a proportionately higher frequency of single car accidents. These included noncollision accidents such as running off the roadway and overturning on the roadway, and fixed-object collisions (18).

Special single-car accident studies by the Wisconsin Motor Vehicle Department and Ohio State University have substantiated the California tabulations (19, 20). The Wisconsin study revealed that fatal off-the-road single car accidents among younger drivers were more predominant than all other types of fatal accidents, and were out of proportion to the number of drivers in that age group. Specifically, drivers under twenty were involved in 28.6 percent of all the fatal off-the-roadway accidents and in 16.4 percent of all the other fatal accidents, while they comprised only 8.6 percent of the driving population. Drivers from twenty-one to twenty-

five years old also had a disproportionately higher percentage of off-the-roadway accidents, but of a slightly lower magnitude than the teenage drivers.

A study of single-car accidents in Ohio in 1956 provided similar data. Furthermore, an analysis of the characteristics of drivers in these accidents indicates that the susceptibility of the younger ones may be due to inexperience. The study revealed that poor roadway features played a dominant role in off-the-roadway accidents for the sixteen- to nineteen-year-old drivers and for inexperienced drivers. Highway conditions such as poor pavement, narrow roadway widths, slippery pavements, and absence of centerline markings were significantly related to the single-car accident experience of these drivers. A study of personal injury accidents in Great Britain for the year 1953 also supports the view that inexperience is the major factor in teenage accidents. In this investigation the age of the driver was related to the errors considered to be primarily responsible for the accident. Errors which sharply differentiated the younger drivers from the others included "overtaking," "losing control," "swerving," "skidding," and "inexperience with type of vehicle in use at the time." Teenage drivers were also responsible for significantly more accidents where the driver was "asleep" or "fatigued" (21).

An analysis of California accidents in 1956 by age group revealed that 61.9 percent of the teenage drivers were considered at fault in the accidents. This percentage was the second highest for all the age groups and was exceeded only by drivers over 70. Speeding was considered the prime factor in the driver-at-fault accidents accounting for 44.4 percent of the teenage driver faults. The next important errors of teenage drivers were: failure to grant right of way, improper turning, and driving on the wrong side of the road. The accident involvement of teenage drivers because of these latter faults, however, was lower than in the case of older drivers. Excessive speed has also been demonstrated by the Vermont Motor Vehicle Department (17), as well as in Great Britain (21), as being the major cause of teenage driving accidents.

The data bearing on the frequency or severity of violations of the motor vehicle laws by youthful drivers are inconsistent. They do not permit any clear conclusions about whether youthful drivers are more or less likely to be arrested and reported for violations than are other drivers. The is-

sues are confused by different attitudes on the part of law enforcement offices towards youthful and adult offenders, differences in reporting practices, and differences in the severity of actions taken in different areas so that there are variations in the deterrents to violation. An example of the difficulties of interpretation is a study on the detection of speeders by radar. Of 419 arrests made on radar evidence during a four-month period, only 8, or less than 2 percent, were drivers under eighteen. The two interpretations suggested are that the young drivers may be responsible for fewer speed violations than their elders, or, as has been suggested, the young drivers may be more alert to the presence of police and do their speeding when or where they are less likely to be apprehended (4).

There is some suggestion that among youthful offenders, there is a group, ranging up to about one-third of all youthful offenders, who are repeatedly being apprehended for violations.

IMPLICATIONS OF THE HIGH ACCIDENT RATE OF YOUTHFUL DRIVERS

It is well known that the best scores on tests of physiological functions, sensory abilities, psychomotor coordination skills, and mental ability are made during the young adult period of life. Reaction times for example, are shortest, night vision and glare resistance are best, and the ability to learn coordinated skills is highest in the late teens and early twenties. Thus, evidence that accident rates among young drivers are disproportionately high presents the paradox that the driver is most susceptible to accidents at the time of his greatest potential operating skill. Hence "youthfulness" rather than age per se has been cited as the important factor. The factors underlying this "youthfulness" have usually been interpreted as inexperience, and various factors of immaturity and attitudes particularly characteristic of youth (22).

Experience

Since increasing age and increasing experience go hand in hand, it is almost impossible to separate the experience factor from the other concurrent changes which may be occurring on the basis of age, and to state

definitely how great the influence of inexperience may be in the safety record of young drivers. It is well known that in industry accidents are characteristically most frequent during the early phases of learning a new job or skill, and become fewer with increasing time on the job. It would be reasonable to assume that the same situation would prevail on the highway. Certainly, in the process of learning to drive, there are many accident-potential situations which are never encountered, and experience in handling such situations is not gained except during the course of acquiring further experience. One writer has pointed out that the judgment of traffic situations is perhaps the most important factor in whether or not an accident occurs, and developing this judgment in turn depends on actual experience on the road. This writer has also commented that the young driver may often operate with insufficient margins of safety simply because his experience has not yet been sufficient to appreciate completely the consequences of his actions in terms of the speeds with which emergency situations develop and his own limitations in regard to the time relationships and physical forces involved (23).

Training

Closely allied to the factor of experience is that of training. Adequate training has been shown to be a very important method of keeping accidents low in many different types of activity. In regard to highway safety, many studies have been made of the effectiveness of driver training. The results substantially show that drivers who have taken formal driver training tend to have fewer accidents and violations than do those who learned to drive in other ways. The results of a number of these studies are combined in Figure 2 (15).

Although it is clear that trained drivers initially have better records than the untrained, the studies so far made do not conclusively indicate that the better record is solely the effect of the training. The studies do not eliminate the possibility that those electing to take driver training may be those who would have better attitudes towards safety and be safer drivers anyway. Experimental evidence on this point has been entirely lacking until very recently. One study of teenage drivers, tested by psychological tests prior to their being old enough to learn to drive, has

indicated that those who later elected to take driver training were indeed different in respect to several personality traits and adjustment tendencies from those who later rejected driver training and learned to drive in other ways (24).

The latter point should not be interpreted as an indication that driver training has no beneficial effect. The control it can provide the driver

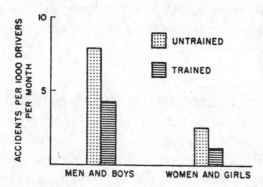

2. ACCIDENTS AMONG TRAINED AND UNTRAINED DRIVERS.
BASED ON 1,226 ACCIDENTS DURING 300,536 DRIVER-MONTHS.

and the development of attitudes appropriate for safe driving are in themselves justification for the program. More research needs to be carried out, however, on the content and methods of driver training, and the possibility of including training in the recognition and handling of emergency situations.

Attitude

A wide variety of sensory, psychomotor, psychological, and physical characteristics have been investigated in relation to the accident frequencies or accident rates of drivers and groups of drivers. Although highway accidents are usually attributed to human failure of some kind, close and invariable relationships between particular characteristics of drivers and the frequency of accidents have not been found. Some traits have been of importance in some accidents, but not in others. Thus far no single characteristic of drivers has been isolated which appears to be outstanding in accounting for a large proportion of accidents on the highway. Those attributes of drivers bearing a gross statistical relationship to

accident frequencies include low intelligence, youthfulness, and a personality make-up in which social responsibility is weak or lacking. As the evidence now stands it appears that attributes most likely to show a sufficiently high relationship to the safety of driving for an application in preventive measures probably relate to variables of personality and adjustment. Research emphasis in this area seems to be justified, especially efforts to develop better methods of assessing temperamental qualities, attitudes, and personal reactions. There is great urgency for studies emphasizing this approach (22).

THE ACCIDENT-REPEATER DRIVER

Most of the studies which have been carried out on relationships between personal and emotional adjustments or attitudes, and tendencies to have accidents, have been concerned with adult drivers. One of these is described below, however, since it resulted in a very promising concept concerning the adult accident-repeater, and one which may also be applicable in understanding the high accident rates among certain younger drivers.

In Canada, Tillman made an intensive psychiatric study of accident-repeater taxi drivers, and noted the frequency of various kinds of personal and social maladjustments, as compared with the personal histories of taxi drivers who were free from accidents. Of particular interest was the fact that the data included information on such items as school truancy and disciplinary incidents, juvenile court records, and disturbed family relationships.

Based on this, a thesis was developed that "a man drives as he lives"— that is, if he makes mistakes in adjustments to the personal and social demands of living he will make repeated errors in his driving. Undoubtedly this concept applies to youths and young adults and studies using this approach should be made.

The validity of this thesis was tested in an objective manner. The names of 96 accident-repeater drivers and two groups of 100 accident-free drivers, matched for driving experience and from the same geographic

region, were checked for a record of contact with a variety of judicial
and public-service agencies. These included the juvenile and adult courts
(non-traffic charges), credit and collection agencies, venereal disease and
public health clinics, and social service agencies. The results are shown
in Figure 3. Sixty-six percent of the repeaters were known to one or more
of these agencies, as compared with only 9 percent of the accident-free
drivers (25).

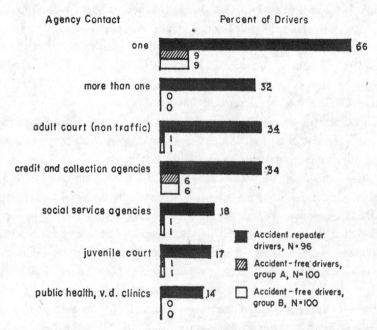

3. COMPARISON OF PERSONAL AND SOCIAL ADJUSTMENT OF ACCIDENT REPEAT-
ERS AND ACCIDENT-FREE DRIVERS

Two recent studies are of interest since they were concerned with persons in the military services and included large numbers in the early
adult age range. The first was an analysis of the off-duty, private motor
vehicle accidents at a large military base. Several interesting findings came
from this investigation. It was shown that, contrary to the widely held
opinion, off-duty accidents did not primarily involve servicemen driving
long distances on weekend passes. They occurred predominantly during
evening hours of freedom and in connection with short trips nearer the

base in quest of recreation and entertainment. The analysis also indicated that the personnel chiefly involved in the off-duty accidents were the young, low-ranking, unmarried servicemen living on base (26).

The second study was an intensive psychological, physiological, and psychiatric study of airmen, comparing those who had had motor vehicle accidents with their accident-free counterparts. It was found that of all the comparisons made, the one area where differences were consistently found, between those having accidents and those who were free of accidents, was in the field of personal values. Accident-prone drivers consistently tested lower on scales measuring religious values, and higher on scales of aesthetic and theoretical values. When this test was applied to other groups of airmen, the accident-prone drivers could be identified with an accuracy of 75 percent on this basis (27).

This study is now being extended to a long-range study of teenage drivers. The test of personal values, along with several other tests of personal adjustment and attitudes, was given to all the male sophomores in the high schools in and near Denver, prior to the time they were old enough to obtain a license. These students are being followed with respect to their subsequent driving records of accidents and violations for a period of at least three years. Their test scores and other data from school administrative records will then be analyzed with reference to their driving history to determine whether, on the basis of personal and attitudinal variables, those likely to have accidents can be identified ahead of time in order to apply preventive measures. Already, with an average driving experience now of about 17 months, 16 percent of these youths have sustained one or more major accidents for which they were responsible. With regard to violations, 4 percent have incurred two or more hazardous driving citations, and 7 percent have already had license suspensions as habitual violators.

It is only in recent years that systematic studies in this area have been undertaken which have been specifically directed toward the teenage driver. Some of these are not yet completed, and the results are not yet available. In one study which has been reported, two groups of students from various high schools in Pennsylvania were selected. The drivers in the first group had had two or more traffic accidents. Those in

the second group were chosen to match the individuals in the first group with respect to geographic location and length of driving experience, but had had no accidents. Both groups were given a standard psychological test of emotional and personal adjustment, and a Driver Attitude Inventory. The investigator found that the youthful drivers having accidents tended to score high, and those youths free of accidents tended to score low, with regard to each or a combination of several attitudes, as follows:

1. An attitude toward driving as activity which relieves psychic tension.

2. An attitude toward driving as a form of behavior by which youthfulness can be compensated and the role of an adult can be assured.

3. An attitude toward driving as a form of behavior in which confidence in one's ability can be manifested.

4. An attitude toward driving which does not consider speed an element of danger or, if it is considered as dangerous, an attitude manifesting desire for danger.

5. An attitude toward driving which places greater emphasis on the power of a vehicle than on its style or utility. On the personality tests it was found that the accident-prone youths showed more disregard of social mores and more defiance of authority and more of a tendency to excessive activity and enthusiasm (28).

On the basis of items in the various scales of this test, the investigator concluded that persons who had had the following experiences are more likely to manifest behavior which results in accidents.

1. A drive to leave home.

2. An urge to do something harmful or shocking.

3. A tendency to be influenced by people about them.

4. Association with peers to whom parents object.

5. A desire to frighten other individuals for the fun of it.

6. A tendency to become readily impatient with people.

7. A tendency to be somewhat suspicious of overfriendly people.

8. Prior trouble with the law.

A study carried out in Michigan involved the analysis of the case histories of 100 teenage drivers deemed the "poorest drivers" by their driving instructor. Unfortunately, no comparisons were made with "good"

or "best" drivers in this investigation, so the interpretation of the results is limited. The investigator observed that four-fifths of these students were working below their level of ability in school, two-thirds were discipline problems in school, three-fourths had poor relationships with their teachers, and half were considered aggressive. He also collected information on the family relationships of these students and on their driving habits. There was a large amount of family disruption in this group, and they tended to have driving habits characterized by show-off behavior, reckless driving, and habitual speeding. He concluded that these problem drivers either do not learn rapidly enough to accept responsibility, or have strong antisocial urges and unstable personalities, and thus will accept little or no responsibility. He suggests that maladjustment may be expressed in driving habits; an extreme need for recognition may lead to reckless driving; feelings of escape may be manifested in excessive speeds; and active hostilities toward control may be expressed through rejection of the responsibilities involved in driving and disregard for the social controls of traffic rules and regulations (29).

CORRECTIVE AND PREVENTIVE MEASURES

Various programs and procedures have been developed in attempts to reduce accidents and improve safety on the highway. Those which are of particular relevance to the improvement of driving and of safety among teenagers and young adults can be roughly grouped as follows: 1) safety education and driver-training programs; 2) youth safety conferences and driving clubs; 3) driver clinics and retraining schools for violators and accident drivers, court actions, and penalties; 4) administrative policies of motor vehicle departments centering about control over the license privilege.

The influence of driver-training programs on accident frequencies and on violations has already been discussed. It is apparent that much remains to be done in the way of research aimed toward the improvement of driver training, particularly with reference to what is most important to teach and the most effective methods of teaching. It appears that classroom training plus supervised behind-the-wheel practice is more effec-

tive than classroom teaching alone and unsupervised practice (30). The possible role of synthetic trainers and simulators is now being explored. It seems likely that if training in more aspects of traffic situations can be provided through such aids, the results would be reflected in improved driving on the highway. The teaching of driving techniques to prevent or control skids, for example, or to take evasive action in rapidly developing emergency situations, could be more systematically developed than at present.

Apart from the many studies which have been carried out to measure the influence of driver training on safety and violation rates, there have been very few adequately designed investigations to test the influence of preventive and corrective measures. As has been pointed out by various writers in the safety field, the effects of safety campaigns and propaganda, and various court and administrative practices are largely unknown, not only in regard to younger drivers, but also for their elders. Some statistics have been presented to suggest an improved performance on the part of those violators and accident drivers who have attended driver clinics and retraining schools. Most of these studies, however, entail technical weaknesses which render the findings inconclusive. There is also very little evidence available about the relative effectiveness of various actions taken by judicial or administrative authorities.

One study (which included both young and adult violators) was the analysis of the accident records prior and subsequent to the re-examination of some 4,000 drivers with poor driving records. The conclusion was reached that in general, when pre-examination records were not heavily weighted by the more serious offenses, educative and persuasive procedures were more effective than more drastic actions. If pre-examination records were extremely poor, no type of action seemed more effective than any other (31).

One study (which for obvious purposes should not be identified while in progress) is currently being carried out on a group of several thousand teenage drivers. The purpose of this experiment is to test the influence of various kinds of corrective procedures on subsequent driving habits and accident and violation experiences. Some of the procedures being compared are: 1) participation in special group discussions designed to clarify and improve driving attitudes; 2) attendance at standard traf-

fic violator schools and driver clinics; 3) fines, probation, and other court actions; and 4) administrative actions, such as withholding licenses.

Several procedures which are being tried or proposed for the improvement of youthful driving and safety emphasize: 1) the extension of driver training to all youth of high school age; 2) the improvement of driver training; and 3) a greater emphasis on rehabilitation and educational procedures in the disposition of cases made by courts and administrative agencies. It has been proposed that driver education must be directed nót just to impart knowledge of good driving techniques and traffic laws or to develop the physical skills required to operate the car. Developing attitudes which will insure safe driving will require special instruction beyond stressing the importance of attitudes. Procedures should be developed to help young drivers to understand their attitudes towards driving in a therapeutic sense and to aid them in solving personal problems (32).

The importance of having young persons themselves participate in efforts for the improvement of safety in driving habits has also been recognized. Several Youth Highway Safety Conferences have been held on a statewide basis under the sponsorship of state and civic organizations. No systematic evaluations of the effectiveness of these conferences have, as yet, been made.

Mention should also be made of those driving clubs and "hot-rod" organizations sponsored by civic groups or individuals. Such sponsorship is believed by many to be an important factor in eliminating hazardous driving from the highway (4).

Several recent proposals are focused on control over the license privilege as a means of enforcing good driving and safety. Many administrators believe that the threat of the loss of one's license is a greater deterrent than are fines or other penalties. In most states the motor vehicle administrator has discretionary power to suspend the license, and the current trend seems to be toward an increase in the exercise of this power in regard to the teenage group. In this connection, some states are now considering the first license to be a probationary one, to be held and replaced by a permanent license only through the demonstration, on the part of the licensee, of a satisfactory driving record.

At present there is an active controversy about whether safety records can be improved through raising the minimum age for licensing. Current opinion seems to be that requiring a minimum age of more than sixteen years might well introduce more difficulties than would be solved. Perhaps the most serious drawback to a minimum age of eighteen would be that the high school driver-training programs would then be available only to a few students who are older than the average (4).

SUMMARY

In this presentation an attempt has been made to indicate the role of the automobile in American culture, with particular reference to adolescents and young adults. It was shown that the vast majority of young persons in the United States have become drivers during their late teens. The influence of the automobile on the behavioral and cultural patterns of youth was reviewed.

Problem areas related to the use of the automobile included school adjustment, social adjustment, and delinquency. The data on automobile accidents showed a high incidence of injuries and deaths in the younger age ranges. Youthful drivers as a group were also shown to have disproportionately high accident rates. Causes of the high accident rates in youth have usually been given as inexperience and lack of training, but in recent years there has been growing evidence of the influence of attitudes and personal adjustments on driving behavior.

Several studies of adult and youthful accident-repeaters were reviewed for their implications regarding the improvement of the safety record, and especially the quality of driving by the teenage group. It was also pointed out that there is very little information available on the effectiveness of the various measures employed in an attempt to improve safety. The need for research to supply factual information was stressed throughout. Such factual information is required for the design of effective educative, corrective, and rehabilitative measures in regard to the use of the automobile by youth.

INTERGROUP RELATIONS

Hilda Taba

INTERGROUP RELATIONS have been and continue to be an important issue in American life and American education. In many ways Myrdal's dramatic statement that the problem of race relations in our country represents the "vast and ugly reality of our greatest failure" still holds, even though much progress has been made since his study. For educators and for community workers the improvement of group relations still remains a major task, and for several reasons.

First, the improvement of human relations among the various cultural groups in our society is essential to preserving and extending democracy, to promoting a way of life which maximizes human worth, and to minimizing conflict, tensions, isolation, and inequality. It is as important today as it has ever been to square our treatment of minority groups with our professed democratic ideals.

Second, the quality of intergroup relations at home is a mirror against which our efforts as a nation abroad are measured. It is difficult to hold up the image of democracy to the newly developing nations if this image is marred by cleavages and prejudices and by the denial of human and economic citizenship to certain groups in our own society. The effectiveness of our leadership in the other parts of the world depends in no small measure on the quality of the group relations we can demonstrate at home.

Third, the current emphasis on the cultivation and preservation of tal-

Hilda Taba is Professor of Education and Associate Chairman, Division of Education, San Francisco State College.

ent and excellence in the human material, in order to preserve and enhance economic strength and cultural vigor, makes it mandatory to study the corrosive factors which prevent or block the fullest development of the potential in all individuals everywhere, and to eliminate them wherever possible. These corrosive factors are not limited to cleavages and tensions in community life. They include also all practices in our communities and schools which limit access to the opportunities to develop potentiality, to develop a cultivated mind, to achieve an articulated citizenship and a healthy self-respect.

As one reviews the current scene, one finds different levels of perception of what intergroup relations mean, what problems are crucial, and especially what causes them. The programs of education and action, either actual or proposed, usually correspond to those levels of perception. They are either more or less mature, depending on the maturity of the perception that underlies them.

THE RACIAL CONFLICT

The simplest and the least mature perception is that which equates the problems of intergroup relations with overt conflict on racial grounds.

The racial conflict, of course, is also nationally the most difficult one. However, this level of perception leads only to the type of program of improvement which involves trouble-shooting or legislative measures to control public conduct. It does not provide a platform for education or for preventive measures, both highly necessary. It also permits many communities and school systems to assume that they need no program of improvement in intergroup relations because they either have no minority groups or because on the surface these minorities live together amicably. School administrators and community workers whose perception of intergroup problems is on this level even insist that a closer analysis of intergroup relations problems is dangerous, because it engenders conflict: let the sleeping dogs lie.

As the thinking on intergroup relations becomes more sophisticated, the

assessment of "problems" changes also, and with it the perspective of what needs to be done. A more sophisticated emphasis on intergroup relations includes interreligious, interclass, and interage relationships. The problems attacked and studied include not only the phenomena of overt conflict and discrimination, but also those of covert prejudice, rejection, fear of differences, lack of communication, participation in community life, and ethnocentricity in judgment.

For example, many studies have documented the fact that minority status is connected with low socioeconomic status, especially in the case of the racial minorities, and that the characteristics and behavior which in naive view appear to be racial, are actually generated by the lower class conditions and style of life. Therefore, many of the difficulties regarding integration of Negroes, Puerto Ricans, and Mexican Americans are encountered not solely because of racial or ethnic differences, but also because a large number among these groups carry a rural or a lower class cultural pattern, and it is these behavior patterns rather than the racial and ethnic backgrounds that are the objects of rejection, suspicion, and discrimination. Scarcely anyone today is unaware that the differences in socioeconomic status not only intensify racial feelings, but also produce cleavages and create prejudices on their own.

Anthropological and psychological studies have enlarged the perspective on intergroup relations still further by throwing light on the genesis of the attitudes which operate in intergroup relations. One useful concept is that of cultural or social learning. According to this concept many of the attitudes and behavior patterns which are crucial in intergroup relations are learned: individuals *learn* to resort to overt aggression as a way of solving conflicts, just as they *learn* to regard themselves as either capable or incompetent, to fear differences or to see them as enriching possibilities, and so on. Individuals learn these things according to a style of life which surrounds them in their families and neighborhoods.

Viewed from this angle, improvement in intergroup relations could be brought about by the development of a broader and a more cosmopolitan sensitivity on the one hand, and by providing opportunities for overcoming culturally induced handicaps on the other. Instead of berating preju-

dice, it would seem important to change social conditions in order to immobilize prejudice, while at the same time providing laboratories for democratic interaction in order to change attitudes.

INTERGROUP RELATIONS IN EDUCATION

The material in this section is based on a survey. The survey was conducted by the author for a working paper in a seminar on the status of intergroup education, held under the auspices of the American Jewish Committee, January 1960. The survey contained samples from the following: 1) an elementary and a high school district with Mexican-American population in southern California; 2) a large Eastern industrial city with a large minority population; 3) a Midwestern city with a stable minority population; 4) a large recently desegregated border city; 5) a Northwestern city with no pressing minority problems; 6) seven suburban areas, two near an Eastern city with a large minority population, one near a Midwestern city, and the rest were around a Northwestern city with an incipient minority population.

School personnel were asked: 1) what they consider to be the current status of intergroup education; 2) what new problems they are experiencing; 3) how intergroup relations materials appear in teacher training; and 4) what they would like to do if they are given a free hand. The perception of the problem of intergroup relations depends in a large extent on the perspective of the viewer. However, among the multitude of problems, ranging from difficulties surrounding the celebration of Christmas in schools to the conflicts raised by desegregation, a few stand out as common perceptions.

THE EXTENSION OF DE FACTO SEGREGATION

Currently a new area of stress is created by the new migration of minorities within the urban areas: from slums into residential areas of the city and from the city into suburbs. For example, in many large cities the Negro population is extending into formerly white residential areas

of the city. This phenomenon is at once a fruit of the new openness in economic status and in housing facilities, and a source of new problems.

First, new transition areas are created, that is, areas which are changing from all white to all Negro. These areas are beset with the same problems which used to characterize neighborhoods adjacent to slums. In cities in which urban renewal is in progress, this movement has an added momentum, because the destruction of slum dwellings creates new pressures on dispersion of minority population. Usually a great deal of misunderstanding, cleavage, and resentment attends this process, especially when relocation is not well planned and prepared for, or even sufficiently understood. Continued in-migration compounds the racial problems with those of socioeconomic class differences. The new neighborhoods combine not only the newcomers from rural areas with the older residents, but families of low economic status with those of higher income, better education, and greater "acculturation" to the city life.

Many middle-income white families are moving to suburban areas in large numbers, areas usually not available to nonwhite families. The out-migration process often occurs extremely rapidly when Negroes move into an urban neighborhood which was formerly all white. This situation creates a whole series of new problems. One of these is the extension of *de facto* segregation in schools.

The cities which have undergone a fairly successful desegregation (such as St. Louis and Wilmington), are facing a spread of *de facto* segregation. Schools which only a few years ago were completely white or mixed are now nearly 100 percent Negro or Spanish American. While some effort is made to block this segregation, both the community agencies and the schools are baffled by this spread of residential segregation due to the flight of white population, and can do little more than watch it. Nor is this phenomenon limited to special transition areas in large cities with a large Negro, Puerto Rican, or Mexican population. The movement is perceptible also in smaller cities, though not yet on a serious scale.

Tensions are all the sharper because they involve no longer the voiceless immigrants from rural areas, but families "who are on their way up," who know what they are about, and who, therefore, make demands on the schools and the community agencies.

Organized minority groups are more articulate about their lack of opportunities and privileges than in the past. They are less and less willing to accept a role of inferiority in the life of the community. They have high and informed expectations regarding services they need and their role in the community. This "aggressiveness" is resented by some school and community people and interpreted by others as an expression of insecurity. Whatever the real or imputed causes of misunderstanding, the newcomers threaten the aspiring parents in school communities, and the prejudices of the old residents, which include business groups and service as well as social clubs, are aroused.

Both schools and community agencies are unprepared to deal with these new problems, or with the old ones on a new scale. The new transition areas often lack the amount or the type of social services that the new population needs. The large cities, for example, face the problem of extending the work of social agencies to schools in areas which formerly did not require them.

Teacher placement is a cause for friction in many areas. While teachers from minority groups are hired with a greater frequency than before, the practice still persists of assigning them to schools with a large minority student body, and this practice pleases neither the white nor the Negro parents. The practice of placing the least capable or the newest teachers in the most difficult areas still persists and leads to high turnover of personnel. It creates the problem of teacher and pupil transfer. Policies on drawing school district lines are affected also. In some communities, for example, the majority of parents want new schools placed so that the newcomers will be concentrated in one school, while organizations such as the NAACP want the minority students scattered throughout the city, even if it involves transporting a large number of children. In some instances such transporting is resorted to as a deliberate measure to avoid complete segregation. At any rate, to the extent that the "minority" schools are identified as ones with the least competent staff and the most problems, it is natural that both parents and teachers regard assignment to these schools as discrimination.

In mixed communities friction is further intensified by a lack of communication between the different factions, whether socioeconomic or ra-

cial. Schools report difficulties about achieving a balanced participation in the PTA membership and difficulties about explaining the school's program to parents in the minority groups.

Intergroup agencies find it difficult to generate a balanced participation in solving community problems, partly because of the resistance of the dominant group to including minority members, and partly because of the failure of the minority group members to respond to situations involving community problems. Evidently, while the possibility of participation is more open, as yet there are no effective techniques of inducing mixed participation.

The teachers who face this new student population and the new problems are largely unprepared. Success stories about desegregation were possible because a fairly intensive orientation preceded the official act of desegregation. The teachers in the new conflict areas have no systematic preparation. They attack symptoms rather than causes, because they do not understand the cultural conditioning of behavior. They are appalled by behavior which may be new to them, such as talking back, resentment of control, aggressiveness, lack of good work habits, and poor motivation.

Since the transition is taking place in the general atmosphere of stressing ability and achievement, teachers are even more upset by the low level of ability and achievement. The general tenor in schools makes the lack of achievement on the part of the newcomers more startling, and the exercising of pressures for achievement more mandatory. By insisting on high standards of achievement and conduct, without understanding the psychological and social causes for the deficiencies, these teachers add fuel to the fire. All of which forms a vicious circle of hostilities, misunderstandings, and tensions.

The reactions to this vicious circle vary, depending on the level of perception of the problems and the orientation. The less sophisticated cannot accept the fact of low level of achievement. They either try their best to keep up the standards by whatever means, including physical punishment, or else they give up and say, in effect, what one Negro teacher said: "You can't do anything with a dish like that."

Those who are sympathetic or dedicated make an extra effort to help these youngsters achieve through individual instruction. But these efforts

leave them defeated, tired, and frustrated. Those who have had sufficient training see the whole problem as that of differences in cultural values, and in patterns of acculturation. They understand that these lower-class children suffer from low motivation and self-expectation because of their cultural conditioning. Consequently, they feel duty bound to challenge ability, to help these youngsters to "acquire enough of a common culture to live together with the whites as good citizens."

Even the most dedicated and understanding teachers find it difficult to accept children who fail to understand the critical role of cultural advantages offered by education. They are surprised and discouraged that these students do not easily live up to their new role—that of living in a community which offers them vastly expanding opportunities.

Ten years ago to be a Negro or a Mexican made one an object of rejection. Now the focus of rejection, in schools at least, seems to lie in low achievement. This, of course, reflects the improvement of attitudes towards minorities, as well as the change in the tenor or educational outlook in the country.

It must be pointed out that segregation in schools is not now, and never has been, a Southern monopoly. As Dodson points out, many forms of segregation occur in the North. We segregate in schools because residential living is segregated and because various neighborhoods are zoned for segregation. We segregate in school programs by ability grouping, and we segregate by ignoring students (1).

There is evidence that much progress has been made in integrating teaching staffs: more schools have mixed staffs, Negro teachers are more frequently placed in all white schools, and more Negro teachers hold high school, supervisory, and administrative positions.

Paradoxically, though, while desegregation is a legal fact—an actuality in many border cities, and a token act in many areas of the South—integration seems to be on the way out. The phenomenon of the spread of de facto segregation in cities that presumably have been desegregated successfully has already been mentioned.

To bring about integration in the mixed schools is an extremely difficult task. Desegregation was a dramatic gesture in many border cities, and as such commanded united effort and goodwill. School systems which

had had training and experimentation in intergroup relations accomplished desegregation with a degree of aplomb. In St. Louis, for example, during the desegregation the whole community joined in a united action, which left the schools free to deal with technical matters. The new problems of integration are less dramatic and it is more difficult to mobilize the effort for them. It has also been hard to face the unpleasant reality that desegregation, instead of solving all problems, has created many new ones.

In the newly desegregated cities the good behavior shown in the initial stages of desegregation soon wore off, and hostilities have appeared because the expected integration did not take place. The Negro community groups, helpful and patient before, now are beginning to accuse schools of discrimination because they fail to stem the widening *de facto* segregation. Even the actual steps forward, such as the hiring of Negroes in administrative positions, have their negative consequences, because the act of hiring has not been followed through with other integrating moves: these new administrators are assigned to the so-called Negro schools. In one city, for example, the Negro principals feel more hemmed in because now they work almost exclusively with a Negro administrator and thus feel cut off from the white staff.

Hostilities and other difficulties are increasing in schools also, seemingly partly as a consequence of the community turmoil, and partly as a reaction to pressures for achievement and for the middle-class standards of conduct. Grouping according to ability has generated a rejection of the less able and an intensified competition, which adversely affects relations between teachers and children, teacher and teacher, teachers and administration. One principal reports, for example, that a group of "talented" minority students deliberately made poor grades in order to "return to the anonymity of their former group," because they feel out of place in the accelerated group.

Integration as an educational policy involves steps that go further than simply putting students from different cultural backgrounds under the same roof. It involves, first of all, a careful study of the difficulties and the problems to discover their psychological and social causes. Among the many reports of the procedures of desegregation, only one school

system in southern California indicated that a systematic effort has been made to analyze the causes underlying the rejection of the newcomers by the majority students, and the presumably "aggressive behavior" among the minority students. This school system not only studied the records of their minority students, but also analyzed the leadership patterns and studied interaction in clubs and activities.

Secondly, integration means adjustments and changes in the nature of curriculum offerings. In schools in which group relations problems prevail, it would also be important to introduce materials throughout the curriculum which are helpful to the development of a broad, cosmopolitan, cultural sensitivity, and to the development of adequate social skills for dealing with cultural differences. Some offerings may be addressed to filling the gaps in home training, such as discussion of personal grooming, of methods of coping with interpersonal problems and cleavages, and of ways that are helpful in dealing with developmental tasks. It is also necessary to study the psychological phenomena and processes which underlie intergroup relations to develop rational understanding of and effective solutions to these problems. Above all, to "take in the minority students," the materials of curriculum need to reflect the fact that they too are part of the mainstream of American life.

Integration means minority group participation and interaction with the majority group: the minority must be able to participate in school life and activities, and have a share in the leadership roles and there must be interaction among the groups in the classroom (2).

And finally, integration means that many minority students must undergo a severe process of acculturation. In entering a school dominated by white middle-class standards, those who have been deprived must learn new habits, behaviors, and values. The greater the distance between the requirements for conduct and achievement, the style of life, values and skills required in school, and the social learning of the children from their own culture, the more severe are acculturation problems. A successful integration therefore involves providing appropriate pacing of expectation and ego support during the process.

These are demands which are difficult for schools to fulfill, especially in a period when the importance of social education has the lowest value

among the educational objectives, and when the importance of developmental learning and of building readiness as a principle of good learning seems to have been repudiated. Education for all American youth seems to have been replaced by education for "the able and willing only." Unfortunately, many minority youth cannot demonstrate their place either among the able or the willing without special help.

IMPLICATIONS OF GROUPING ACCORDING TO ABILITY

On the surface the stress on achievement and grouping according to ability is a far cry from problems of intergroup relations. Actually, according to many accounts, the problems of integration and of intergroup relations are greatly affected by the difficulties generated by the current policies of serving "the able and willing" first.

Reactions to grouping according to ability as a way of fostering excellence vary sharply. Some view it as a new opportunity for individualization of instruction and even as a boon to students from minority backgrounds. Others consider ability grouping as a measure which inadvertently reintroduces and reinforces in school a pattern of segregation prevailing in the community. Research points out, for example, that generally under present conditions minority group children have a higher incidence of low IQ. Ability grouping in schools, therefore, segregates the minority groups from those of the majority culture. Assuming that the social and cultural learning is accomplished by contact and interaction, such grouping closes the gates for acculturation in our schools. According to some it introduces an educational caste system, adds to the army of neglected talent, and serves to extend segregation (3).

The validity of the concept of the intellect and of the intelligence tests on which the grouping is based is also subject to question. Empirical and research evidence suggests that the current intelligence tests measure only a limited range of abilities and are culturally biased, and that the concept of static intelligence has prevented us from considering the role of cultural impact on the development of functioning ability. If these limited measures are used to fix the position of children as either slow or fast

learners, the schools not only cease to be the means for supplementing cultural deprivation, but reproduce within their own walls the very conditions of inequity of exposure to learning which cause the differences in the first place.

This issue becomes especially sharp when one considers that the cultural environment affects not only the shaping of the native potential, but also the motivation to learn and the mental system with which students approach learning problems and tasks. Research points out vast cultural differences in mental and motivational systems, Frustration is encountered in part because of the lag between knowledge and practice. Teachers tend to use motivational devices which are ineffective with the lower-class minority children (4). Minority children, therefore, suffer a double handicap: the lack of cultural advantages at home and the inappropriate methods, materials, and motivational devices used at school.

Ability grouping is also reported by many as having a destructive effect on the general climate of human relations and on good education. Many observers see the emergence of a new group of "have nots," namely the "dummies," and a new cleavage between the "dummies" and "the brains," in which context the minority status is underscored with an increasing force. Rejection of nonachievers is increasing, and this rejection falls more heavily on the shoulders of minority children. The stress on acceleration of achievement, namely "teaching this year what should be taught the next," makes many teachers resent the slow learners, whatever the causes of their slowness.

And finally, ability grouping creates an atmosphere of competition among students, teachers, parents, and schools, which is detrimental to human relations all the way round. Several school systems report new difficulties with parents who either insist that their children be placed into higher ability groups or require explanations regarding such placement. The more severe consequences of segregating the minorities within schools, the consequent blocking of acculturation of the lower-class minority groups, and the sharpening of prejudice towards those who are not able are yet to come.

At any rate, more consideration is needed if the measures employed to raise the achievement level are not to replace the aim of "education for

all American youth" with one of "education for the able and the willing." The consequences of ability grouping on segregation and on the creation of new inequalities in learning the common culture especially need serious consideration. Schools may ignore the aims of human relations and social development only at the cost of great danger to democracy.

CURRENT PROGRAMS

Assessment of current programs shows that the programs have not kept pace with either the new problems or the new knowledge about group relations.

There is a wide range of ideas which suggest how the schools and community agencies can best contribute to the improvement of intergroup relations, and there is a wide range of practices. Each is somewhat tied to a special perception of what constitutes an intergroup relations problem, and of what the causes and factors are that contribute to the difficulties.

Some programs and proposals are limited to what could be described as missionary efforts: exhortations of good will, decrying of prejudice in others, or passing on information about races and ethnic groups on the assumption that lack of information causes prejudice. Many units in school curricula currently are on this level, as are many special programs, such as the Brotherhood Week observance, the special celebrations of Christmas, the UN days, the assemblies on the contributions of the ethnic and racial minorities to the American culture, etc.

Still others stress humanistic studies and the analysis of the democratic values and of the role of minorities in our society. Many in this group include anthropology among the school subjects. Surveys of the school practices indicate that this emphasis on extending the intellectual horizons, whether relevantly or not, is by far the most widely accepted practice.

Some teachers and curriculum workers are concerned with helping the minority children in their acculturation, such as by helping them learn certain indispensable aspects of the common culture. These programs

stress units on grooming, on personality development, help in coping with interpersonal conflicts, and give special aid in English and reading.

Still others tie the emphasis on intergroup education with the efforts at improving mental health in our schools. The assumption that underlies these efforts is that insecurity breeds prejudice and intolerance. Developing secure and healthy personalities, therefore, is an insurance against prejudice and intolerance. Still others suggest making the teaching and administrative group much more broadly representative by enforcing the fair employment practices in the hiring of school and community personnel.

There is less emphasis in actual programs as well as in expressions of opinion on using the school as a laboratory of democratic human relations. Producing such a laboratory would imply a greater effort to eliminate segregation outside the school and within it by redistricting, and by initiating cross-district activities as an adjunct to maximizing the school's contribution. Fewer reporters include in this idea of a laboratory a careful use of the school life—of the formal and informal association of the students—to reintroduce heterogeneity of contact and of interaction in clubs and activities. Currently, while the school activities are presumably open to anyone, actually prestige clubs and activities are semi-segregated either because of the rules which limit admission or because of hidden selection and exclusion practices.

Practically no mention is made of the use of guidance and counseling as a way of helping individuals and groups in school, especially those who may have difficulties because of living in a double culture—that of their home and neighborhood and that of the school.

This range of practices and of views regarding desirable programs is not in itself disheartening. However, the wide range of maturity of perception reflected in them should cause concern. These descriptions suggest that the interpretations of the group relations problems and the quality of programs have not kept pace either with the changing problems or with the growth of knowledge in this area. For example, while psychological and anthropological research has demonstrated that there are cultural differences in motivational and mental systems, these facts are overlooked in the efforts at acculturation, or at "raising the achieve-

ment levels." Teachers use the same old teaching techniques and motivating devices which have already proven so ineffective with the lower-class minority groups in the past. While the lower-class minority groups seek to adopt middle-class standards, there is little appreciation of what this might imply by way of charity, ego support, and pacing. The available knowledge on group dynamics is not being utilized, as for example, using small groups in classrooms or in the community for building bridges across differences, for enhancing motivation, or for changing attitudes. Nor is there a clear enough appreciation of the ways in which certain aspects of the school as a social system influence intergroup learning either negatively or positively.

This failure to keep pace is partly caused by the fact that there is no agency, similar to the intergroup education projects of a decade ago, whose task it is to translate research into educationally usable ideas and experiments.

As new information regarding the nature of intergroup relations, especially about the psychological and social dynamics of groups becomes available, new assessment is also needed regarding which problems are most crucial, and which methods of education and action are the most effective. For example, a different pattern of education is required if the concept of "prejudice" is replaced by the concept of "frustration" or "cultural deficiency." This would suggest that one way of revitalizing intergroup education is the dissemination of new concepts, facts, and research and stimulation of new experimentation with educational and action techniques.

Possibly a renewed effort at training is also needed. However devoted the efforts of the past decade have been in leavening the education of teachers and administrators with human relations emphasis, there is agreement that at present there are not enough skilled administrators and teachers to advance intergroup relations wisely. There is no doubt that generally this training has produced an increment of knowledge and sophistication about human relations. This effort is now slackening under the pressure of the movement "back to the fundamentals." Inservice education in this area is quite sporadic today. Training is also too narrow and isolated to provide a continuing resource of trained skills. It pro-

vides some knowledge, but too little of subtle sensitivity which work in human relations requires. The isolation of such training programs as have persisted from ongoing experimentation and active field programs has added to their sterility and alienation.

In many respects work in the community agencies shows a greater progress than that of the schools. Human relations agencies in many parts, of the country have become a permanent part of the community structure. This assures a continuity which has been lacking in school work. The personnel is more professional and the activities more systematic and better organized. There is a clearer delineation of roles and less overlapping. Evidently the machinery for the communication with schools has improved also. Supported by legislation the work has become more stable and pointed and the leadership more sophisticated.

But the interesting fact is that while the organization has improved, there is scarcely any change in methodology. The devices and techniques used in schools, community agencies, and teacher training institutions have remained practically the same. There are no new inventions. The schools employ the same curriculum units, conduct the same type of programs, and generally depend on the same devices. The community intergroup agencies, while bolstered considerably by new legislation, have not changed their programs to any considerable extent. While psychological and anthropological studies are finding new facts about group processes, and about the nature of the groups, these have not yet sufficiently percolated into the action technology of schools and social agencies (5).

While in the 1940s, national and systemwide programs, research and experimentation flourished, now such training is spasmodic, and experimentation is all but at a standstill. Although some new teachers in some areas get a better preparation, background in human relations is as yet not a part of all teacher-training institutions, nor are these programs located in areas that most need them. Such experiments and studies as those conducted in New York City with the education of Puerto Ricans are an exception rather than a rule. While workshops in human relations are still carried on, there is no concerted effort either for attendance or for relating the workshop training to ongoing programs. This recession in experimentation and invention is partly caused by a lack of a

stimulation in the form of experimental projects and the absence of a national forum.

There is especially a need for continued research on the problems of intergroup relations and intergroup education, and for continued experimentation with social education. We need to know more about the processes of acculturation, about the role of contact and interaction in developing desirable attitudes and skills, about the consequences of many current practices on human relations, and about the role of small groups in shaping the orientation toward differences.

New inventions are needed to deal with the hardening of the racial lines since the Supreme Court decision. New inventions are needed also for dealing with problems of acculturation in those schools that have a mixed population. It should be on everyone's conscience that developing new technology in human relations is as important to survival as is technical proficiency.

NEGRO YOUTH ON DEMOCRACY'S GROWING EDGE

Frederick D. Patterson

IN 1942, nearly twenty years ago, the late Edwin R. Embree, president of the Rosenwald Fund, in a contribution to the special issue of *Survey Graphic,* "Color: the Unfinished Business of Democracy," wrote, more in regret than in anger, that we keep overlooking "gross discriminations (against minorities) . . . in a nation publicly devoted to . . . brotherly love, eager for progress and prosperity, founded on democracy, and now engaged in a life and death struggle . . . throughout the world." He averred, "Changes would come even more surely if we recognized that true democracy would benefit our public health, our law and order, our culture, our wealth, and military effectiveness" (1).

At the end of the Civil War, the newly freed Negro was essentially illiterate, Southern, largely rural, and lacking in property or significant income. Four million then, and 16 million now, the Negro population is today literate, distributed nationwide, predominantly urban, and markedly improved in income and property holdings. Changes in the American economy, the improvement in minority group status, the necessary influences on U.S. domestic policies of her leadership role in international affairs, the emergence of new nations in Africa, and the new surge of colored peoples of the world generally have given American Negroes the opportunity, and in fact have forced them, to reappraise not

Frederick D. Patterson is President, Phelps-Stokes Fund.

only lags and potential but also their identity as American citizens.

The U.S. Supreme Court, in the school decision of May 17, 1954, ruled that segregation is inherently unequal and therefore unconstitutional. The Court thereby overturned the "separate but equal" doctrine which had prevailed since the *Plessy v. Ferguson* ruling of 1896. In other decisions since 1954, notably in recreation and transportation cases, the Court has again affirmed that segregation *per se* is unconstitutional. These decisions offer basic protection to all Americans; their significance to date has largely been in improved opportunity and improved morale for the Negro group.

There can be no doubt of the progress and increased opportunities over the past decade. Occurring in all spheres of American life, change has been in the direction of full American citizenship for Negro and other minority youth. The nature of that progress and the nature of the obstacles within the economic and political systems, as well as within the Negro group itself, are indicated in the following review of the Negro minority's status in education, public facilities, employment, housing, and citizenship.

EDUCATION

American Negroes are still facing discrimination in schools today, whether they live in the North, in the South, or in border states.

In the seventeen Southern states and the District of Columbia, there are nearly 10 million white and over 3 million Negro children. Of these, 2½ million white and a half million Negro children are in school districts which have undertaken programs of desegregation (2). In most of these situations, desegregation has been initiated on a token basis. In many, only a handful of Negro children are affected. In some approved plans, the desegregation programs are designed to take as long as twelve years to complete. Many have taken token steps with no indication of when, if ever, new steps are to be taken.

Most of these districts still maintain separate schools for Negro students, and only allow a highly selected few transfer into formerly all-

white schools. Desegregation by such rules has been accomplished not by positive action of school boards in placing students, but by initial action on the part of Negro children and their parents, requiring unusual perseverance, patience, and courage. The United States is still a long way from the goal of education without regard to race.

Even in those city school systems where relatively extensive programs of desegregation have been undertaken (such as St. Louis, Washington, Baltimore, and Louisville), practice has tended to settle into the kinds of discrimination, subtle but unmistakable, characteristic of Northern schools.

In the North there is an endless variety of ways in which Negro children become segregated from others, and ways in which they are treated differently from other children. When housing is segregated by race, a considerable number of schools for only one race become inevitable. School segregation is often intensified by the practice of establishing boundary lines which place the children in "white" blocks in schools separate from those in "Negro" blocks. Often school zone lines are so drawn that the term "gerrymandering" is wholly applicable.

Many Northern cities and towns still have one or more "Negro" schools which have been there many years, which Negro children, even if they live some distance away, attend by custom, and often by subtle guidance from school officials. Very often only Negro teachers are assigned to these schools. In many, many towns and in areas of virtually every large city, there are Negro children as isolated, as removed from vital school activities and programs, as surely segregated from the community at large, as in any formally segregated community in the deep South.

Discrimination is felt in school situations most poignantly by the attitudes of teachers, guidance officers, and principals. When they expect less from Negro students, they will inspire less and they will find less.

Negroes in Northern cities tend to attend the older schools in the crowded and less advantaged areas of the city. They have the least experienced teachers, the highest rates of teacher turnover, the least money spent, and the largest classes. Children having most need for something creative and dynamic at school do in fact have least. Thus is built the

vicious circle of poor education, low job potential, low aspiration, and low incentive for school achievement. Can the school begin to reverse the circle?

The nation still little realizes the extent of the disadvantage experienced by those 2½ million Negro children who are still attending the wholly segregated school systems of the deep South. Despite extensive programs to equalize white and Negro schools, the latter come out the poorer on virtually every count. In 1956–57, Mississippi spent $187.33 for each white child (based on average daily attendance) and $107.34 for each Negro child. The comparable figures for North Carolina were $183.59 and $166.89, and for Arkansas $150.59 and $112.85 (3). In each state such contrasts are to be found, vastly greater in rural areas than in urban.

In the field of higher education, some breakthrough toward making public facilities available to all citizens has been accomplished in all states with the exceptions of Mississippi, Alabama, South Carolina, and Georgia. However it must be realized that with notable exceptions, such as Oklahoma, Missouri, and Kentucky, even this breakthrough is of the token, escape-valve kind. The starkness of the discriminatory pattern in some states is suggested by the fact that Georgia in 1958 expended nearly $35 million on higher education for all, but $94 out of every $100 spent was for white youths exclusively. The research expenditures at institutions for whites in Georgia in 1958 were over $6 million; expenditures for research at institutions for Negroes were just over $13,000 (4).

PUBLIC FACILITIES

The past decade has seen substantial improvement in restaurant and hotel accommodations in nonsouthern cities. Airport waiting rooms and restaurants are becoming largely nondiscriminatory throughout the South. Where segregated facilities exist, it is claimed that only state monies were used in constructing the segregated unit while federal funds were employed elsewhere.

One of the vagaries of discriminatory behavior is that golf courses and

parks are open in cities that have not desegregated their schools; yet it is the children of the South that often play together on a nondiscriminatory basis.

The following description of recreational facilities in Atlanta indicates the nature of the still present problem.

A gentleman who has labored long and hard for improvement in the recreational facilities available to Atlanta's Negroes recently summarized the situation in these words: "Better than it was; worse than it ought to be." Parents, teachers, and citizens concerned with crime and juvenile delinquency rates in our community understandably feel that the situation is a whole lot worse than it ought to be. The public golf courses are open. Negroes who wish to read for pleasure may now enter Atlanta's Main Library without being ushered out onto the street again. But Negro Atlantans can't help smiling wryly when the Chamber of Commerce says: "Atlantans and their visitors have amusement facilities in abundance."

What does the city of Atlanta actually provide?

42 major parks for white Atlantans; 3 for Negroes.
92 small parkways for whites; none for Negroes.
20 football fields for whites; none for Negroes.
16 recreation centers for whites; 3 for Negroes.
12 swimming pools for whites; 3 for Negroes.
22 baseball diamonds for whites; 3 for Negroes.
119 tennis courts for whites; no more than 8 for Negroes.

Not only are some of the facilities listed above for Negroes substandard, but the tensions and frustrations brought on by overcrowding tend to convert some of these recreation centers into potential trouble spots.

Though some of the programs and activities for whites sponsored or co-sponsored by the City are duplicated for Negroes, there are others for which no parallel program or activity for Negroes exists.

Except for the necessarily-limited fare provided by the modest budgets of the local Negro educational institutions, Negro Atlantans who are interested in first-run movies, opera, concerts, live theater, and the dance are either excluded altogether or restricted to participation on a segregated basis.

Except for the YMCA and YWCA, only a few agencies in the Negro community have been able to provide facilities and personnel for supervised recreation and guidance on a continuing basis; the Citizens' Crime Committee has said that such guidance is an important deterrent to juvenile delinquency and crime (4).

The desegregation of transportation in most Southern cities of size has been an important gain of the past decade. Some cities have moved swiftly once court orders were made final; others have moved ahead of the filing of suits in their communities. These have moved quietly and often without an announced change of policy. Thus, an uneconomic policy which served largely to humiliate and inconvenience Negro passengers is on its way out.

EMPLOYMENT

The ability of minorities to get jobs for which they are qualified or can be trained, and which they should be able to aspire to realistically, is probably the most crucial and pragmatic single test of progress. The job is the long arm linking and supporting the citizen and his family in every sphere of community life. What is the current picture? And what are the prospects for minority youth?

The decade 1950–60 has been one of comparatively full employment. This has been especially beneficial to the Negro for it has moderated his position of being the "last hired and the first fired." However, the fact that the Negro has become more unionized and that most of these unions have a policy of "no discrimination" has but slightly reduced the hazard of race since the Negro's recent union status confers only a low seniority in the event of work shortage.

The most significant improvement in the Negro worker's condition is that of substantially higher earnings from urban jobs, with minimum wage floors, particularly compared to farm and non-farm employment in rural areas. The handicap of a low level of literacy and the absence of skilled training have added to the influences which keep the Negro at the bottom of the employment ladder.

Industry has moved slowly in upgrading Negro workers even when they have the requisite skill. Limited improvement in this regard has come in industries holding federal contracts. Many of these have acted under the urging of the President's Committee on Government Contracts. Since several of these industries are located in the South, integrated em-

ployment at all, or at least several, skill levels has had the value of demonstrating the feasibility of Southerners working together on a racially nonrestrictive basis. The experience has been similar in the growing number of states and cities with fair employment practice laws and enforcement commissions.

One of the most difficult barriers to fair employment on government contracts as well as in other areas has been the restrictive policy of recalcitrant international and local unions. This has been dramatized in the nation's capital where "Negroes have been blocked from getting jobs on Capitol Hill construction projects because the locals supply the workers but won't admit nonwhite members" (5). Very recently, the President's Committee on Government Contracts announced a double-barrelled attack in which federal contracting agencies will demand immediate compliance with the non-discrimination clause; and President Meany of the AFL-CIO pledges cooperation and promises to "meet head-on" any problems with local unions.

Lest we become too sanguine even about cities which have good reputations and significant evidences of advance and enlightenment, the following description of the employment picture and prospects for Atlanta Negro youths is sobering.

In a modern city such as Atlanta, any group which is economically handicapped is straitjacketed as it attempts to achieve its full potential in education, in health, and in creative citizenship. Every third man in Atlanta's million is a Negro—though it would be difficult for a visitor to believe this if he surveyed the offices, the labs, the mechanized production lines, and the counters from behind which the goods which help make Atlanta's wealth are sold. Often a porter—seldom if ever a production assistant; often a handler of bundles or crates—seldom if ever a driver; a taxpayer supporting his city, his county, his state, his country—but seldom on their payrolls above the janitorial rank—the Atlanta Negro as a jobholder is indeed a "marginal" man.

Policies and practices of governmental agencies, private employers, and labor unions in Atlanta are reflected in such white-to-Negro employment ratios as these: social welfare and recreational workers, 9 to 1; bookkeepers, 200 to 1; electricians, more than 20 to 1; overall professional technical and kindred workers, 13 to 1.

In addition to locally owned and operated concerns, over 3,300 of the coun-

try's leading business organizations have branches in Atlanta for manufacturing, warehousing, and distributing. Many of these provide on-the-job training. Again, the prevailing pattern is to adopt discriminatory employment patterns and to exclude Negroes partially or wholly from the training programs.

The following are but a few of the 55 Atlanta-based federal offices and agencies employing over 18,000 people, whose clerical and white collar staffs either contain no Negroes or provide token employment related to "advisory" or "consultant" positions: Department of Health, Education and Welfare; Housing and Home Finance Agency; Department of Labor; Veterans Administration; National Labor Relations Board; Small Business Administration; Department of Agriculture; Civil Service Commission.

As thousands of Negro householders pay their light, gas, electricity, and water bills they find little comfort in the fact that there are no Negro meter readers, technicians, or white collar workers employed by Atlanta's public utilities agencies.

Although Negroes provide a sizable proportion of the dollar income which sparks the growth and expansion of Atlanta's department stores, food chains, factories, etc., the typical employment pattern is one of little or no adequate job opportunities for the graduates of Atlanta's Negro high schools and colleges (4).

Since it is anticipated that enlightened employment practices will increasingly prevail, important attention must now be given to alerting Negro and other minority youth to this trend, to the end that they are motivated to seek better training and better jobs.

A problem in securing adequate motivation has been that of getting teachers with Negro pupils to become aware of new employment trends. Often teachers advise Negro youth in their classes to enter noncollege preparatory areas regardless of the interests and aptitudes of these youth. Thus, teachers who should be revealing opportunities to Negro youngsters in keeping with their potential often do nothing to counteract the influences of low motivation exerted at home by parents whose horizons are limited by the common labor jobs they perform. Far too many Negro youth fail to prepare for skilled jobs or professional opportunities because they believe these jobs do not exist for them, and employers therefore are often unable to employ Negro youth because they are untrained.

The National Urban League has reported that only 200 of 28,000 engineers graduated last year were Negroes. A part of the reason for this

lay in the fact that only 5 percent of Negro high school graduates enter college as compared to 25 percent for white youth. Moreover, a disproportionately large number of Negro youth leave high school before graduation. These youth feel that additional education will be of small value for the kinds of jobs they will be forced to take.

Segregation results in the twin evils of substandard performance and isolation from growth-inspiring contacts. A recent meeting of Medical Fellowships Inc. (6). revealed that the chief bottleneck in efforts to increase the number of Negro physicians is not at the point of finding available openings in medical schools or even the monies required for a medical education but that of finding college graduates interested in medicine who have the requisite high academic standing. Since Negro youth possess the normal distribution of native abilities, the problem is placed squarely at the door of poor preparation beginning in grade school and extending through college. The quality of preparation in primary and secondary schools, and the associated motivation or lack of it, is probably a more important determinant than the college years, or by that time the pattern of attitudes and achievement levels has been set.

Those who see in the desire of the Negro youth for integrated public schools merely the social aspiration to be with white youth fail to note that the major point at issue is the poor quality of work which characterizes segregated public education.

HOUSING

The growth in home ownership among Negroes provides a significant index of the rising income level. Home buying represents the Negro's most extensive investment. The low rate of default in payments testifies to the high value which Negro Americans place on home ownership. This has been attributed in part to the role of the home as a refuge from the many forms of discrimination encountered in daily contacts outside the home.

The limitations which Negroes and other minority groups experience

in efforts to obtain homes in keeping with their means and desires in locations that provide wholesome surroundings for their children are especially regrettable. It can be said that because of the unusually great importance minority groups attach to their homes, privations involving their homes work a greater degree of harm on their function as a major influence in child nurture.

In the United States, the American principle of freedom to move and to choose one's place of residence is taken for granted by most people. Yet, the Report of the Commission on Race and Housing states:

Housing is the one commodity on the American market that Negroes and persons belonging to certain other ethnic minorities cannot purchase freely. A complex of forces and pressures operates to exclude members of these groups from residence in the majority of the nation's urban and suburban neighborhoods. The result is to segregate them in certain limited districts. In consequence, a minority person typically has fewer alternatives in housing than does a white homeseeker with comparable purchasing power. The latter may choose any location and compete for any available dwelling that suits his needs, tastes, and pocketbook, subject only to the general laws. The minority person, however, can compete freely only within circumscribed areas. Elsewhere he confronts formidable barriers because of his race, color or ethnic attachments (7).

The inevitable result is that, in the market for shelter, a dollar in a non-white hand will buy less housing value and less financing on more costly terms than will a dollar in a white hand. This situation generally obtains in the market for both rental and sales housing.

Extensive and rigid discrimination in housing is a phenomenon of the past two decades. It has spread during a period of extensive migration and during a time that housing has become a matter of public policy and federal assistance. Prior to this period, the South, where Negroes then lived in greatest numbers, operated on a basis of random choice at moderate and especially low income levels.

With the development of extensive federally aided housing projects, public and private, came also the development of organized management of realty groups. These groups have formulated codes, written and unwritten, based on the assumed desirability of housing developments of

exclusively white ownership or occupancy. Thus, for reasons primarily of assumed financial expediency, there has developed a ruthless abridgement of the right of members of minority groups to exercise the freedom of choice in the selection of a place to live which is the common and unquestioned experience of white Americans.

The location of the home bears a crucial relationship to schooling, employment, and general wholesomeness of environment. Those who determine, for whatever reason, where others shall live exert an influence far reaching in its consequences. It may very well be that considerations based on a concern for property values stultify the lives of countless minority group children by forcing them to live in slum areas, inimical to proper growth and development, when their parents are fully able financially to provide them with homes located in healthful environments. In no other single area of American life do minority groups find their rights and immunities so freely and ruthlessly violated. If wholesome intergroup contact, especially among American youth, is desirable as sound preparation for an adult society of increasingly diverse human contacts, present patterns of housing discrimination with minority group isolation is a trend whose dire consequences will be felt for many years to come.

Equally unfortunate is the fact that in public housing and publicly assisted private housing, as in other areas requiring substantial federal aid, discriminatory practices exist. In 1954 the President of the United States enunciated the principle soundly and unequivocally to the effect that "where Federal funds or Federal authority were involved, there should be no distinction or discrimination based upon any reason that was not recognized by our Constitution." Yet, today, some six years later, no concrete steps have been taken to implement the policy the President so distinctly stated.

Because of the extensive and serious consequences of housing discrimination, the challenge to government at all levels and to voluntary agencies to seek wise solutions through intensive and persistent study and experimentation and, equally important, to put them into action is both clear and mandatory.

CITIZENSHIP

Our Constitution contains provisions designed to protect the basic rights and privileges of citizenship of all. Yet, while the legal base is there, there are still serious impediments to the full enjoyment of these rights by Negro citizens. In states in the South where programs of "massive resistance" to desegregation of schools have been undertaken, a new series of legislative acts and administrative measures continues the attempt to keep Negroes "in their place."

Southern Negroes are still partially disenfranchised. The report of the U.S. Commission on Civil Rights has instances of techniques used to discourage or prevent registration for voting in a number of situations which the commission investigated. In a vast majority of rural counties of heavy Negro population, intimidation and a lack of tradition of political activity prevent even the effort to register. Thus Negroes are hampered in the basic democratic process of participating in the election of local, state, and national officials.

Southern Negroes are finding many barriers in the way of making protest and obtaining redress of grievances. Those who have signed petitions seeking school transfers for their children have often been the victims of reprisals: loss of job, refusal of credit, and threats or violence. Anti-barratry laws are designed to make it much more difficult for Negroes to take cases into the courts.

In some cases, teachers or other state employees have been asked to sign statements that they do not believe in integration and do not belong to the NAACP. A variety of measures, ranging from tax investigations to the revival of obscure laws about registration of organizations, have been taken to render it virtually impossible for the NAACP to function in some states. There are even some state laws which render it illegal to hold an interracial meeting!

It is clear that the democratic process itself is negated in these islands of resistance and repression. What is intended as a repressive measure to keep a minority powerless becomes the process by which the democratic

values of free speech, free assembly, the right of petition, and access to the courts are threatened for all.

A NATION MATURES

Not only the well-publicized youths of Little Rock, but also the hundreds of anonymous Negro youths involved in the transition to integrated facilities have demonstrated courage, poise, and the best qualities of Americanism—and often under exceedingly trying circumstances. More recently Negro college youths, frequently in company with white counterpart supporters of democratic practices, have dramatized the discrimination in public eating places.

The recent visit of President Sekou Toure of Guinea to the United States and his reception in North Carolina gave to Negro residents of North Carolina and elsewhere deep satisfaction and pride along with a new awareness of the worth of people of color. It is understandable that the youth of Greensboro's colleges, and those of other cities should, as a result of this awareness, seek an end to discrimination in ten-cent stores which denied them lunch-counter service while accepting their patronage elsewhere in the store. A great need exists for full recognition of the contemporary forces impinging on the consciousness of all youth, white and Negro, which are shaping their image of America and their roles in it. Negro youth will grow increasingly sensitive to those circumstances and barriers which mark them unfairly from other Americans.

A crucial question is: Can white youth as well as minority youth properly prepare for their necessary and expected roles as Americans in today's world, in the face of local and national happenings which make a hollow mockery of human dignity and the democratic ideal? It was heartening and significant that some white college youths of Greensboro and Durham joined Negro youth in a protest against discrimination at the same time that a teenage rabble and the Ku Klux Klan sought to uphold the practice of discrimination.

In the past two decades, the United States, confronted both abroad and at home with the most serious threats to its unity, existence, and identity

as a leader of the democratic world since the Civil War, matured as a nation. It did so in large measure when it assumed greater and renewed public and private responsibility for equalizing and improving the chances and opportunities of all citizens—and particularly its minorities and youths. Much improvement has occurred in the status and in the opportunities of all ethnic minorities in the United States, although all still suffer some disabilities—but to different degrees, in different aspects of the nation's life and economy, and for different reasons.

The Negro is the largest color minority in the United States, and remains the most disadvantaged. Yet, color as such is not the really decisive factor in discrimination against minorities. Historical and cultural factors are. There are numerous minorities on the American scene with the distinctiveness if not the handicap of color—the American Indian, those of Asiatic extraction, many Puerto Ricans, for example—who on the whole fare better than the Negro, even in situations where their economic status is lower.

The decisive fact in the continuing discrimination against the Negro minority is not that they are of different color alone, but that their forebears were at one time slaves in America. The persistence of this image in the dominant group, rather than any presumed persistence of a slave heritage or plantation tradition in the Negro himself, is the really decisive "cultural" factor in discrimination and the Negro's status. This and the remaining state laws that attempt to fix that status and to exclude are lingering barriers. They are no longer defensible on constitutional grounds; they have never been affordable on grounds of national interest or morality.

An important sign of change is that the arguments or rationalizations defending discrimination or supporting the delay in change are now hardly ever based on ideological or racial (in the biological sense) grounds; the reasons now given are pragmatic in character, based on the need for time, the economic costs, and the frequently distorted use of the phrase "cultural differences."

The promising and heartening feature of these times is that the nation in its new maturity is taking a sober look at both the bad and the good about the present status of its minorities, particularly the Negro, and at

what minority youth expect from and can contribute to an expanding American democracy. It is particularly timely and appropriate that assessment and reassessment of the position of minorities should be occurring now, with the centennial of the Civil War and of Emancipation occurring during the first half of the 1960 decade.

A most significant measure of democracy's growing edge and of the improved status and prospects of all youths is revealed through another look at Embree's statement of 1942. What he said about the extent of discrimination is appreciably less true, what he said about the consequences of discrimination against minorities is more true, and neither he nor anyone else could have then anticipated the degree to which the nation now recognizes, concerns itself, and acts to solve these problems for all of its youth.

PART THREE

Values in Transition

TRADITIONAL VALUES IN TRANSITION

Liston Pope

NEVER HAS THE NEED for attention to the problems of childhood and adolescence been greater. Goethe's words, which he called "wisdom's last fruit," fall on our ears with special insistency on an occasion like this: "What you have inherited from the past, that earn in order to possess. He alone deserves freedom, life as well, who daily conquers them anew."

To generalize about the ideals and values held by today's young people would be a very dangerous undertaking. Which young people? Those of the United States, or South Africa, or India? Of what age? Pre-school, high school, college? In what social environment? Rural, suburban, or inner city? From what economic level? Rich, middle class, or that substratum including one fifth of the nation's children, where income is less than fifty dollars a week for a family of four? It is quite clear that ideals and values vary a great deal in relation to national and other differences. Generalizations are therefore very difficult.

One can speak with a greater degree of confidence about the levels of aspiration and status of values in the society in which children and young people are growing up. Their own values and ideals will be shaped profoundly by the moral atmosphere in which they spend their most flexible years.

Liston Pope is Dean of Yale University Divinity School.

In general, we are presenting a blurred image of our American ideals and values to American youth today, and to the entire world as well. Young people in the United States and Europe are maturing, or failing to mature, in a time of indecision, equivocation, and paradox—a time when ideals are clouded and values are confused. At the same time, young people in many of the newly independent nations of Asia and Africa have a new sense of mission and hope that augurs well for the future of their countries.

In the Western world the answer to nearly every important question is both affirmative and negative. The attitude of the public toward most significant proposals is ambiguous. Our approach to life itself is a curious blend of response and withdrawal. We seem to be living Jekyll and Hyde lives in a schizoid world.

We do not know where we stand, for example, with regard to the great ideal of peace. Wistfully and technically we are at peace, but it is a peaceless peace, as filled with apprehension as the warless war of 1940. If war is defined as organized conflict, as has been said, peace must now be defined as conflict organized. The children and young people of 1960 may spend all their lives in the half-light between the darkness of war and the dawn of peace. Great patience and devotion to the ideal of peace will be required to keep alive the conviction that peace is a greater value than war, whether or not it is a greater value than freedom.

A comparable confusion attends most public issues. The spirit of nationalism is stronger in the world than it was at the beginning of this century, just at a moment when we are painfully aware of the necessity to achieve international peace and concord and of the need for a world community. Here in America, belief in democracy is our official creed, but our treatment of minority groups often belies our public professions. Racial integration in the public schools is the law of the land, but it is openly defied in several states. We affirm that we will rise to the defense of freedom in the world wherever it is threatened by an aggressor, but we are often unwilling to tolerate, much less encourage, unpopular views here at home.

We present to our young people a hazy picture as to the very ideas on which they will base their lives. Belief in the essential goodness of man

is tempered by recognition that man is a selfish creature capable of almost anything. Belief in social progress is still widespread in America, but we doubt that we are making any net gains except possibly in the field of mechanical gadgets. We continue to teach that hard work is a great virtue, but the work week grows ever shorter. We praise virtues of frugality, temperance, and modesty, but we live as the most spendthrift and boastful nation in the world. Religious faith is widely advocated, but the object of that faith and its consequences for daily life are either undefined or described far too simply in psychological terms. We plead for the unity of the family and the sanctity of marriage, but births out of wedlock continue to increase and more children than ever before are growing up in broken homes.

In our personal lives as well as in public matters and social philosophy we give confused answers to life's challenges and opportunities, and our young people sense the confusion. We know that we ought to give liberally of our time and energy and money for the improvement of our communities and the world, but our altruistic and civic impulses are often restrained by personal caution and fear. We know that we ought to oppose evil, in high places and in low, but the evil is so vast that we are reluctant to become involved. In a day of great issues we know that we ought to declare our convictions—to stand up and be counted—but our convictions themselves are so tentative that we are most often prompted to be careful and to remain silent.

In contrast, Americans who were born near the turn of the century grew up in an atmosphere in which ideals were rather clear and certain values seemed to be established. World War I, to be sure, burst on the world in the formative years of many of us—but even that could be interpreted at the time as "a war to end war," and it was turned into a great idealistic crusade. The future of human society seemed to be clear and bright: men were to progress or evolve into a new golden age; those who thought in religious terms called it "the Kingdom of God on earth." Specifications for its establishment were often formulated. In the 1870s the Reverend Jesse Henry Jones of Boston, by no means an eccentric, declared: "Intelligence agrees with density of population in pointing to the neighborhood of Boston as the place where to found the True Chris-

tian Society." He may have been provincial and overly optimistic, but he could at least look to the future with confidence and hope. So could most of his contemporaries; their formulas changed from time to time but they shared a positive faith and a dauntless hope.

The traditional values of America were still regnant when few persons disputed them. A righteous God was in his heaven, and if all was not right with the world, at least men knew how to make it so. Each individual was precious in God's sight. The family was closely knit and performed innumerable functions subsequently to be taken from it. Science and technology were thought to hold the keys to knowledge and to the future. Government existed for the benefit and at the direction of the governed, and each individual had natural and inalienable rights, including the rights of freedom of speech and assembly. Public office was regarded as a public trust. Government was thought to be "a government of law and not of men." The church was to be kept separate from the state. In international affairs, it was agreed, America should stay at home and mind her own business. Economic enterprise was almost entirely in private hands with a minimum of government interference, and the rewards of a man's labor and ingenuity were almost entirely at his disposal. The right of property ownership was sacred—as sacred as the rights to life and liberty. Civil authority was superior to the military establishment.

Many other values traditionally accepted as axiomatic in American culture could be listed. But a recital of these basic ones reveals that nearly every one of them has been modified or challenged during the last half century. The basic values presented to children in the first decades of this century are no longer taken for granted or really reflected in the conduct of American affairs, though there are many echoes of them.

Compared to the certitude at the turn of the century, doubtless all of us except the most simple minded and the most dogmatic are somewhat uncertain and confused about the issues of our own day and the prospects for the future. After two world wars, a debilitating depression, and disillusionment over so many hopes—hopes centering in the League of Nations, prohibition, isolationism, the peace movement, and what used to be called the "Noble Russian Experiment"—after such disillusionment

many members of the older generation have taken vows of disbelief in simple belief. The complexity of contemporary issues is overwhelming, and programs of action are undertaken with the expectation that they will be only partially successful. We have adopted as our own Alexander Pope's version of the "ninth beatitude": "Blessed is he who expects nothing, for he shall never be disappointed."

The contemporary hard-headedness and realism are doubtless to be preferred to the sentimentality and wishful thinking of fifty years ago. But we must not be surprised if our young people seem to deserve the labels so often applied to them recently—that they are apathetic, silent, "the beat generation." They can be rallied only by clearer ideals, not by a set of reservations. They cannot be inspired by foghorns; they need the sound of a trumpet. Communism, with a few simple—too simple—ideas artfully aided by revolutionary skill, has reached out to engulf a third of mankind within a single generation. Its deplorable success thus far demonstrates the truth of Carl Sandburg's promise: "Men are ready to die for a living word on the tongue."

Most likely, the young people of this generation will work out their own systems of faith and morals with a minimum of help from their perplexed elders. Their response to confusion will probably be quite different from that of their predecessors who faced similar uncertainties. They are not going back to the trivialities of the "Flaming Youth" of the period just after World War I, or to the crusades and easy answers of the depression years in the 1930s.

Rather, I think that American youth will redefine traditional American values in terms more appropriate for our country's changing nature and its new place in the world. Most of the young people of my acquaintance put a high premium on independence of thought and action, despite all the sentimental talk about "togetherness"; they seem to sense that they are a new type of frontiersmen in a world of hydrogen bombs and the exploration of outer space. In an era of mass media, Madison Avenue, and organization men, they seek almost fiercely to find their own identity; perhaps this search helps to explain the value they put on security. Their search for integrity may produce a new version of the doctrine that every individual is precious in God's sight, even in a world in which individ-

uals beyond number have recently been sacrificed, whether on battlefields, in gas ovens, or in impersonal corporations.

It seems obvious that the coming generation will be far more sophisticated about social possibilities than their parents were. Today's young people begin with the assumption that the results of science can be either greatly beneficial or vastly destructive. They know that they live on the brink of disaster, and that, as one teen-ager put it, the fourth world war will be fought with rocks. They understand that government must be big and must accept responsibility for the welfare of its citizens and for peace in the world. They take it for granted that the economy of an advanced industrial society must be complex.

Despite the necessity of facing the facts of the world in the 1960s, the problem of young people remains the same as for their elders, namely, that of finding ideals by which life's motion may be made meaningful and values by which intelligent moral and ethical decisions can be made. No blueprint of the future ethos can be made. It is likely to be clearer in its features than the present one, for better or for worse. The next ten years will be crucial ones for determination of man's aspirations and ethical standards.

I am confident that young people will rise to the occasion. Despite the ominous and continuing rise in juvenile delinquency, I think that I detect a new stirring among young people in general that may lead at last to a new moral atmosphere in America. It may be that the leadership taken by college students in the struggle for racial justice is a symptom of a wider reawakening. Young Negro students, with the support of countless white students in many parts of the country, have gone out into the streets and into segregated eating places to make a peaceful and courageous witness for the proposition that America was conceived in liberty and is dedicated to the proposition that all men must be treated equally. At no time since the end of World War II has there been so much moral excitement among students as at the present moment.

A new concern about religion is also undeniably emerging among young people. There is no great religious revival in America among either old or young, in the accepted sense of that term (which is the nineteenth century sense). But there is a significant revival of interest in religion,

and this seems to be especially true of young people. On many campuses a higher percentage of students is enrolled in courses in ethics and religion than at any time in the last fifty years. Hard questions are being asked about the fundamental objectives of life and about the legitimacy of values and the standards for morality. If students are less extensively concerned about public affairs than they were in the 1930s, they are far more deeply seeking an adequate basis for their individual lives. It is not likely that very many of today's children and youth will be able to look back from the perspective of later years and exult with Wordsworth: "Bliss was it in that dawn to be alive, But to be young was very heaven."

Perhaps our children will be able to remember this present period with a happy glow; England was at war a good part of the time during Wordsworth's childhood and young manhood, and the French Revolution and subsequent Reign of Terror kept France in turmoil across the Channel. Age generally looks back with nostalgia toward a long lost youth. In any event, today's young people, growing up in a world of stress and confusion, may learn the lesson that Justice Oliver Wendell Holmes was taught by the bitter struggles over slavery during his childhood and by the horrors of the Civil War during his young manhood. "Through our great good fortune," he wrote in later years, "in our youth our hearts were touched with fire. It was given us to learn at the outset that life is a profound and passionate thing." Our parlous times appear to be teaching that truth to us all, and possession of it may be the greatest resource for the young people of today as they fashion the ideals and discern the values of the future.

CREATIVE DISCIPLINE

Kenneth B. Clark

DISCUSSIONS OF DISCIPLINE may emphasize theoretical explorations of definition and dynamics (1, 2); empirical studies of types of discipline and effects (3, 4); and practical advice to parents and teachers on how to discipline their children most conveniently and effectively (1, 5, 6). The extensive popular literature which has been devoted to discipline probably reflects, among other things, the desire of Americans to obtain from their "experts" workable formulas and devices for resolving complex problems of interpersonal relations. Certainly if it were possible to develop simple tools and techniques for effective discipline of children, parents, teachers, and others who are charged with the responsibility of training young people would have a significantly easier task. The demand for simple, convenient, and efficient tools and rules seems to account for a substantial amount of the "how to" literature in the field of child care, marriage and morals, and house and garden maintenance. These desires and demands account for many fads and fashions in child rearing practices, oversimplified delinquency prevention schemes, and, occasionally, a new and effective insight or method.

The literature on effective forms and techniques of discipline is rather extensive. Understandably, the problem has broken through the traditional boundaries of academic and professional journals and has invaded the pages of the mass media. Fritz Redl has published an article on discipline in *McCall's* Magazine. The editor's introduction to this article

Kenneth B. Clark is Professor of Psychology, College of the City of New York, and Director of Research at the Northside Center for Child Development.

may be reflective of a major new trend in the "experts'" advice to parents: "And why is discipline so hard for modern parents? Maybe, says a famous child psychiatrist, because we're using too much 'psychology' and too little common sense" (7).

Dorothy W. Baruch has written a pamphlet entitled "How to Discipline Your Children" (5). In this pamphlet the methods for disciplining children are summarized with the usual explanation that children should be disciplined in a manner which both satisfies the parents and at the same time fits the needs of the child. The traditional stress on the role of love, frankness, and willingness to understand the child as factors which prevent persistent misbehavior are also found in this discussion.

Certain points are consistently found throughout the literature dealing with discipline. In addition to the general admonition that discipline must be exerted within the context of love and understanding on the part of the parents for the child, the following suggestions are offered to parents and teachers:

1. The discipline of children must serve some positive and useful purpose and must not be just an outlet for the disciplinarian (8).

2. Discipline should not be used to intimidate the child but should have the more positive function of teaching him that there is a moral orderliness in the world. It should help him to develop self-control, self-direction, and a reasonable degree of social conformity (9).

3. The primary function of discipline is to teach the child to discipline himself (10).

4. Discipline involves the inevitability of the child's conflict with and rebellion from the standards and values of his parents. This point is complicated by recognition of the necessity for the parents to maintain a firm and stable role in order to provide the child with the stability he apparently needs (11).

Generally implicit in articles dealing primarily with the mechanics of discipline or suggestions for increasing its effectiveness are assumptions concerning the definitions and goals of discipline. Among the more common of such assumptions is that discipline should be used to promote the optimum development of each child (12). A frequently stated goal in these articles is that discipline should lead to self-discipline (13). One of

the clearest statements concerning the goals of discipline within the context of the larger purposes of a democratic society is to be found in the works of a Swedish author who states: "In a democratic society, discipline ought to help a child become a citizen conscious of his responsibility toward society with respect and love for other people" (14).

Sheviakov places the problem of discipline within the even larger perspective of the complexity of contemporary civilization:

In a complex civilization, the individual often has to subjugate his personal inclinations, whims, comforts, even some of his liberties, to bigger goals than personal ones. . . . If the democratic philosophy is to flourish, our ways of living and believing, the ideals of generations must be preserved. For this we need children and young people who cherish these ideals above all and who, therefore, are ready to endure privation and to exercise the utmost self-control (1).

Fritz Redl also approaches the goals of discipline within the accepted context of the democratic ideology (1). Implicit in his approach is a definition of discipline as synonymous with the maintenance of order. Redl's definition, however, is complicated by his concern with the concept of the actuality of democracy as a necessary condition for effective order. He therefore poses the problem—which he does not discuss as a dilemma—for himself and the classroom teacher in terms of translating "the principles of democratic discipline into daily action in the classroom." The "how to," practical approach is exemplified by Redl's presentation of an eight-point guide post which he hopes will be helpful "to the hurried practitioner on the job."

An examination of a sample of the available literature reveals that while there are some common assumptions, topics, emphases, and admonitions which run through these discussions of the problem of discipline, there is no fixed, generally accepted set of definitions, techniques, perspectives, or situations in which discipline is discussed. Rather, it seems that each author tends to write about discipline in terms of the particular emphasis with which he is at that time concerned or for which a request has been made. Discussions may emphasize techniques for the control of the behavior of children by parents in the home or techniques for the maintenance of order by teachers in the classroom. There is a growing

literature on the problem of discipline in terms of the larger social and community problem of the control, prevention, or cure of delinquent behavior.

It may be helpful to attempt to extract from these varied approaches and suggestions some common factors which may help us understand the essential problem posed by any discussion of discipline. This task necessarily must start with an attempt to answer the following questions: Discipline for what? By whom? When? What are the conditions which determine the degree of severity? By what standards does one judge the various techniques?

A DEFINITION

Implicit in an attempt to answer the above questions is the need for some working definition of discipline. Such a definition, if it is to avoid the disadvantages of the too loose or the too specific, must seek its base in the fundamental social and interactional process of which discipline is merely a single manifestation. From this point of view, it is possible to view discipline as one of the techniques of social control—one of the methods by which an individual's behavior is influenced by the desires or demands of others or by external conditions which are either inevitable or structured by others.

This approach makes the specific problem of discipline an aspect of the larger problem of the *socialization* of the individual, those processes whereby the human organism becomes a human being. Socialization is made possible only through the capacity of the organism to modify its behavior according to external demands—that is, to be able to learn. In its most fundamental sense, the learning process involves the capacity of the organism to internalize and have its behavior influenced by external imperatives.

A meaningful discussion of discipline, therefore, must concern itself with the specific problem of controlling the individual's behavior in terms of the prevailing and acceptable standards, values, and attitudes of the culture within which he is developing. From this point of view, prob-

lems of discipline, when they arise, are essentially the problems of conflicts between the propensities of the individual and the demands and standards of external forces.

Applied discipline may then be seen as a technique by which the external forces seek to resolve such conflicts by directing the individual toward the external goals and values. The standards of the agents of the society, the social institution, or the subculture become the molds within which the individual must be shaped by the necessary and appropriate techniques of discipline. These external, social goals are valid by virtue of their general acceptance and their power to reinforce themselves by discipline applied to individuals who seek to disregard them. It is necessary to understand these reality imperatives which give substance to the fact of discipline as a powerful cohesive force in human society before one is able to understand the more specific problems which may arise in the dynamic interaction between the individual and the restrictive social forces.

This approach reduces discipline to a problem of power and the use of power as an instrument of social control. In fact, the individual who is being disciplined is being subjected from infancy through adulthood to the power and control of others—being molded, directed, rewarded, persuaded, pushed, punished, or in some other way being coerced toward some standard or pattern of behavior which is considered desirable by other individuals who control this power.

It would seem to follow, therefore, that the degree to which the individual must be so influenced or the severity with which his behavior must be controlled is a function of the degree to which his existing behavior is congruent with or deviant from the values and standards of the power controlling individuals in his environment—parents, teachers, police, or significant others.

The consequence of discipline must necessarily, therefore, be some degree of conformity. The so-called dichotomy between individuality and conformity becomes meaningless in the light of this approach to the understanding of the nature and dynamics of discipline. The only meaningful dimension within which the concepts of individualism and conformity may be discussed in terms of discipline would be to evaluate the degree

of conformity on some hypothetical continuum varying from absolute, uncritical, and rigid conformity reinforced by intimidation and severe punitive discipline, through some more balanced accommodation between the demands of the external power forces and the needs of the individual, with some room for socially acceptable forms of individuality and opportunity for optimum creativity, to extreme Rousseauian permissive individuality functionally indistinguishable from personal and social anarchy. Viewing the problem in terms of this continuum, it would be difficult for one to become a partisan, confident that any given point on this scale is in itself more or less conducive to mental health or personal stability.

The bounds of individuality permissible in a given culture may be arbitrary and inconsistently defined. The risk to individuals who break the definite or ambiguous boundaries of permissible individuality, even when such transgressions are interpreted as essential to creativity and originality, may be great. Such individuals run the risk of social punishment or varying types of discipline, threatened or actual, such as ridicule, loss of status, ostracism, physical punishment, imprisonment or some other form of institutionalization, and, in extreme cases, death.

THE TREND AWAY FROM PERMISSIVENESS

There has been increasing concern about the psychological and psychiatric implications of permissiveness. Redl argues against permissiveness in the clear language designed to appeal to his mass audience: "Nor is it any kindness to the poor child who's allowed to run wild at home and drive his teachers to distraction at school. Even though behavior is what psychologists call 'age typical' a youngster still needs control and support from his parents" (7).

One of the most articulate critics of the permissiveness extreme is Melitta Schmideberg (15). Dr. Schmideberg states categorically that permissive upbringing has not succeeded. As evidence, she points out that our high schools have turned out thousands of illiterates and that "delinquency is steadily rising; juvenile drug addicts probably run into tens of thousands . . . ; we constantly hear of infantile schizophrenics, and the

number of neurotics is certainly not less than it was under the sternest Victorian upbringing."

However, Dr. Schmideberg does not advocate the reintroduction of extremely severe punishment as the corrective discipline. In fact, she states that: "Punishment is not discipline, though it may be one of the means of achieving it. Discipline is the subordination of immediate impulses to a purpose or to moral values." She does not say how such subordination of impulses to moral values may be achieved except that "learning, working and organized sports" or "any sustained activity that presupposes concentration, perseverance, acceptance of defeat, or realizing one's ignorance" are means toward self-control and discipline. This clearly does not answer the question of how one obtains these laudable ends.

The crucial questions concerning the relationship between permissiveness on the one hand and creative discipline and personal stability on the other are not disposed of by eloquence or generalizations which blame such varied problems as inadequate secondary schools, childhood schizophrenia, and adolescent dope addiction on an undetermined amount of an unclear "permissiveness."

A danger inherent in the present trend away from permissiveness is that overgeneralized rejections may lead to sweeping demands for a return to more severe punitive forms of discipline in the home and at school. In the quest for the simple solution, oversimplified punitive attacks on already vulnerable, confused, disturbed, and defenseless human casualties may attract wide popular support. A member of the New York State Legislature (Corso) has introduced a bill in the 1959 and in the 1960 meetings of the state legislature which would permit teachers to inflict corporal punishment on their pupils. A recent issue of the *New Yorker* (February 6, 1960) reprinted the following item without comment concerning its obvious Freudian implication:

This action on the part of the school districts follows legislation last year which permits each school district to make its own decision on capital punishment.   Walnut Creek (California) *Sun*

The not-too-well disguised hostility toward young people, particularly those who are seen as different or deviant, which seems involved in some

arguments against permissiveness is illustrated by the following comments of Melitta Schmideberg:

A generation ago reformers and sociologists still saw the main cause of delinquency in the slums and in extremes of poverty. Even today, of course, the majority of offenders come from the poor. The troubled or delinquent Negroes and Puerto Ricans are the poor of the nation, and the discrimination against them is as much due to middle-class horror of squalor and uncivilization as to dislike of their color or language. The poor of today are not starving any more. They do have the necessities of life; if they steal, they do not steal bread, but cars. . . .

Yet while we should continue to fight discrimination and corruption, strive to improve social conditions, and in particular provide help for the poor in difficulties, at the same time people must accept social inequalities and even injustices, since no social system can ever be perfect (15).

It is difficult to understand how Dr. Schmideberg could counsel us to accept social inequalities and injustices, and presumably the human tragedies which result, in the same article in which her polemic against the personally responsible delinquent is found. By this same argument she should advise that delinquency be accepted "since no social system can ever be perfect."

This type of hostility sometimes takes more subtle forms. For example, Dr. Margaret Mead has taken the position that the present increase in the rate of juvenile delinquency is due to compulsory education laws. She suggests that these laws, requiring reluctant adolescents to remain in school, result in feelings of frustration which these children then tend to act out destructively (16).

Related to this argument is the contention that our public high schools have become extremely heterogeneous—with a large proportion of lower status individuals such as Mexicans, Puerto Ricans, and Negroes, who are intellectually incapable of profiting from the type of education provided in urban high schools.

This point of view confuses the role of the public schools with the snob appeal role of private schools. Traditionally it is the function of the public schools in a democracy to provide for each child, without regard to his social class background, the type of education and intellectual stimulation which would make it possible for him to function up to or

near the maximum of his intelligence. The public schools were not initially intended for only one type of children. It is questionable whether at any time in their history, American public schools ever consisted of a homogeneous group of students, unless homogeneity were defined in purely arbitrary terms such as color. For more than a century northern urban public schools have been charged with the responsibility of assimilating waves of Irish, Italian, Polish, German, Russian, and Scandinavian immigrants. The contention that the present public schools consist of a more heterogeneous school population is based on the arbitrary emphasis on color or the assumption that one native language brings a more significant type of difference than does another.

That prejudice against and rejection of minority groups are closely related to discipline has been documented in *The Authoritarian Personality*. Studies of the personalities of bigoted and intolerant individuals reveal that these individuals were subjected to severe parental discipline in infancy and childhood:

Prejudiced subjects tend to report a relatively harsh and more threatening type of home discipline which was experienced as arbitrary by the child.
Of even more relevance to the present analysis is the finding:
The goals which such parents have in mind in rearing and training their children tend to be highly conventional. The *status-anxiety* (scoring added) so often found in families of prejudiced subjects is reflected in the adoption of a rigid and externalized set of values: what is socially accepted and what is helpful in climbing the social ladder is considered "good," and what deviates, what is different, and what is socially inferior is considered "bad" (17).

The compatibility of this approach to discipline and its goals with a creative and empathic character structure is questionable. Harsh and rigid parental discipline which is status-dominated leads to the development of an obsequious worship of and submission to those who are seen as strong, and to contemptuous hostility toward those who are seen as weak. It also involves a deep resentment against parents and other authorities who imposed these demands for rigid conformity and who are responsible for their inherent frustrations. Cynicism, a fundamental disregard for the validity of any human and moral values, may be one of the reactions to this pervasive conflict and confusion.

DISCIPLINE AND THE SOCIAL HIERARCHY

We must now examine the complicated relationship between discipline and other socialization processes, on the one hand, and the social value system on the other hand. It can be assumed that a given society communicates to and reinforces for its young people its hierarchical system—the relative status of defined groups of individuals—through a complex pattern of discipline devices. It can also be assumed that the status of a given group within the society will be maintained and reflected by the severity and types of discipline that can be inflicted upon the individual members of that group with impunity.

The above assumptions may be clarified by relevant illustrations. A college student recalled that he first seriously questioned his parents' ethical sincerity when they forbade him, under threat of punishment, to continue his friendship with his best friend because "he is not like us—he is a Jew." He was twelve at the time, and could not understand his parents' logic, since prior to this conversation he had seen them as the embodiment of kindness, sensitivity, and justice. The severity of his parents' demand, its unexpectedness, and the necessity to give the impression of compliance while he maintained a clandestine relationship with his friend made this a highly salient experience which this individual was unable to repress. What is more, his disrespect for his parents has continued.

White and Negro children in American society are taught at an early age that whites are considered superior and Negroes inferior (18). Initially this social fact may be communicated to the young child by the sum total of his observations and experiences—his contact with the prevailing attitudes expressed in overheard conversations, mass media, and so on. If, however, these normal means of socialization do not appear to affect the child's behavior then more definite techniques must be used. It is not uncommon for an American parent to tell his elementary school child that he must not play with or invite to the home another child because he is a Negro, Jew, or lives across the tracks. If this admonition is not readily accepted by the child, it can then become an early source of conflict between parent and child. Since the parents are in control

they may exercise the necessary discipline and force the child to comply with their wishes, subordinating and probably eventually eliminating his own desires.

This type of conflict becomes even more complicated at the adolescent stage since it involves or arouses the parental anxieties concerning sex. At this stage it becomes even more imperative that the child give evidence in his behavior and attitudes of the acceptance of the prevailing status distinctions among the various groups which comprise our total society. The higher status child cannot be permitted to jeopardize his and his family status by free and spontaneous association with lower status individuals. This cannot be permitted even under the guise of freedom or individualism. If the adolescent persists in violating this social dictum he runs the risk of severe parental and social discipline. At times this discipline may be severe enough to threaten the very status which the parents initially sought to preserve, suggesting a vengeful retaliatory force involved in the dynamic complexity. A recent example of this was found in the widely publicized incident wherein two parents, the father an educator, permitted their eighteen-year-old daughter to be brought before the court on the charge of being a "wayward minor" because she dated and claimed to be in love with a Negro student.

Negro students in newly integrated schools are told by their parents, friends, and school officials that they must be exemplary in their behavior. Implicit in these admonitions is the idea that the behavior of the individual Negro child must be determined by the fears, anxieties, or hostilities of others. The acceptance of this assumption even by Negroes indicates the degree to which the existing patterns of group status distinctions have permeated the thinking of all segments of our society. This is further illustrated by the fact that most school officials believe they are justified in expelling—a most severe form of discipline—any Negro boy against whom a white girl lodges a complaint. In some cases such complaints need be no more serious than the type of banter which has existed among school children from the beginning of coeducation. It is enough that the white girl complains for the Negro child to be severely disciplined.

Minnijean Brown's expulsion from Central High School in Little Rock shows that lower status individuals are not immune from severe discipline

by the controlling forces in our society even when there is such justification for their behavior as self-protection in the face of flagrant injustices.

E. Franklin Frazier and other observers have described the processes by which Negro parents prepared their children for their inferior status in the larger society. The possibility of conflict between the normal self-esteem needs of these children and their parents' desire to protect them from the more punitive discipline of the larger white dominated society is indicated by the following observation by Frazier: "Although in some middle-class families the children have been told to avoid conflicts with whites and to use such techniques as 'jiving' or flattery in order to get along with them, one is likely to find that the children will not accept wholeheartedly such advice" (19).

One boy's parents had told him that he should always "be clean, stop being common, treat them with respect and do as you are told." The boy replied, however, "You can do all these and not get along with them."

The task of the Negro parent in providing the appropriate preparation and discipline, if need be, in order to protect his child from the more harsh and severe discipline which awaits him if he transgresses the racial status taboos and etiquette is made more difficult by the social reality which imposes more severe punishments on minority group children. An examination of delinquency statistics reveals that incidence of arrests, court appearance, and institutionalization is disproportionately higher among children and youth of minority groups (20). Many interpretations, ranging from suggestions of inherent racial inferiority to emphasis on the role of sociological and psychological factors, have been presented to explain these findings. So far, however, there has been relatively little emphasis on the possibility that a substantial proportion of this higher incidence of delinquency among minority group youth reflects the greater tendency of the police and other law enforcement agents to be more diligent and literal in the enforcement of the law when relatively powerless and defenseless minority group individuals are involved. It is probable also that courts tend to be more severe in their punishment of a minority group person, particularly if the offense involves some explicit or implicit violation of the racial status pattern. It is generally known among Negroes in the South and certain Northern states that an assault against

Negro by Negro is not likely to be punished with the same severity that a relatively minor incident involving a white person would elicit.

The problem of a differential severity in terms of status may be illustrated with equal clarity by incidents involving white middle class youths in urban and suburban communities. In spite of attempts to keep these children from overt antisocial behavior by formidable family and community supports, some of them do come in conflict with the law.

The chief of police of a suburban community described a situation in which a number of boys from upper middle class, professional, and executive families were discovered engaging in acts of vandalism perpetrated on public and private property. This behavior was sufficiently reprehensible to bring these young people before the court on a charge of juvenile delinquency. Indeed, the chief of police indicated that "if they had not come from such good families, I would have taken them down to the police station." Instead he went to their families to tell them of their sons' actions and to obtain from the fathers of the boys an agreement to pay for the damage. Not one of these boys was listed on the police and court records in spite of evidence of repeated vandalism and other forms of antisocial behavior.

Certainly these more privileged children, as well as the victims of more harsh social discipline, soon learn that the standards of the larger society are flexible, arbitrary, and status determined. They learn that their own parents are required to be the agents of the larger societal inconsistencies and must adjust their own standards and techniques of discipline to protect the child and/or the tenuous status of the entire family. The privileged child must learn that while parents and society might be lenient or even permissive in their discipline in some areas of behavior, they will be most severe when the child's behavior threatens the existing social patterns, values, attitudes, and aspirations of his parents and his social group. The privileged child must be taught that there are certain realities of social interaction and distance which he will not be permitted to violate. If he seeks to violate these, he subjects himself to the most severe forms of discipline from his parents and the group with which they are identified.

These harsh facts remove the discussion of the essential problem of

discipline from the level of whether the infant or the child should be spanked or not spanked—whether discipline should be severe or permissive—to the more fundamental level of the function of discipline in molding young people into the social image of their parents. The problem of discipline then becomes crucial to understanding the problem of social change—will it be progress or deterioration?

The use of discipline as a technique for the maintenance and reinforcement of a given social status hierarchy can be understood not only in terms of what children and young people are punished for, but also by looking at the types of personality and behavior patterns which are rewarded.

It may be most difficult for persons within a culture to analyze objectively those patterns of behavior which are rewarded, since they generally reflect uncritically accepted norms of that society. To question these norms places the individual in the role of social critic with all its associated risks. What may be even more disturbing is that to question these norms is to question the validity of some important aspects of ourselves.

Serious questions must be raised, however, about the type of education and general socialization processes which reward those children and young people who are adept at "adjusting" to the norms of the group and who are able to suspend or eliminate their capacity for critical, independent thinking. If this is necessary for acceptance by the group or by those in authority, it may be that such an approach is sometimes justified by institutional conveniences or by other social imperatives, or it may even be that the capacity for this type of flexibility is evidence that the individual has been subjected to the type of constructive discipline which is essential to effective and socially realistic functioning. Serious problems arise, nevertheless, when such a pattern becomes dominant in the individual's character structure, reinforced by parental authority, education practices and procedures, and by other social institutional patterns.

Among the relevant questions which must be asked and answered for an imperative understanding of this problem are: To what extent do our parents, teachers, and other authority figures encourage constructive or discourage independent critical thinking and social sensitivity in our young people? Are those students who are able to accept passively and

retain whatever they are told the ones who are more likely to be re-warded? Are those students who are engaged in the tortured, and at times bungling, search for values more likely to be judged, discouraged, and labeled as "odd" or "difficult"? Have our schools, wittingly or un-wittingly, become a chief agent in transmitting to individuals the high value placed on the "noncontroversial" approach to human values—and particularly to those problems related to social justice?

The answers to these and related questions will determine whether our society is using its power and its discipline to develop a significant and necessary proportion of human beings with the dynamic creativity and integrity essential for major social contributions. The alternatives to such individuals are the passive, conforming, desensitized, human automatons, or those gray-flanneled adolescents whose present and pro-tective identification with the power sources and norms of their society masks a pervasive cynicism, conscious or not, and a generalized personal flatness and moral emptiness. This is the essence of the privileged delin-quent.

The term "delinquent" is in general use to describe children who come before the police or the courts because of behavior which violates certain legal norms. Yet the very word suggests something beyond the purely legal, namely the lack of something which society considers essential. The author has elsewhere defined the concept of the privileged delin-quent:

If delinquency is to be defined in terms of its essentials of the lack of sensi-tivity, lack of empathy, the callous disregard for the humanity and dignity of others, a punitive approach to others who are considered weak and de-fenseless, then these privileged individuals must be considered delinquent in spite of the fact that they are not part of the court records and the presently available delinquency statistics. The fact that we do not, at present, know the number of such young people who are developing in our schools; that we do not have the theoretical framework and the methods for recognizing them; and that we do not know whether their numbers are increasing or decreasing does not necessarily diminish the social gravity of this aspect of the delinquency problem (20).

The relationship between the privileged delinquent and his social environment is essentially exploitative and opportunistic. His behavior is

not bound by stable principles of right or wrong, nor is he likely to be concerned with problems of fairness or unfairness, justice or injustice, unless they directly involve him personally or someone immediately close to him. His standards of justice vary according to closeness or distance of the individuals involved in the issue. He is primarily concerned with maintenance of his own status and reinforcing his chances of personal success without serious concern about the means by which these are obtained.

The privileged delinquent does not come before the courts because his family generally can and does protect him from these forms of social discipline. It is difficult to obtain objective data on this form of delinquency because this form of pathology is so inextricably woven into the fabric of the valued and privileged aspect of our society. The behavior of the privileged delinquent may go unnoticed because it may be seen merely as a "normal and natural" pattern of a discriminative middle and upper class way of life.

Like the underprivileged delinquent, the privileged delinquent too is a victim of his society. His personality has been shackled to the competitive values of the quest for status and success. He has been disciplined and rewarded in terms of these goals from the competition for grades and approval in the elementary grades through the hectic anxiety in awaiting the competitive examination scores which will determine his admission to or rejection from a privileged college. Under these conditions others are likely to be seen as threats, competitors, or inferiors.

The privileged delinquent may be a product of rigid and severe discipline or of permissive, overindulgent parental reactions. The particular form of discipline may be less relevant than the fact that most effective forces in the society mold individuals in such a way as to reduce their human effectiveness. Future research may well support the hypothesis that the corroding social insensitivity of the privileged delinquent is inimical to the maximum development and use of his intellectual and artistic creativity.

It is hereby suggested that the goal of creative discipline—parental and social—is to provide for the child and adolescent those social conditions within which he may develop the type of character structure which is

consistent with his maximum creativity, a respect for his own humanity, and a functional identity with other human beings—an integrity of self and social empathy. These conditions are obtainable; the product is also obtainable through the most rigorous form of discipline—the discipline of the human ego, its pretenses, and its distortions.

If discipline is directed toward these goals it can be neither punitive, harsh, and rigid, nor chaotically permissive. It necessarily will come with the human sensitivity, flexibility, guidance, and structure which are essential to human creativity, and which reflect a self-perpetuating respect for the inviolable dignity of all human beings.

TEACHING VALUES TO OUR CHILDREN

Henry Enoch Kagan

TO SURVIVE A SOCIETY must have values in which the majority of its members really believe. The study of the rise and fall of nations should teach us that this area of values will indicate the first sign of a nation's decadence. The first symptom of decay is the decline of confidence in those ideals and values. As Joad observed, we can identify decadence when people begin to value their personal experience "for its own sake, irrespective of the quality of the experience, the object of the experience," when they leave out the end which the experience is to serve. It may be ironic, but a person can be so preoccupied with himself that he can be totally unaware of where he is going. Has today's hedonistic pursuit of pleasure so comforted us that we are not alert to the direction our changed situation has already taken us?

Power, personal or national, does destroy itself if it has no more purposeful use or control than the enjoyment of itself. This was the conviction of the classical peoples upon whose culture our Western civilization rose. For their arrogance or "hubris," the Greeks declared, men would meet their "nemesis" at the hands of the gods. The Hebrews stated it more succinctly: "Pride goeth before destruction." We can never allow ourselves to forget for a moment that atomic annihilation can become a fatal reality. Nevertheless, these ominous portents of doom are less cause

Henry Enoch Kagan is Rabbi and Counseling Psychologist, Sinai Temple, Mount Vernon, N.Y.

for anxiety than the more subtle self-doubting, the more corrosive wearing away of faith that what we, as Americans, are doing has no significance for the morrow.

THE "NONDIRECTED" AMERICAN

That too many Americans have lost the feeling that what they do has lasting importance or any importance at all has become the focus of attention of the honest critics of our day. Their argument that the average American is too much "other directed" has been amply documented. As an organization man, grey flanneled and executivized or white collared and unionized, or as a mere commodity personality to sell or to be sold to, or as a status seeker frightened into conformity, or as a rootless nomad with amnesia wandering from apartment to apartment among the faceless masses of the city, or as an anonymous, mobile, suburbanite shuttling from station to station, or as a rubberstamp brainwashed by the mass media of communication, in the opinion of some critics the average American has become an unthinking robot.

These critics plead for more "inner-directed" persons interested in the independent thinking a democracy requires. For the more a person becomes "other directed" the more is he amenable to the eventual control of totalitarian dictatorship. Dangerous as the absence of "inner-directed" persons is to a democracy, probably more dangerous is the presence of "nondirected" persons who do not care whether they are "other" or "inner" directed. To them it makes little difference because they do not believe or do not realize they possess any freedom to choose between being "other" or "inner" directed. The world's problems are too big for their little "me."

Democracy is not a system that can survive on calloused cynics or on deterministic disbelievers in free will. Democracy is a system for those who believe a man can reason and make a choice between alternatives—and choose the more valuable in terms of the durability of its truth, goodness, and beauty. If we are not merely to be changed by the changing times but make our own changes to meet the challenge of the times, we

must become more aware of what we are doing and why we are doing it. Such an awareness of the object of our acts can best be stimulated when we stop to think about what we hope for our children. Should we hope for a better future for our children?

Do we have the right to bear children if we do not believe they have a future? The question is not asked to engage in a discussion of the "population explosion," acute though this problem increasingly will become and related though it is to the destiny of our children in the 1960s. The answer to the question, "Do we look upon the child as an accident or as a purposeful commitment to the future?" is the fundamental premise of teaching value. Unless we first place the proper value upon a child we cannot instill values in him.

In our times a child need not be an accident. Therefore, we can more easily choose purpose and emphasize the purpose of the child—but purpose for what? Because man can reason as well as feel, this purpose need not be just the blind animal instinct of the herd to preserve itself. An animal instinct to survive in the human would certainly be healthy for it could countervail suicide, seldom found outside the human species. But we are humans and not animals because we are conscious of time and have acquired a scale of values. Thus we want our children to have a better tomorrow as well as to be alive tomorrow.

Self-preservation is a strong motive for imitative training of children to do what their parents do as persons, as members of a particular socioeconomic group, as citizens of the nation, and as communicants of a religious group; but self-examination will reveal that in each of these multiple roles we ourselves play we are constantly being confronted with the choices of right or wrong, true or false, beautiful or ugly, just or unjust, kind or cruel. Frequently, our varied roles are in conflict with each other and what we choose to do in private we might not choose to do in public, and vice-versa. Even if our main purpose were to train children to maintain the status quo, to keep things exactly as we bequeath them, we would still have to teach them to believe that choosing a certain set of values is better than others. How much more, then, will a conscious awareness of values be necessary for our children, when the changing times force them to make new decisions?

VARIATIONS IN VALUES

The training of another person can never be entirely impersonal. Objective though the educator, parent or teacher, should try to be, there is always the emotional residue of subjectivity which puts a value on what is being taught. This subjectivity applies to ideas and ideals. It even applies to pure facts, as for example, when some scientists say nuclear "fallout" is not too much while others say any "fallout" is too much. In the more aware and honest adult the personal purely emotional evaluation is smaller. It is greater in the partisan who conceals this fact of emotion by declaiming his objectivity and insisting he has "the whole truth and nothing but the truth." It is just because the value of an experience is implicit in the emotional reaction we have to it that it becomes all the more necessary to subject our set of values to a reasoning awareness. This is important lest systems of beliefs, personal, social, national, and religious, each demanding loyalty and sometimes inconsistent with each other, become so obscured by emotion as to create an "inherited conglomerate" of conflicting feelings beyond the approach of reason.

To be ethical, an act should be more than a conditioned reflex. It should be more than a rationalization of an emotional need. Nor is morality merely a matter of personality to be equated with the acceptance or nonacceptance of self. A decision made in the area of the moral should be a true decision based on the eternal verities. Since democracy is predicated on the ability of an individual to make choices based on reason, the fate of democracy will be determined by the success we have in creating decisionmaking values that are ethical, meaningful, consistent, and consciously chosen.

The challenge of teaching decisionmaking values can best be approached by a clarification of their emotional origin and content which will reveal more clearly the delicate balance of intellect, will, and emotion. We can do this on many levels. For the purpose of definition, we can speak of personal values, social values, and religious values. For the purpose of locating where these values are learned, we can speak of personal values learned in the home, social values learned in school and

society, and religious values learned in church or synagogue. For the purpose of analyzing techniques for teaching values, using Herbert C. Kelman's classification, we can speak of learning values by compliance, learning values by identification, and learning values by internalization. For the purpose of measuring the effectiveness of values, we can speak of the proposed content of values (what we say), the emotional attitude toward values (what we mean), and actual behavior regarding values (what we do).

The fact that we can discuss our values on so many different levels is in itself disturbing. A person truly kind, honest, and tolerant does not talk about it. His actions speak for themselves, for as Rabbi Ben Azzai said: "The reward of virtue is virtue itself." A society which really lived by its values would not be embarrassingly conscious of them as we here apparently are. Furthermore, that we are able to differentiate value learning on so many different levels may well be the major reason why our young are the victims of so much inner conflict about what is the right value. The father kind in his home, but impersonal in his business, intolerant in his politics, and prejudiced in his religion, can scarcely effect consistency in the behavior of his child. Ideally, we would welcome an integrating continuum of values through home, school, society, and religion; but realistically, we must face up to the hard fact that there is as much contradiction as there is congruence between the different values our young confront in so many different places.

The absence of a strong sense of value continuity in our society is a primary cause of the difficulty we face in helping the child to become personally ethical, socially democratic, and spiritually religious so that the ethical, the democratic, and the religious are consistent with each other. Anthropologists tell us that some small tribal groups produce mentally healthy children because, early in their life, these children are made conscious of their intimate connection with the adult community. In some, as early as the age of six, the children organize themselves into groups exactly modeled after the adult group. This does not mean that they become mechanical conformists, for competition between the children is encouraged. However, they compete not merely for personal success but primarily for an achievement which will enhance the whole group. The

children are approved and praised not for the triumph they have over a rival but for the discipline they impose upon themselves in order to be better achievers.

Unfortunately, we do not have this advantage of continuity of an isolated homogeneous group. Our society is pluralistic in more ways than one. While economically the norm is increasingly middle class, we have the upper middle, the middle middle and the lower middle groups as well as religious, racial, and geographic groups. The more these separate groups become conscious of their identity, the more they compete with each other. Furthermore, unlike a simple, settled, agricultural group, our industrial, multigroup society is highly mobile.

In fact, in our democracy we boast of a fluidity between our groups which enables a member of one class to move into another. Whether the move is considered to be "up" or "down" fluctuates. In this situation, competition is not for achievement to enhance one's group but for the success of an individual in moving up into another group. Since in our land a very high premium is placed on individual success, measured by the material gains and status of the most successful of the competing groups, this end all too often will justify questionable means. This all pervasive compulsion to be individually successful aggravates the difficulties involved in teaching the ethical, democratic, and spiritual ideals our society must value to survive.

We have the evidence that idealism among our youth declines where personal success is the only motivation. Contributing factors such as low salaries and low status of teachers or the length of time needed to become physicians and discriminatory practices of medical schools should not obscure the fact that the dangerous drop in the number of our youth desiring to enter the helping professions of teaching or medicine is also due to the unwillingness of these youth to make personal sacrifices. If the observations of the college teachers are correct, the concern about making college students take loyalty oaths is unwarranted for the only "ism" they are interested in is "privatism." What is disturbing about the college-trained future leaders of our nation is that they have no adventurous enthusiasm for any cause. For a comfortable berth in industry they are prepared to conform without loyalty oaths.

The apathy of our youth to ideals is not a conscious philosophy based on the cynical "beatnik" question: "What's in it for me?" Long before they enter college, our youth are infected with the contagious germs of security and success.

On the one hand, the increased welfare aid necessary for the aged, the sick, the unemployed, and the retired, creates an atmosphere in which social security becomes a goal all too soon for vigorous young people. This premature desire to be settled may be a more potent reason than passionate romance for the present rash of immature early marriages. On the other hand, success-motivated parents do not accept their children unconditionally. The child is approved only if he performs in a manner which the parent expects will move the child up. Frequently, depending on the degree of his need to compensate for his own frustration, the parent may even expect to move up himself through the child's success. With such unhealthy parental pressure the child may feel compelled to find the successful vocation in a secure job at the expense of his own interests and his own conscience. The debilitating effect that this smog of security and success has had on the ethical values of our young is painfully exposed by the participation of their "heroes" in TV quiz-rigging and "payola"; and even more so by the apathy of our young toward or acceptance of such immoral behavior as natural.

Home, school and society, church and synagogue, will have to make yeoman efforts to reverse this process of decay in values. The challenge does not come from the educational and technical successes of the Soviet Union and of China where desire to enhance the total group is the motivation and where achievement is inspired by nationalistic enthusiasm and by a passionate belief in Communistic values. Because we are not committed either to what we ought to do for the state or to what the state ought to do for us, but because we are committed to the sanctity and dignity of the individual, we ought to be challenged to do that which is ethical, democratic, and spiritual for its own sake. A nation which will not discipline itself will have discipline imposed upon it. We must recognize that the difference between liberty and license is self-discipline. Otherwise, a democracy may also be compelled to legislate every act of existence.

TEACHING VALUES IN THE HOME

Only as the child grows in self-discipline does he emerge as a responsible citizen. To teach values successfully we must emphasize the concept of growth. We must constantly be aware that, like all other learned experience, learning values is also a developmental process. A young child does not instinctively, and certainly not generally, know what is moral, what is the correct democratic attitude toward the different, nor that the Lord doth require of us "to do justly, love mercy and walk humbly."

Learning a vocabulary from parents which includes a "yes" and a "no" is the beginning of the semantics of morality. Because the child wishes to be approved and loved by parents, he welcomes the affective judgment they project by gesture and tone of voice as well as by word. Furthermore, contrary to the popular misunderstanding of progressive education and psychoanalytic theory, the child is healthier when he feels the safety of parental boundaries. Nevertheless, the best-intentioned parent should not be surprised if the child's behavior is not consistently reliable.

Teaching Principles

An adult may handle specific situations in terms of a general principle; but a child handles general principles in terms of a specific situation. Therefore, a parent may sincerely teach honesty as a supreme general value, but when the same parent instructs the child to tell an unwelcome telephone caller that the parent is not at home, the child looks upon deception as honest. A parent may sincerely uphold the general principle of the constitutional doctrine of equality and the religious doctrine of the brotherhood of man but when the parent makes disparaging remarks about a minority or about a majority, the child begins to think like the triumphant pigs in Orwell's *Animal Farm* who claimed "all animals are equal but some animals are more equal than others."

To learn merely the meaning of the words, honesty, equality, religion, the child must have a specific reference that is reasonably stable. Learning values in the family becomes more complex, because there often are

variances in ethics among its adult members. As Swiss children learn three languages without knowing it, German from a grandparent, Italian from a mother, or French from a father, so specific types of conduct are unknowingly picked up from a variety of adults in the family which can make for conflicting behavior in the child. A child who complies with the command of any one parent at any one given time will incorporate this reaction only superficially. He adopts the behavior temporarily because he expects to gain approval or avoid disapproval in that specific instance. For consistent moral behavior a method more effective than a parental order must be used to create and reinforce a positive attitude of the child toward desirable behavior.

The Father's Critical Role

It is at this point that the role of the parent, especially of the father, becomes the critical factor. Because the father's drive for occupational success has been so consuming that he has little time left for family relations, much has been written about the absence of father authority and the consequent dominance of the mother in the typical American middle-class home. However, it is not the time spent but the image of a parent which the father imprints in the mind of his child which is significant. The former patriarchal family with certain disciplinary advantages as well as handicaps will not return. In the modern home of the emancipated woman, authority shifts to the more dominant or the more compulsive of the two parents. Yet, a healthier coequal authority could exist between them if both parents, professing belief in the sanctity of the family, would also accept the religious point of view that the authority for authority should be love and should exist for the well-being of the governed. Tyrants in the home will command obedience, but only understanding parents will elicit the response of the fifth commandment: "Honor thy father and thy mother."

If the matrix of the family is to be a love relationship, the father must be no less loving than the mother, whatever may be other differences between the masculine and the feminine. The father who loves his child will assume his role of authority without being authoritarian, and if he is consistent he need not be coercive. It is only when the child identifies

himself with such loving parents, father as well as mother, that he begins to believe in his act of conforming. Good behavior becomes good because it sustains for him a desired relationship.

A cause for child misbehavior and also a cause for juvenile delinquency is either the absence of any father authority or the presence of only an authoritarian father who incites infantile rebellion. As far as boys are concerned, when they are disciplined only by mothers, they develop, as a reaction formation, an identification of goodness with femininity and to prove their masculinity their behavior may run into antisocial directions. On the other hand, a failure to make any positive identification with either parent can lead to the serious psychopathic delinquent who has no moral system at all to which he can refer in order to distinguish between right and wrong. A careful psychological experiment designed to induce the feeling of guilt in such hardened psychopathic delinquents failed.

Of course we must be on guard against instilling neurotic guilt by making normal children overly concerned about the inconsistency of their developing behavior, however, this does not relieve us of the responsibility of teaching the child right from wrong. For normal children, it has been found that guilt feelings can have a healthy purpose when punishment is accompanied by the full acceptance of and affection for the child. To tell a child "I won't love you unless you do as I say" is a betrayal of trust as well as nonproductive. The parent wishes to be wanted as a person; so does the child. Since responsibility and decisionmaking in the group is the need of a democracy, training in both should begin in the home by encouraging the child as a wanted member to participate in family decisions including the matter of punishment. In this context of mutuality and respect for person the foundations of the child's ethical, democratic, and spiritual values are being built.

TEACHING VALUES IN SCHOOL AND SOCIETY

Wherever a child must grow without parents or with parents who are inadequate for the task, society is compelled to provide substitutes.

Whether these surrogate parents be the personnel of an educational, a religious, or even a penal institution, all must become aware of the therapeutic nature of their relations to that unloved child. Social worker, guidance expert, psychiatrist, probation officer, teacher, or clergyman will not only have to do what parents failed to do but what is far more difficult, undo what the parents did.

As for the average child, loved and an active participant in a home of coequal and consistent parental authority, his growing sense of values needs constant reinforcement and enlargement. This responsibility now rests upon the school and society. If they are not to undo the good which good parents have accomplished, school and society must continue those positive patterns of value learning already set in the home. The principle of the ego-involvement of the child applies in the classroom as much as it applies in the home or, as the Talmudic teacher put it, "not he who begets but he who teaches the child is the father." In the school, too, values are not memorized like facts nor do they last long if they are ordered by fiat.

When it comes to moral and democratic behavior, identification is superior to compliance in the classroom as it is in the home. The child will identify favorably and feel secure in his new group situation when a feeling of belongingness with his classmates is stimulated and when the teacher recognizes the significance of his or her role in the group. The teacher should remember that the child is not a receptacle into which information is poured, but a thinking, acting, and feeling person. In such a frame of reference, the teacher becomes more successful in communicating any information when he acts as an exemplary democratic leader in any democratic group by enlisting the participation of the student in making decisions and thus overcoming any emotional resistance by the individual member in decisionmaking. This applies even more to values than to facts just because so much feeling is involved in values. When the teacher holds the child's level of aspiration too low, the result is listlessness; when the teacher holds it too high, the frustration may result in cheating.

Because of our growing knowledge of motivation, our educational philosophy has passed from the stage of learning by memory to learning

by doing. But if the goal of learning by doing is just to socialize a child by the introduction of cumbersome activities and projects at the expense of his thinking, this pragmatic program is no improvement. Good citizenship is not good unless it also produces knowledgeable citizens. To think, one must believe in the value of curiosity. On the elementary level, the teachers convey this by empathy with the child's natural curiosity; on the secondary level, the teachers convey this by an inspirational approach. To learning by doing and learning by thinking, we must now add learning by feeling which moves the student to feel the worth of honest learning. A teacher failed this threefold process when she, with the best intentions, expressed her anger with a class of six-year-olds because so many of them copied each others' answers. When one mother asked her child why the teacher was angry, he replied, "Oh, because we copied the wrong answers."

Rabbi Jochanan ben Zakai said the purpose of education was the development of "a good mind"—intellectual achievement; "a good neighbor"—social development; but necessary for both was "a good heart." This is equal to our idiom "putting your heart" into an action because you believe in it. The three "R's" are more readily learned if they are approached with the three "H's" of motivation—head, hand, and heart. The classroom is the joint venture of leader and group who prefer doing together that which is ethical, democratic, and spiritual.

VALUES DURING ADOLESCENCE

This effort faces greater obstacles as the student becomes an adolescent just because society imposes upon him greater frustrations by postponing his adulthood. Since moral value, especially in a democracy, should be the result of decision, the adolescent must grow toward independence. The adolescent must pass through a period of rebellion against both home and school. This rebellion should not be discouraged, but it can be guided. A real problem in moral values arises in the area of sex mores because the adolescent's biological maturity precedes his social maturity. Because adults themselves have so much unnecessary conflict about sex education

of the adolescent, in this area the home and school is much too handi-capped by secrecy, fear, and ignorance. To prevent the degradation of personality through sex, it is important that the emotional response and ethical aspects be not neglected while teaching the biological facts. Lov-ing parents could do this more effectively than the school if they could overcome taboos and be properly trained on how to teach sex. Even so, the adolescent is more affected or influenced by society outside school and home than is the younger child, just because he wants so quickly to be an adult.

Will the adolescent want to be more than a well-paid technician if the intellectual is an "egghead"? Will he approach his work in dedication if so many adults approach their work just as a necessary vocation? Will he emulate heroes of American freedom if we have debunked them all? Will he be sensitive to kindness if our mass media daily make cruelty and violence more exciting? Will he respond to sexual maturity if he is entertained publicly by infantile immorality? Will he believe in de-mocracy, when taught in the school, if the very same school is prevented by outside pressure, by government law, or by popular tradition from being democratic?

It is this very conflict within adult value interests which drives the ado-lescent to seek groups of his own in which he may create values within his own group which are consistent and frequently more idealistic than those of his adult environment. Because values do become more firmly anchored when approved by one's peers, probably the most fruitful area to counteract the decay of values in our day is in the self-organized youth groups under a democratic leader who is himself highly motivated by ethical, democratic, and spiritual beliefs.

At any rate we should once and for all cease making a scapegoat out of our schools for the sins of our society. Because our schools are more and more emphasizing the quality of the things and ideas their students learn, they are teaching ethical, democratic, and spiritual values by ex-perience, sometimes more effectively than home, church, and synagogue. In this sense, the schools are already inculcating religious values even though they do not, as many groups feel they should not, actually teach religion.

TEACHING VALUES IN CHURCH AND SYNAGOGUE

Throughout this essay, I have emphasized the supreme importance of consistency in teaching values. Therefore, I have consistently used the phrase "the ethical, the democratic, the spiritual" as though they were synonymous. In the noblest expression of our American beliefs they are certainly harmonious. With great insight, our founding fathers separated the church and the state because they believed the ethical and the spiritual must also be democratic. This is not to imply that religion is not democratic, for within each religion there is a doctrine of brotherhood which welcomes converts from all groups. But with reference to each, different religions do not accept the principle of absolute equality. In a democracy which gives freedom to all religions, the introduction of religion into the public school could produce divisiveness because so many different religions have the right to exist here.

Furthermore, since it is the nature of religion to believe it has the right way and, to some, the only way to salvation, instruction in religion can never be purely informational and objective. To teach a religion as mere fact without faith, which is a feeling of conviction, is useless. This can only be done by believers in a particular religion. Since religion above all other experience is a value judgment, it is an educational error to think it can be effectively taught by didactic information with no reference to a personal decision or commitment.

There is still another powerful reason why one may hold that the religious values of a religion should not be involved in or beholden to the school systems of the state. The great independent undertaking of a religion is to develop the independent man who can make decisions on the basis of his religious commitment that will reflect his confidence that it is God's will that he should love his neighbor as himself.

The observations already made on the home, school, and society that values are truly learned if they are consistent, anchored in identification, and measured by actual behavior likewise apply to the teaching of specific religious values. Therefore, authoritarian compliance with religious doctrine will only mildly affect the actual religious belief and be-

havior of children if their parents are only indifferently identified with their religious heritage. Psychological studies of the family have shown that those homes in which religion is too strict or too little seem less stable than those homes in which an understanding loving religion is a cooperative venture in which parent as well as child participates. As some child guidance clinics require the attendance of parents, would the religious instruction of the Sunday schools become more dynamic if they refused to accept children unless their parents attend? However, the major avowed purpose of religion is not merely to change attitudes in order to achieve better behavior but to make the new attitude and behavior a welcomed integral part of the inner life of man. Therefore, to achieve this goal religion needs more than compliance and more than identification.

Religion hopes to have its value system so internalized that satisfaction in it comes not from approval or conformity but from the inner content of the experience itself. While preaching and exhortation create a favorable climate, we know that people best recognize their inner needs by self-discovery. Religion today, therefore, is searching for new strategies for teaching the ideal of love, for making prayer more meaningful for youth, and especially for the most effective way of initiating religious faith in children.

In the case of love, religion is discovering through the psychodynamics of prejudice that love finds no room in the soul that is already unwittingly filled with hate-producing dogma. Hate must be talked out and confronted before love is extended.

In the case of faith, just because it must be instilled very early in the child, religion is discovering that a courageous faith is best strengthened by fortifying it in the home. The child wishes to feel protected by God as his loving Father. In this strange world filled with so much anxiety the child wants to feel "wanted" in a cosmic sense. There is little doubt that the child desires to believe in a Protecting God and sometimes desperately at a very early age. The little child of three begins to ask "Who made me and the world I live in?" just because he is so small in such an immense universe. To put off the answer as childish is to frighten the child.

If the child is frightened he does what the human race did when it was

a primitive child, namely, the child manufactures in his mind magical powers to see him through this strange universe, which are conjured up by just wishing, or he will think that he is a powerless puppet pulled around by magic. This is unhealthy for the child and for the decision-making values both democracy and religion wish to inculcate. It deceives the child with one of two false notions; one, that there are easy substitutes for work, and two, that one has no free will to make decisions.

The Piaget studies in child development show that little children grow out of an infantile frightened sense of the magical omnipotence of everything around them and begin to develop a healthier, realistic idea of cause and effect by the answers given to their question "Who made me and this world?" Failure to make this step to reality can have damaging psychological effects in meeting later the crises in adult life which do call for decision. Children intuitively express this basic need to believe there is an intelligent cause for life, and this is why the Gesell statistics show that interest in religion reaches a peak in the average child before the age of six. Therefore, many of our organized religions, Jewish, Catholic, and Protestant, are now wisely directing their energies toward family life religious education.

I conclude with a reference to Moses, one of the world's great, inspired teachers of ethics, democracy, and spirituality. He deeply experienced all three of these values by fashioning a moral code, freeing a people from political slavery, and finding his God. At the close of his long career, Moses came to the conclusion that all three values, including religion itself, could best be learned by the child in his home. In that home, the parents become the best teachers when these ethical, democratic, and spiritual values are not superficially upheld by them but when they are so internalized that in private and in public the parents' behavior is consistent with them. Thus, at the end of his life Moses said: "And these words which I command you this day shall be upon thy heart. Thou shalt teach them diligently unto thy children and shalt speak of them when thou sittest in thy house and when thou walkest by the way."

A SOCIOLOGIST'S VIEW

Talcott Parsons

THIS CHAPTER will concentrate on values for society and its sub-sectors, rather than for individuals as such, important as the latter subject is. In this light the value system of a society is the conception held by its members, with varying degrees of unanimity, of a *good* society, and hence the standards by which they measure the good things and the short-comings of their own society. The central pattern, then, will be specified in terms of its applicability to limited subsectors of the total society; child-hood and youth constitute one of the most important of these.

ACHIEVEMENT

In these terms I think there has been a notable consistency in the basic orientations during almost the whole period of our national existence. I like to characterize the American value system as one of *instrumental activism*. The use of instrumental here means that neither the society as a whole nor any aspect of it, such as the state, is elevated into an "end in itself," but is considered to be instrumental for "worth while" things, with a very wide range of what may be considered worth while. The element of activism, however, narrows this range. For the unit of the society, whether it be a collectivity or an individual, it means the *achieve-ment* of something important. So far as these achievements are contribu-

Talcott Parsons is Professor of Sociology, Harvard University.

tions to the society, they must be the maintenance or, better still, the improvement of the society as a base and environment for achievement.

The spelling out of this abstract formula brings up a number of familiar themes. If we value achievement, we must value the conditions which are essential to it. From the point of view of the achieving unit we may speak of freedom and opportunity as the essential parts of the environment. Freedom here implies absence of unnecessary hampering restraints, while opportunity is a structuring of positive possibilities. Indeed we may go a step further and suggest the importance of positive rewards for achievement which are in some respects involved in the somewhat maligned "success" complex. This essentially is to say that if achievement is valued, people must be given freedom and opportunity to achieve; moreover, if they in fact achieve admirably, this should be recognized.

A strong emphasis on achievement, however, raises inevitably the problem of equality; because achievement and its rewards are inherently uneven, they create positions of power and privilege. Hence we not only value achievement as such and the freedoms, opportunities, and rewards that go with it, but also access to these good things. The basic formula in this respect is equality of opportunity. Opportunity in turn, however, is a relative concept. What is an opportunity for one trained or financially able to take advantage of it may not be an opportunity at all for others. What is realistically an opportunity depends on the capacity of the individual to use the opportunity. Capacity is the potentiality for achievement which in turn is partly a matter of innate ability and probably even more of the "advantages" or handicaps which an individual has experienced.

The activism of our values indicates that we do not value a static, unchanging society. Rather we value one which is continually changing in a "progressive" direction, which is to say in accord with the central values. Above all, it may be said, this is defined as progressive increase in capacities and opportunities for achievement on progressively higher levels, and in the freedoms necessary to use them. The maintenance of certain equalities—or, of course, improvement of them—goes without saying. We value stability, but a stability in change, not a stagnant absence of change.

This value complex has a very obvious bearing on the problems of

childhood and youth. After all, the capacities of its members to achieve are overwhelmingly the most important resources of the society. In this respect the younger generation is the most important sector because it has the longest period of activity ahead of it. It is also far more flexible than its elders and its bringing up and education requires a very heavy commitment of resources.

Foreign observers have often stressed what is sometimes called the "child-centeredness" of American society. This is sometimes interpreted to imply a heavy, indeed undesirable, emphasis on "indulgence" of the child. In my opinion the more important and just interpretation lies in the concern we have for the future of our society and the training of those on whom its future depends.

Institutionalized values, in the sense in which I am using that concept, establish a certain broad direction for the orientation of members of a society, but they do not determine concrete action. This depends on many other factors having to do with the structure of the society, other aspects of the culture, and the characteristics of its individual members. I should like to attempt to analyze the bearing on the problems of American childhood and youth of the interplay between this broad set of values and certain critical trends in the development of American society.

Though it is my view that the main institutionalized values of American society have remained stable, the society as a whole has been anything but static. It has, as we well know, been changing with great rapidity. There has been enormous economic development, growth of population, urbanization, change in international status, and many other things. For my purposes, however, I would like to stress the process of differentiation which has been going on and the process of upgrading of expected levels of performance in the society which has accompanied this differentiation.

THE CHANGING FAMILY

The aspects of the society in which children and youth are most intimately involved are of course the family, the local—especially the resi-

dential—community, and the system of formal education. Trends in their development, however, need to be seen in the context of the society as a whole with its development of high technology, of large-scale employing organizations, innumerable associations, and the like.

As these structures have developed within the present century, the American family has undergone major changes. In the first place it has become a much more specialized agency, i.e., it has become more differentiated from others. The most obvious phase of this is that many of its previous functions in such spheres as economic production have been taken over by other types of organizations. This is true also of certain financial responsibilities which have been assumed by social security, pension plans, many types of insurance and the like.

Another important development is that of the greater concentration of the nuclear family as a residential unit. In spite of the high divorce rates and the serious problem of broken families discussed by Dr. Eveline Burns (1), there is a larger proportion of the total population than ever before living in nuclear families, and the proportion of persons in the household other than nuclear family members has steadily decreased (2). At the upper end of the status scale, of course, the living-in domestic servant has almost disappeared. At the lower end the roomer is now a rarity, but above all relatives other than nuclear family members are much less common as household members.

But if the family has become more specialized in function, we may ask, for what? The main reference point for answering this question lies in our value system, sketched above. The family is perhaps the most important single builder and conserver of our human resources, in the first place through the rearing and, as sociologists say, the socialization of children, and also through the subtle psychological significance of the relation of spouses to each other, and through their common parenthood. Functions other than these such as economic production, financial security, religious education, and health care, have been steadily transferred to other agencies. But on the other side the intensity of involvement in socialization and mutual emotional attachments has been continually increasing.

Demographic Factors

Two demographic phenomena which have become conspicuous since World War II are important indices of this trend. One is the marriage rate and its consequences. There is today a larger proportion of the total population of marriageable age married and living with their spouses than at any time in the history of reliable census data; this is true in spite of divorces (since most divorced persons remarry) and separations. One of the reasons for this, of course, is increased longevity, which means that spouses have longer married periods before the death of one; another reason is that people are now getting married at an earlier age.

The second phenomenon is the much discussed increased birth rate. This is a noteworthy phenomenon. Its quantitative aspect is noteworthy since it has occurred in a society where knowledge of contraception has been more widespread than ever before, and the methods available more reliable. There are other noteworthy aspects. One of these is the increase in the number of families having three or four children with a continuing decline in the number of large families having five or more children. Another is the concentration in terms of spacing. The average American married woman now has her last child by the age of twenty-seven.

With respect to the birth rate, it is my view that whatever portion may be accounted for by such factors as reemployment and continued prosperity, there is a deeper set of forces at work here. It represents a new phase in the development of motivation for parenthood. In particular for women it represents an impressive new dedication to what is clearly the most central of all specifically feminine functions, namely child bearing and rearing. But the phenomenon of larger families is taking place in a context where women are not going "back to the home" in a traditional sense. Rather we should say it has been occurring at a time when the feminine role as a whole has been differentiating so that maternity is only one, though probably the single most central, component of it.

Masculine and Feminine Roles

Thus women are becoming much more educated than before, as part of the general process of educational upgrading which will be discussed presently. Furthermore there is greatly increased participation of women in the labor force, most notably of married women living with their husbands, a fact which quite clearly is not explained by the pressure of economic necessity. The concentration of the child-bearing period is particularly impressive evidence of this process of differentiation. It, combined with longer life and better health, frees the woman for a variety of other functions in later life.

Associated with these changes in the feminine role has been a set of less drastic ones in the masculine role in the family. Here the conspicuous part seems to be the more active participation of men in family life, their new flexibility about helping with household chores and child care, and their more "companionate" relation to their wives. Generally speaking the American family has become more "democratic" in structure, with wives taking larger shares of responsibility. But broadly, except for reduction of hours of work in the "labor" occupations, this has not meant less devotion of men to their occupational roles, in spite of recent contention about lack of ambition on executive levels. The average man's job is probably on a higher level of competence and responsibility than ever before, and is at least as important to the status of the individual and his whole family, not only in terms of money income but of all the subtle symbolic factors which are involved.

The Children

What then of the children? The really big shift seems to be in the direction of greater emphasis on what is sometimes called independence training as a prerequisite for more responsible adult roles. This seems to depend on a rather special combination of intense emotional attachment in the early years and the use of this attachment to motivate enhanced performance, which becomes increasingly independent of the objects of the attachment. The very exclusiveness of the nuclear family circle facilitates this high emotional concentration. But the involvement,

not only of the father, but of both parents in interests other than their children, and the pressures for the child to participate outside the home, starting with nursery school and kindergarten and going on from there, create a situation in which this emotional concentration cannot be perpetuated in its original form but must give way to a restructuring in terms of an extrafamilial set of objects and standards.

It has been so common as to be almost fashionable for this trend in the family to be deplored, on the one hand as an indication of withdrawal by the parents from extrafamilial responsibilities, on the other as exposing the child to overattention and indulgence. It seems to me that this view fails to take sufficient account of the articulation of the family with the rest of the society. First, there is obviously the participation of both parents in the outside world, most conspicuously enhanced in recent times on the part of the mother.

EDUCATION AND THE SOCIAL STRUCTURE

There is also, however, the position to which the child himself is exposed. After the cushioning preliminaries of nursery school and kindergarten, the child in the first grade enters a new competitive situation. Schooling in our society is, of course, a way of imparting information and specific skills. But much more than this, it is a mechanism by which fundamental character and value commitments are developed, and through which the members of the oncoming generation are selectively allocated within the social structure.

Of course American society has a class structure, though a relatively open one, and children of the upper groups have strong differential advantages. Nevertheless, the educational system is a powerful selective mechanism and, particularly with the general process of educational upgrading, can provide much opportunity for upward mobility; of course, conversely, failure in school can have very serious consequences. The evidence indicates, for instance, that school records in elementary schools is overwhelmingly the primary criterion in the selection of college applicants. College in turn is an increasingly important factor in the

future social status of the individual; it is the main recruiting ground of the higher occupations.

In both of these two major contexts, differentiation and upgrading, the trend of our educational system presents a most striking picture (a convenient summary of the data is given by Eleanor Bernert) (3). The crucial fact is that, even apart from the consequences of the increased birth rates mentioned above, there has been a steady increase in the proportion of children participating in formal education at every age level. At the lower end the increase in the proportions going to kindergarten is striking. In the elementary grades, of course, it could not be great since virtually the whole age cohort had already been attending that level of schooling. But we are rapidly approaching a situation where all but virtual defectives or severely handicapped individuals will be completing high school. The proportion of the age cohort going on to college has ·already reached more than one third, an unprecedented proportion in any other society. There is, then, a steady trend toward completion of increasing numbers of years of college. Finally, the postgraduate and professional levels of formal education are by far the most rapidly increasing of all.

It is sometimes alleged that this enormous quantitative increase in education has taken place at the expense of qualitative standards. While these certainly leave much to be desired, the evidence does not seem to bear out the view that there has been a decline.

OCCUPATIONAL STRUCTURE

Educational upgrading in this sense has been associated with a profound change in the occupational structure of American society. In the first place a larger proportion of the population than ever before is in the labor force, in spite of the later age at which so many enter in order to finish more schooling, and of the growth of compulsory retirement rules at the upper end. But most important is the fact of upgrading in this area. At the bottom of the scale, the proportion of gainfully employed persons classified in the census as unskilled laborers has been cut in half

in the last fifty years. The proportions who are classified as semi-skilled and skilled have not greatly changed, but by far the most rapid rates of growth have occurred in the higher occupational groups. Even the clerical groups, which have expanded a great deal, are undoubtedly being upgraded in levels of skill and responsibility. And semi-professional, professional, and managerial occupations, though a relatively small proportion, have been increasing very rapidly indeed.

It is not adequate to judge the trends of a society in terms of quantitative indices alone. Probably the two most central developments in our society are the growth and spread of large-scale organizations and the development of functions requiring high levels of technical competence. These higher level occupations are demanding greater capacities for carrying complex responsibilities and for developing and utilizing generalized knowledge than ever was true before for a great population.

It seems to me to follow from these very rapidly sketched considerations that the oncoming American generation, even at the levels on which most individuals can exert direct influence and carry direct responsibility (as distinguished from the overall "fate of the nation"), is being subjected to greater demands and, conversely, being offered greater opportunities for achievement than ever before. Because of differentiation these also cover a wider range of kinds of achievement than ever.

The wider range in many respects multiplies the difficulty of choice. The general prolongation of the period of education confronts the individual with a long succession of choice-points. At each of these he is forced to decide what he wants and, in addition, his qualifications are subjected to complex evaluative procedures so that he is more continually, or repeatedly, put on his mettle than were the youth of a more traditional and less dynamic society.

STRAINS AND PRESSURES

Since the society itself is changing at virtually all levels, there are many uncertainties facing not only young people themselves, but the adults on whom they must depend as sources of security, as role models, and as

educators. But even under the best conditions this situation would place children and young people in difficult positions because of the variegated pressures to which they would be subjected in any case. Conditions in fact, however, are rarely the best; adults also are under strain and behave erratically in their relations to the young, especially since these relations bear the consequences of the inadequacies of their own earlier life experiences.

Severe strains in general tend to produce protective mechanisms which serve to mitigate their severity sufficiently so that the majority in fact master them with at least some success. At certain points, however, these mechanisms tend to break down and indeed be "perverted" to antisocial ends. It is unlikely that such drastic processes of social change as have been going on could operate without a considerable quota of casualties. It may therefore be worth-while to attempt to bring these considerations to bear on a few of the more distressing phenomena in our field.

One preliminary point may be relevant—the problem of illness. Illness in general is not merely a physical condition, it is also a socially structured phenomenon, a form of motivated deviant behavior operating through so-called psychosomatic channels. It is my impression that, in the last generation or so, there has occurred not only a very great decrease in mortality in infancy and childhood, but that the phenomena of childhood disease have become much less prominent than they were. Partly this is a matter of "closing the door" to this path of deviance since immunization measures and some curative ones make it impossible to become ill or remain so for long. It may, however, also be a function of child care which is psychologically more adequate than was true for an earlier period. This seems at least to be a suggestion worth considering.

THE PEER GROUP

To jump to another very salient problem. One of the most conspicuous phenomena viewed among American youth is what we call the peer group, the "informal" set of associations which a young person has with others of about his own age. This starts very early, and, with various

transformations, continues as a salient factor through adolescence. Clearly in one respect it is an important protective device. Above all it is the primary repository of the needs for emotional security and acceptance which have been so powerfully fostered in early childhood and then so sharply cut back in relation to the original objects, the parents—particularly, of course, the mother—because of the imperative of achieving independence.

Given the importance of the whole complex which leads toward occupational status, particularly for boys, the peer group has a special set of significances beyond that of easing a difficult transition. For the more successful groups it becomes the principal field for learning skills which in an organizationally complex society must be of the greatest significance, namely skills in "getting along with others." Though the picture is highly variegated, it seems to be broadly true that the leadership of the more prestigeful youth groups, in and out of the school context, coincides broadly with a level of academic achievement which is compatible with higher occupational status. There is, however, clearly a differentiation in that the highest academic achievement tends to be confined to persons who do not strongly "go in for" popularity among their peers.

If I may for the moment oversimplify by stressing a tendency to bifurcation of age cohorts on the basis of achievement, it would appear that for the lower groups the peer culture may be of even greater significance. Precisely because they are gradually coming to be committed to the renunciation of the most highly valued achievement goals, the importance of their peer-group investment must be enhanced. Again, particularly for boys, this is the main structural reference point for the development of the delinquent gang, which is essentially a perversion of a very important positive social institution.

This leads to a set of considerations touching the most serious though not the only important problems of social pathology in this area. There is strong evidence that, in a wide variety of respects, there is an accumulation of factors of disadvantage at the lower end of the social class scale. Among those affecting the child, there are more divorces and desertions, hence many more broken families at these levels. There is lower income, poorer housing, and perhaps most important, lower familial self-respect,

more than for any other single reason deriving from the status, occupational and otherwise, of the father in the community.

For the boy, then, who by virtue of limited ability has somewhat hard going in school, and who does not get strong support for whatever motives to achievement he may have from his parents, the peer group is clearly the most readily accessible social setting in which he can maximize whatever assets he has. Moreover it is likely to be a peer group which is composed mainly of people in the "same boat," who are broadly shunted out of the main achievement channels. They tend to react to their inability to meet school and community standards by denying their validity and from there to act in terms of defiance of the more general social standards.

JUVENILE DELINQUENCY

Given the general trend of educational upgrading and, closely connected with it, the occupational upgrading which among other things downgrades the lowest echelons of the occupational scale, it would be expected that the pressure on the children who do poorly in school would be increased rather than decreased. It is in terms such as these that I would like to see the setting of the much discussed problem of juvenile delinquency today.

It is exceedingly difficult to determine how far or much this problem has recently increased. The fact that it probably has increased may very well be a function of the accelerated educational upgrading process combined, in all probability, with a contemporaneous acceleration of central urban "decay" and concentration of the most disadvantaged groups in particular slum areas. In this situation it is common to attempt to speak of a general "moral decline" in the society, and to assign blame specifically, for instance, to parents. In my opinion this point of view is mistaken in both respects. This phenomenon is the dark underside of a process which, as judged by all our principal values, is one of general advance in the society. To be sure, many families have failed, along with various other agencies of the society. But one of the principal explana-

tions of the phenomenon is that it occurs mainly in parts of the social structure where it is far more difficult than usual to establish sound familial prerequisites for the socialization of children. The problem lies not with particular parents, but with the social conditions which favor particular types of lower-class family situation and other contributory factors; it is futile to attempt to deal with it by exhorting individuals to do their moral duty.

Thus it seems that considerable rates of juvenile delinquency should be regarded as "natural" concomitants of the general process of development of our society, whereby this development is pushed so hard and fast that it engenders strains of such severity that at weak points the institutionalized controls give way. This is not to say that there is a rigid inevitability about quantity, form, or consequences. Certainly the situation would be worse than it is without the devoted and competent measures now being taken to mitigate it, and much more and better can be done. My essential point is that it is naive to assume that the great social transformations we have been experiencing can occur without cost. But it would be incompatible with our values to neglect any opportunity to minimize that cost. Obviously the commitment to equality of opportunity should not be suspended in the case of an individual once he has started down a dead-end road. It is among our deepest obligations to do anything possible to help him back on one which leads somewhere.

It is an important part of the moral complexity of modern society that in the case even of such obviously antisocial behavior as delinquency, there are expressed essential components of our positive values. The most conspicuous are the display of enormous energy and often initiative in skillful doing of difficult things, willingness to take risks, and capacities for cooperation and group loyalty of a high order. This very fact, however, involves an encouraging aspect for those concerned with remedial measures: in a large proportion of cases the delinquent has qualities eminently worth salvaging.

This aspect of delinquency is suggestive for the interpretation of another deviant pattern which is causing a good deal of comment at present—the increase in rates of illegitimacy. To me this relates to the fact that child-bearing and maternity constitute the primary feminine function in

any society. In general terms it has undergone an impressive renascence in our own society in the last twenty years through the baby boom. However irresponsible the bearing of illegitimate children may be from many points of view, the fact of consciously or unconsciously wanting to bear children is interpretable, I think, mainly in terms of the valuation of this central function. It is perhaps significant that in recent years the proportion of illegitimate births to teenage mothers has declined, while the general rate has not. It seems fair to suggest that the older girl who gets illegitimately pregnant is somehow asserting her desire to do a generally valued thing, even though for both social and psychological reasons she, like the male delinquent, does it in a socially unacceptable way.

Unfortunately we cannot here either develop this example more fully or enter into others. The point I wish to make is that even in the pathology of the field, the importance of the central value system I have sketched comes through, however distorted the form its manifestations take.

A VALUE SYSTEM FOR THE FUTURE

Returning then to the consideration of values as such, it is important to distinguish between values for and values of children and youth. There is abundant evidence that Americans have a high valuation of their children. But I have argued that by and large it is valuation conceived in terms of capacity and opportunity for achievement. Certainly we want them to be "happy," but we have a concept of happiness through achievement rather than through avoiding the necessity to achieve. Certainly also, by and large, we want them to be "successful." In spite of much ambivalence over this concept, I think it can be said that underlying most doubt about the success ideal is not a question of the importance of worth-while achievement, but of the attribution of too much importance to "external rewards," lest they seduce one into doing things which are not really worth-while.

It is one of the most important features of a process of structural dif-

ferentiation that instead of giving primary emphasis to one or the other of two interests, there is a way to do some justice to both of two differentiating interests. Children are, in society's eyes, primarily an investment for the future. Concern with the urgencies of the here and now can readily lead us to neglect the future. In American society this has been particularly manifest in the enormous energy which has gone into the building of the great operative structures of the society, the great organizations in the field of industry and government and various others. In a very different connection a manifestation of great interest is concern with the problems of the aged. After all, so far as life in this world is concerned, the problem of older people is one of relatively immediate urgency; these people will have either a good old age in the next few years or a wretched one.

I have suggested that valuation of youth is inherent in our value system. It is, however, part of the general relation between institutionalized values and their implementation, that there should be differential emphases at different times. It seems reasonable to suggest that a new swing has begun in the society in favor of attention to the problems of the young resulting from the types of differentiation I have sketched. The first big manifestation of this swing seems to have been the reorganization of the family to which I have referred, and the voluntary assumption by parents of greater responsibilities, on a new level, for more children. That this is a deep commitment on a massive scale seems to be beyond doubt. The range of concern is then spreading into the field of formal education which certainly in a relative sense has been neglected for some time, even though the educational system has continued to grow. It seems to me that even the Supreme Court decision of 1954 on desegregation in public schools can be placed in this context by the fact that the rights of the Negro child to educational opportunity is a particularly central and ethically sensitive problem.

The educational issue is of course made particularly acute by the combination of the increased birth rates of the recent past with the general process of educational upgrading which has been going on. Various types of public manifestation of concern in this area are already evident, but it is my prediction that this will be one of the main public issues at many

levels for a good many years to come. Both in the interest of its children, and of its own future beyond the life span of the current adult generation, this country cannot afford to neglect the education of the oncoming generation.

Then what of the children themselves? It is one of the most persistent ideological tendencies for adult generations to view with alarm the wayward tendencies of the young, and our generation has its full quota of this sentiment.

It is inevitable that our children and grandchildren cannot be brought up to follow the same paths that we did. If they could, it would negate our national ideal of an evolving society where every new phase places new demands on the people. The question is not whether the younger generation are different; they are and must be. It is whether they have abandoned the central values which have given its main thread of continuity to our society. My own view is that, as a group, they have not done so. Though understandably at certain points hesitant and uncertain, and some, as always, deviant, the youth of today seem to me to be active, eager, and ambitious for achievement. They are exerting great effort to secure training for worth-while achievement and they are certainly as concerned as any generation with the all-important standards of justice and equity. I would think it very difficult indeed to prove that any previous American generation has had higher ideals as our society has defined its ideals.

In particular I wish to question, in the present as in other connections, the validity of the common view that our society is characterized by an "unprecedented moral decline." Part of this derives from applying the detailed standards, as distinguished from the generalized values, of an earlier society, standards which are often inherently inappropriate. Another part derives from confusions about the levels at which it is realistic and appropriate to hold individuals morally responsible for their own and others' actions, as in the case of delinquency.

It is in the nature of so complex and so rapidly evolving a society as ours that it should be shot through with conflicts and tensions and with deviance from our highest moral ideals. I am far from wishing to sanctify the status quo. But I think it essential that we give every effort to rational

diagnosis of the empirical determinants of the phenomena we wish to change and to the realistic empirical conditions of the successful operation of measures of improvement. We should take special care that the more detailed standards we apply are realistically appropriate to the new state of the society and that strength of moral conviction is combined with intelligence. Given some such combination I have high confidence that our values are intact and viable, are being successfully transmitted to our children, and can be expected to play a major part in bringing about a future for our society of which our children or children's children can justly be proud.

THE INTERIOR ASPECTS OF CHANGE

Joseph Sittler

IN A SHORT PREAMBLE I would like to indicate the limitations my own knowledge and experience cause me to impose upon my assignment and to outline how I have garnered my comments. I shall concentrate upon the phrase "changing world," and deal with only the interior aspects of that. The exterior facts of change are fully and competently dealt with elsewhere, and about this I have nothing original to add.

My particular realm of inquiry and discourse is Christian theology, and that activity provides an opportunity more alive than may be instantly apparent to be aware of what I have called the interior aspect of our changing world. For a theologian deals not only with affirmations which purport to set forth the nature and substance of the Christian understanding of life, but also, because it is concerned to lay these persuasively into the contours of man's moving and fluctuating career, with the interior dynamics of the listening ear of each generation.

As I have pondered over what I have seen happening behind the beholding eyes and the listening ears of many young people at this moment in history I have become aware of three major and pervasive determinants of their inwardness. I shall try, in a moment, to designate and describe these. But another preliminary matter must precede that effort: a description of how I have come to the affirmations I want to make.

Joseph Sittler is Professor, Divinity School of The University of Chicago.

That the National Council of Churches has a sense of humor might appear to be a proposition hard to establish, but upon no other ground can I explain why I was asked to prepare this paper. For, in the present area of the enquiry, I have no special competence. No advanced training in the social and "personality" sciences has ever complicated my life and thought. My entire career as a teacher has been at the graduate level —certainly an age group not central to our concern here. And, as my perceptive and generally accurate wife would cheerfully testify, my natural empathy with children and youth is considerably short of astounding. Children and youth are, for me, an acquired taste.

And that, of course, is where the sense of humor comes in. For it is probably the case that, despite the foregoing facts, I have more children than any full-time professor of theology in North America. There are six of them: three are within the category *child,* three belong to the category *youth.* I press this point because if some conclude, as some very likely will, that I am talking through my hat—I wish to make clear that it is a hat full of children and youth. What errors occur will be at the level of interpretation, and not for want of what students in my university constantly call "involvement in the existential situation."

Then, too, what might be called my "research-situation" has been so unstructured, immediate, and so lacking in elements dear to the hearts of academicians as to make it suspect. Three energetic, articulate, and humorous teenage boys gassing around a dinner table, uninhibited by either family tradition or by any feeling of restraint imposed by the presence of a father of (in their eyes) venerable length of days, provide an access to our field of study so rich as to delight the soul of any scholar whose human powers have not been transformed into the likeness of a computer.

All of this is but a way of suggesting that young people are themselves making loud, frequent, and quite clear noises about what is happening to their ideas and values as these are being modified by the thudding of the changing world. With this generation's youth one does not have a "conversation"—at least not in any civilized meaning of that term. What revelations one does get are by way of listening in upon what passes among them as conversation: an oblique but quite efficient form of quasi-

verbal interchange whose only literary equivalent is somewhere between James Joyce and Thomas Wolfe.

What I am about to say is, therefore, gained from specific occasions, but I believe these reflections to have a fair generality. When we talk of ideals and values in change we presuppose some matrix of ideal and value in relation to which change is an intelligible idea. There are such matrices, and among them the Christian tradition is a large one. This tradition has been a fashioner, a transmitter, and a teacher of an entire value-structure. And I think it true to report that neither the venerability, nor the solid institutional embodiment, nor the historical establishment of this tradition in the ethos of the American community spares it from the erosion that presently marks all value-carrying traditions. This erosion has so gutted and gullied the old fields of this particular value and ideal engendering view of life as to expose it, along with other traditions, to that very crisis which is the concern of this book.

What, from within this tradition, its contemporary children must do to reconstruct its terms and recover its powers is another matter. But I refer to this tradition only to make the point that its force is threatened as absolutely as are all the others. And the three large aspects of that threat which I want now to name are neither diminished nor diverted because young people have known and have been to some degree nurtured upon this tradition.

THE NEW VIOLENCE

I stress the adjective. Violence has always been an element in the human community. Violence has sometimes been a tactic in the service of meaning, of values and standards, to protect them, and dramatically to beat down "chaos and old ancient night" meaninglessness. Violence has also been a kind of response to the rejection or destruction of established meanings—but in the name and for the sake of deeper meanings, inarticulate and even inchoate, but felt and served by violence.

But what I here designate the new violence has an utterly different character. The sheer actuality of means of violent action within the

human community, and the knowledge that there is no certainty that it will not be used, begets and nurtures a quite novel situation. A new mental moment came to birth in our time. There is a difference between violence that yields death and damage and a violence whose yield is absolute death and the ultimate damage. There is a qualitative difference between a war which rocks a structure and the envisionment of a war which shall leave no structure at all, nor any men to weep for meanings blasted or to dream of new ones. This violence is not episodic; it is terminal. It is not a fact among facts; it is the all obliterating fact.

This new violence is not a datum in the mind of this generation, it is the silent, sinister, pervading mood of the mind. It is not so much *what* its mind thinks; it is the given theater of thinking. It is not a separate, if horrible, fact; it is the theater within which all facts have a ghostly, unreal, and terribly tentative existence.

Before there is a delinquency of the conscious in terms of order, authority, value, and meaning, there is an invisible and subterranean delinquency. When potential violence is apocalyptical, meanings, purposes, ideals tend to become sardonic. And because that is so, it behooves us to attend to a contemporary poet, because, in the closing lines of his *Advice to a Prophet,* this man is forging images that have a stark actuality for our time.

> These things in which we have seen ourselves and spoken?
> Ask us, prophet, how we shall call
> Our natures forth when that live tongue is all
> Dispelled, that glass obscured or broken,
>
> In which we have said the rose of our love and the clean
> Horse of our courage, in which beheld
> The singing locust of the soul unshelled,
> And all we mean or wish to mean.
>
> Ask us, ask us whether with the worldless rose
> Our hearts shall fail us; come demanding
> Whether there shall be lofty or long standing
> When the bronze annals of the oak-tree close.
>   —Richard Wilbur

THE NEW EXISTENTIALISM

I do not intend by that phrase the recondite philosophical position or the considerable literary output that has been so designated. Both of these are commonly beyond the survey of children and youth. But they exist in those forms because the stuff to call them forth and constitute them a position is alive and general in the common life. The forms of it there are these: traditionless life in adult America—episodic, unreflective, freshly improvised under the blows or before the seductions of a commercial culture; the waning of a national ethos, in the absence of which each moment, event, fact, or decision stands in the nakedness of the immediate; a concept of family in which sheer togetherness is frantically pursued as if propinquity were salvatory; the deepening instrumental evaluation of all things in terms of their tactical service to the moment—possessions for status (the replacement of the family car by the family outboard cruiser is of no significance), education for career lubrication and advancement, knowledge for power without ampler purpose, even religious faith as a personality analgesic or as an adhesive for public order, a moral gimmick with which to secure the persistence of our republic against a strange ideology.

The priorities of the young follow the practice of the adult with absolute seriousness. Protestations are both useless and bitter when the truth about ideals and values is clearly exposed in the satisfactions sought and the deeds done. The teenagers who overrun my house will not take seriously public protestations of concern about the crisis in education when schools disintegrate in the shadow of the new Lakefront Exposition Hall.

THE POWER OF THE PHONEY

By this phrase I intend to affirm two things: that the power of the religious tradition in America to propose, nurture, and solidify the young in ideals and values organically derived from or appropriate to the great

religious traditions which exist here is demonstrably waning; and, second, that that fact may be understood as a tribute to the young rather than as a charge against them.

Instead of making general statements in defense of that proposition I should like to ponder the meaning for my assignment by considering the case of the young man who is the hero of Salinger's enormously and deservedly popular book, *The Catcher in the Rye*. The lad revealed there is lonely, an outsider to the culture which is his familial and school environment. He is sardonic, not because he is tough but precisely because he is tender. He is not basically skeptical about either the values of personal relations or of the reality of commitment to transpersonal purposes and powers. And he is flip, contemptuous and bitter *not* because he despises values or ideals—but because he sees these verbally celebrated by his elders, and regularly betrayed. It is not enthusiasm he scorns; it is the glib and phoney enthusiasm of people saying what they do not mean that makes him snort, "Big deal—cornball—phoney!"

When, for instance, the hero goes to Radio City Music Hall during Christmas Week, and beholds there a grave and awesome moment of the religious story, the Festival of the Incarnation, stripped, banalized, and trivialized into an occasion for tinsel-prancing Rockettes, he utters an apparent blasphemy which is more reverent than the sweetly entranced glee of the adult generation there assembled. His judgment that "Ol' Jesus would have puked!" does *not* reveal a spirit unavailable to an ideal and a value; it reveals precisely the opposite—a kind of holy revulsion before a general phoniness that does not bat an eye in the presence of an abortion. The boy does not affirm the reality of faith or reject it; he is rather in that prior position of saying, in effect, there are various orders of gravity and truth and beauty. Some are proper to an entertainment routine and some are not. And he is saying, in his way, what a great saint of the Church intended when he said: "It is of the heart of evil that men enjoy what they ought to use, and use what they ought to enjoy."

Analysis of *Mad* Magazine, a sort of unauthorized Scripture out my way, is a very sobering experience for adults proposing to be precise about the impact of our reigning cultural patterns upon the young. An

eminent sociologist wrote a book called *Our Sensate Culture*. *Mad* Magazine is the teenage rejoinder to this designation, in the wild and hilarious manner appropriate both to their endocrine system and to the deadly clarity with which they sniff out sober phoniness and give it a picture and a name.

It may be that eventually we shall be able to gain such an understanding as shall better enable us, in our President's call, "to do everything we can to plan ahead and to see that we prepare today's children well for tomorrow's world." But let us proceed with a certain degree of fear and trembling! For youth will not be well served if we assume tomorrow's world as an unchangeable "given"—a mere extrapolation and extension of the world we presently know. Not only must human life be prepared for tomorrow's world; tomorrow's world must be envisioned, in all of its peril and promise, as malleable to the vital requirements of authentic human life. I find no joy in being adjusted to measureless violence, hand-to-mouth and catch-as-catch-can existence, or to a deepening phoniness which embitters the mind, blights the spirit, and saddens the dreaming heart of man.

History is the realm of necessity and freedom. What necessity has laid upon us in this violent, technological, and mass age is sufficiently clear. Less clear, but clamant with the urgency of man's remembered humanity—the impress of Supernal Gift and worth—is his yet unannihilated freedom. A burning solemn anger as we confront a new decade is not a passion proper to the young alone. The ancient apostolic word, "Be ye not conformed to this world, but be ye transformed by the renewing of your minds," is both true religion and authentic humanism. The statement not only exposes the fallacy that a person can be a person in just any kind of a world; it also says at what level genuinely personal life must behold what is right for man, resolve upon a world fit for his habitation and joy, and devise ideals and practices to advance it. The renewing of the mind involves considerably more from adult America than there is evidence to believe she is either sober enough to see or troubled enough to desire.

FREEDOM AND IMAGINATION

T. V. Smith

OUR SUBJECT IS "beliefs," but in orienting ourselves to pursue the subject we may remark three domains of human behavior. First, there is overt action, in which childhood specializes. "The boy," said former President Herbert Hoover, "is an animal who takes exercise on every possible occasion." We may add the girl, too, who is his close second in activity. Both are as bouncy as Winnie-the-Pooh. With time comes thought, our domain of belief, and speech. The domains, at first glance, may be poorly distinguished. A three-year-old was implored by his distraught mother, "Please, please, sit down awhile and think without talking." Replied he: "I'll sit down, Mommy, but a boy must be much older before he can think without talking." Speech is akin to both action and thought but is not the same as either.

These several domains indeed differ in many ways but most significantly in the degree of freedom which each permits and rewards. Action allows least freedom, belief most, and speech something in between, leaning toward the larger leeway of thought.

WHAT IS FREEDOM?

Lest it be thought that I am inventing distinctions to amuse myself or to beguile you (a philosopher is said to be a man who makes a distinc-

T. V. Smith is Maxwell Professor Emeritus, Syracuse University.

tion whenever he meets a difficulty), let me remind you that these three distinctions are the basis of our American Bill of Rights, that constitution of all our liberties. In action nobody is freer than the laws and customs allow, and that is not very free for either youth or adult. We do mostly what we have to do—and that is that. In thought, however, we are all rightly free without limit, though adults discount this when it is applied to youth. Speech comes in between. As a form of thought, speech is largely free, but as a form of action, speech is subject to the laws of libel, nor is any Tom, Dick, or Harry free enough to cry "Fire!" in a crowded theater whenever he pleases.

We see then that freedom of action is largely limited for all. When youth forgets this, we have juvenile delinquency, if not youthful crimes. Limitation of action on any individual or group, whatever the age, arises from the fact that action provides only narrowed options. Collective action requires majority consent, and individual action is limited to what is legal. Where something has to be done, and especially has to be done collectively, there are only two or three, or at the most a few, possibilities open to choice. To forget this is to curtail liberty in the name of liberty. Willy-nilly, then, the sphere of action is the domain of limited freedom. Plato observed two thousand years ago what he called "a law of nature": that it is easier to hit the mark in theory than it is in practice. In thought alone is the sky the limit.

It is literally nobody's business what anybody believes so long as he merely believes it. What another man believes, even about sacred matters, said Thomas Jefferson, "never picked my pocket nor broke my leg." The further notion that belief may lead others to break something is vastly overrated. The freedom which thought naturally has may rightly be exercised, and without fear. Such freedom is not only good in its consequences but also is good in itself. And that goes for speech as well as for thought. But it goes, as we say, without limit for thought.

Now we come to the core of the matter, and to the sad part. Since we cannot be free altogether, we ought all the more to be free where we can. We can be, and can afford to be, free in thought and mostly free in speech. But shall we not weep when those most narrowed by action be-

come the most fearful of thought and even the most distrustful of free speech? This creeping sadness is even drearier when it inundates youth.

THE TWO DELINQUENCIES

We have juvenile delinquency when the young overappraise freedom in action. They believe that because they can think it, they can do it—no sooner thought than done. We have *adult* delinquency when the custodians of culture underappraise freedom in thought and speech. They believe that because they cannot do it, the young should not do it, or even think it. The adult variety is the worst, for it strangles the life of imagination, the fountain, veritably, from which all values flow.

Why, what is science save imagination disciplined into scrupulosity? Without free imagination science sinks to technology and loses the potency to reproduce. What is art save imagination disciplined to manual knack and professional pride? Without imagination art becomes imitation and sinks to respectable display. What is politics save imagination disciplined to allow as duties what it claims as rights, each to count for one and nobody for more than one? Without imagination politics becomes a power game in which men are but pawns. And what is religion save imagination draped across neutral skies in folds of everlasting mercy? Without imagination theology would indeed become what a divinity dean once taught me to call it, "transcendentalized politics."

George Santayana, the greatest philosopher of our time and one of the greatest cultural (as distinct from theological) Catholics of any time, complains in his autobiography that his parents taught him that religion is a work of human imagination but tied to that the conclusion that religion is therefore bad. "I agreed, and still agree," said he, "as to what they taught me, but could never accept their conclusion. No, said I to myself even as a boy: the works of imagination are good, they alone are good; and the rest—the whole real world—is ashes in the mouth." No wonder it was this man who lived to voice the immortal wisdom which only children seem to know: "Give me the luxuries and I'll not grieve

for the necessities." I recommend that you accept this wisdom, not as religious doctrine but as deserved appraisal and emancipation of the life of imagination.

Since children are not present to hear what I say, I speak to adults about our own worst delinquency. Impoverishment of curiosity, the firstborn of imagination, is not a crime, and so cannot be controlled by law. But the desiccation of imagination is so lethal to all values that it is everywhere to be discouraged by education and custom. It is wrong anywhere, at any time, and in any name, for any adult needlessly to impair or lessen any child's imagination. Without exercise how can the youth toughen the fibers of his reverie? If reverie must be at times redirected, the operation must be approached as though an heir to the crown were involved in the surgery. As Emily Dickinson cautions—and this child of fancy ought to know—

> Surgeons must be very careful
> When they take the knife!
> Underneath their fine incisions
> Stirs the culprit,—Life!

I believe the most common cause of this metaphysical malpractice against youth is misapprehension of the relation between belief and action—therefore, my repeated stress upon it. Thoughts of murder seldom lead to murder, and no men, perhaps few women, would be saved if thoughts of fornication more than seldom led to bed. Upon this vast discrepancy between what men think and what they do we can afford to trade with creativeness as the beneficiary. Sometimes reverie is secret practice in vice, but more often it is indulgence in what if not a virtue is nevertheless a great good in itself. Even if we say with a great philosopher that all thought is dramatic rehearsal of action, we know from experience how few rehearsals budge the play to Broadway. This reflection might at least lessen the fear that we are doing wrong when we encourage in childhood the life of fancy. With fear made illusory, the great intrinsic good which imagination is might become progressively apparent. If we can stop drawing "the shades of the prison house upon the growing boy," we can begin to appreciate with Wordsworth, that "Heaven lies about us in our infancy."

IMAGINATIVE EMANCIPATION

The misapprehension of which I have spoken seems often to be most rampant in the relation between religious belief and moral action. If God were not so often used in childhood as a policeman, he might in later life be sometimes "enjoyed" as the creed prescribed "forever." And wholly beyond the sad transvaluation of values which sometimes makes the divine into the diabolical, there is the observation that morality, which ought to remain stable for the sake of action, loses its foundation for action when theological beliefs undergo their great but normal proliferation.

Now such beliefs are highly changeable, not only from culture to culture but also from childhood to youth and from youth to age. Jefferson called Calvin's god a devil, and René Descartes both recognized the fact of theological proliferation and profited from the recognition. While doubting all beliefs he could, he would—he resolved—keep on acting in the same old stable way. Morality rests, when we let it, on much more earthy foundations than changing theological beliefs. George Santayana who, as we have seen, made religion free because imaginary, damned the morality that flowed from merely dogmatic religion. "I ask myself sometimes," confesses he, "is not morality a worse enemy of spirit than immorality?" Freedom is indivisible, though relative to its proper domain. To be free with impunity is to be free indeed. Thomas Jefferson advised Peter Carr, his ward, to be what we might think cavalier in religious beliefs, even advising him boldly to question the existence of deity: "If there be [a god] he must more approve of the homage of reason, than that of blindfold fear." That is one belief about deity, and there are a thousand others. It is hard to prove what any or each over-belief produces in action. Let us enjoy such beliefs as luxury increments of freedom, but observe meantime our duties as defined by our stations or as otherwise tied to the home base of morality.

Think what perturbation of spirit, not to say what loss of confidence in adults, might have been spared the writer of the following letter, if she had been less literal in accepting promises from the pulpit. The author,

now a young lady, allows me to quote here the following letter written when she was eleven.

Sunday night
10:30 about

Dear Mother:

I heard a sermon about letting go and depending on God, this morning at church. Tonight we played bridge. I played with Grandmother W. We were losing but I wanted GMW to be dummy. I depended on God that we should win. I was sure that we would win because the preacher said that if you depended on God he would do it. We lost. GMW wasn't dummy so now what should I do? Believe in God and what the preacher said or say you can't depend on God. I had to write now and I am writing with a pencil I found and some paper that was at the bottom of the drawer. I was so disappointed. Please write quickly.

I love you so.

L.

That is part of the natural history of the suspicions of adults held by children, almost universal by adolescence. Such suspicion could be mitigated by a more imaginative treatment not only of religious beliefs but also of our inherited moral maxims. Few of them are to be taken without a lump of sugar. Let me illustrate.

PLURALISTIC MORALITY

Our duties toward others can be divided into three beliefs, stated here as the Golden, the Silver, and the Iron Rules.

The Golden Rule

Nobody lives strictly according to the Golden Rule; nobody, that is, who survives. To start with, we may rule out such perfection. What, however, cannot be *in toto* may still prevail in part. If we are to live with the Golden Rule, we must find some path wider than strict obedience. Up to some point, and in ways definable, we may indeed accommodate ourselves to the belief that we ought to do to others as we would have others do to us. We may suggest the limit by saying that

the Golden Rule is for golden-hearted people. To be golden-hearted means, among other things, to be like-minded. It is indeed easy enough to see ourselves in the lives of others if these lives are, as it were, already projections of our own lives. It is not impossible to find people who share significantly our notions of morals, our convictions about religion, and even our tastes as to beauty. To do unto such people as we would have them do unto us is to take ourselves as standard—and this is not too hard. To this extent the Golden Rule is a self-referent rule, and is available to *selfish* men.

Its real test begins where we commence to differ about significant things. This starts earlier and persists longer than men like to think. To accept irremediable differences as to important matters is to put ourselves beyond the reach of the Golden Rule. James Madison, one of the framers of our Constitution, not merely formulated the opposite rule but based our Constitution on it—the rule that so long as men are free, they will differ crucially; and so long as they are honest they will contest their differences to the bitter end. Nor is this merely in matters economic. Indeed, Madison makes the statement historic and lethal: "The most frivolous and fanciful distinctions have been sufficient to kindle [men's] unfriendly passions and excite their most violent conflicts."

It is hard to admit that the Golden Rule takes self, rather than others, as the point of reference. We cannot know what it requires of us as touching others until we have referred the matter to our own preferences. Where we differ significantly from others the Rule ceases to have much meaning, or indeed changes its meaning to the opposite. Take the proverbial savage chieftain who has been converted to the Christian way. Knowing what *he* likes he comes to the missionary to offer him a harem. The missionary found himself faced with the irrefutable logic: "You have been teaching me to do to others what I would have others do to me. I would expect this courtesy of you if I visited America. Yet when I proffer the harem, you disdain it and reprimand me. How come?"

You see, the relevance of the Rule implies a widespread similarity. That lacking, the Rule does not neatly apply. To generalize this insight, the Golden Rule applies fully only to golden-hearted people; its greatest value is when we need it least. Wide differences in culture, or even in

wealth, lessens the relevancy of the Rule. Now the saddest thing is to be added: Not only can we not go beyond golden-heartedness, but when we do, we often produce its opposite. To treat men as Christians is not a sure or even dependable way to make them Christians. We have to start where we are in human relations as in traveling. Nor is a straight line the shortest distance between two points when the points are persons. Remember Roosevelt at Yalta; he thought that "Uncle Joe," as he called Stalin, would act like a Christian if treated like one. But Stalin disdained weakness as despicable and took glad advantage of the generous leeway allowed him by the application of the Golden Rule.

The Silver Rule

There is another ethical belief much wider in its ambit than is the Golden Rule. Since positivity betrays us, let us try accentuating the negative. The Silver Rule can be formulated as follows: "Do not do to others what you would not have others do to you." The reference is still to self, but the negative form offers a wider leeway. It is easier, and freer, not to do than to do. Inaction connects us with many more people than does action. And millions of men to whom we do not owe a positive duty we do owe absence of malevolence. The least that strangers can ask of us, and the most that we can accord them, is to "let 'em alone." Indeed, said Justice Brandeis, "The right to be let alone is the most comprehensive of rights and the right most valued by civilized men." So the Silver Rule makes up in extension what it lacks in intention. It applies to millions to whom we do not owe anything more positive.

The Iron Rule

There is still another rule required by the presence of another type of man. There are those (and it may be any one of us at times) who will not only not do good but will not even let other people alone. Since they are not golden-hearted and not silver-hearted, we must treat them for what they are, *iron-hearted*. For their obduracy we must have a rule befitting: "Do not let them do to you what you would not do to them." We owe a duty to ourselves to stand up for our rights.

A weakness of our Christian culture, in the harsh clinches of history,

is the difficulty we have in believing that there are iron-hearted men. If once convinced of that, we can negotiate the next hurdle: that they must be treated for what they are if they are to become any better than they are. We could not believe Hitler's own words because they made him out to be worse than we believed any man could be.

AN APPEAL TO FANCY

So much for moral beliefs imaginatively treated. We boast that we live in a pluralistic society. Let us mean it by opening windows upon all the skies of ideality, upon highlands of beauty as well as lowlands of truth. We need not only to train youth for action but to educate them for speech and for thought. If we do not prize and cultivate freedom where it is easily accessible, as in thought, how can we extend it where the gorges of life are narrow, as in action? Nor can education for freedom begin a day too early or extend a day too late.

A negative way of furthering this appraisal of pluralism is to attack the narrowing but traditional notion that every belief is either true or false. Why, not all beliefs even claim to be true; and of those that claim it, how few can prove it! There are other categories of value such as the beautiful and the good and the useful. Because it is both narrow and hard, this domain has been called the "Tragic Realm of Truth." When it is required, nothing is more important than truth. But it is not as often required as many men seem to think. To say that a story is true, that it actually happened, is to lower its interest, even if it heightens its usefulness. A plethora of beliefs, if freed from the exaction of truth, is normal and wholesome in youth and age. Truth is the intellectual virtue nearest to the life of action, and as such it partakes of the narrowness of this domain. You can see for yourself how little of truth is required when you observe that men and especially women prefer gossip to science. Literalism easily turns into dogmatism.

Little dogmatists grow up to be big dogmatists, and big dogmatists spell defeat for "the open society," the democratic way of life. The surest path away from dogmatism begins in youth, and is the lustrous highroad

of fancy. Imagination is the roomy space where we store, as it were, all beliefs which have reality but are not due, and may never be due, for embodiment in practice. They are too precious to be compromised in politics, and too dear to be mutilated in any form of overt action. But there they are, rich beyond compare—beliefs that encompass Santa Claus and mermaids and classless societies. Even when they do not inform action—as they seldom do—such beliefs are islands of refuge, reached through reverie, when the comings and goings of actuality get too rough.

Let me try to tie all this together with three anecdotes climaxed with a prayer to youth.

I asked a former student, who confided in me that he had lost his belief in hell, what happened thereupon to his moral life. "Nothing," he replied, though he admitted that at first he had been worried. He had not only discovered, he said, that there are other and better foundations for practice but also that he had never really founded his conduct on mere fear, however metaphysical.

I asked a young matron which was the best memory of her childhood. "A room of my own," she replied, "where I could lock the door against mother." Recently, I asked a college girl what provision the college made for solitude. "None," she replied, not even a place where she could cry alone. Adult delinquency, what robbery is done in thy name!

> Let me be
> Swift wings to bear you on your skyward journey
> A sword to cleave your bonds and set you free!
>
> Then, though you drop both out-worn sword and pinions,
>   I shall not care,
> Knowing I gave you wider skies to wander,
> And of my love made freedom—not a snare!
>   Jamie Sexton Holme

REALITY AND RESPONSIBILITY

Reverend Laurence J. McGinley, S.J.

AS WE ENTER a new decade whose explosive forces either promise a far better world for all of us or threaten our very survival, national concern for the spiritual, mental, emotional, and physical well-being of our young people becomes enhanced. There are some 75 million of them: in infancy and childhood and adolescence and young manhood; at home, at school, at work, in the armed forces. They vary from poor to rich, from healthy to handicapped, from retarded to very bright, from the delinquent to the heroic. Most of them are normal, average. All of them are important.

For brevity, and so that my main theme may be presented more clearly, I shall set down at the start certain premises.

The first is: the problems involving children and youth cannot be basically solved by legislation as exploitation of child labor was fifty years ago. They are too deep for merely legal remedy.

My second premise is: we also cannot solve these problems simply by more research, more statistical data, or new remedial techniques. We already know "how" in great measure. We also know it will never be possible to supply enough professional help for the remedial services required. We must concentrate on prevention.

My third premise is: the major problems of children and youth in the 1960s involve values, and these values are derived from adults. In a very real sense, I believe that this is a problem of adults. For every adult is a

The Reverend Laurence J. McGinley, S.J., is President of Fordham University.

teacher, most often simply by attitude.) And we cannot communicate values we do not have and have clearly. A father can give his son the car keys whether he understands the motor or not. But he cannot inspire an integrity in which he does not believe.

I mention one more premise. There are three great human transitions: birth, death, and the growth from the dependence of childhood to autonomous maturity. Each of these involves human travail. Our role is not to make the struggle easier for youth but to make it more worthwhile. This, again, involves values.

And now to my central theme—the impact on children and youth in 1960 of economic, social and cultural factors. We know that the problems are manifold and global. I can only endeavor to identify and appraise those factors in each area which I believe specially condition the values of adults in 1960 and, therefore, of children and youth. Briefly stated, I see the central problem of our day to be this: the difficulty of attaining fulfillment of the individual in the increasingly complex organization of our economic, social and cultural life.

THE IMPACT OF ECONOMIC FACTORS

There are two striking facts about the American economy: it is highly organized and it has given fantastic abundance. The complexity of our economy is startling—its expanse, its multiplicity, the delicacy of its interrelationships. Standard Oil with 9½ billion dollars of assets, General Motors with 520,000 employees, American Telephone & Telegraph with the electronic intricacies of its far-flung web—hundreds of agencies like these mesh into a system which touches on employment, on the flow of money, on where men live, on their health, their schools, their leisure time recreation. Bricklaying in Chicago stops when there is a steel strike in Pittsburgh. A boom in Detroit affects orange sales in Clearwater. Even within a single city, the failure of electric power in an autumn storm plunges homes into darkness, shuts off the furnaces, disrupts traffic control, and spoils the baby's milk in the refrigerator. Ten thousand people can only sit and wait.

This complex economy has given us fantastically varied abundance. Since the end of World War II, our gross national product has risen to a breathtaking $479,000,000,000. This bounty has placed a dazzling array of conveniences within the aspiration and reach of an ever widening circle of Americans. Nine of every ten wired homes in the United States have television. Three out of every four families have at least one car. Sums spent on such items as cosmetics and beverages are astronomical. Even our children are bigger, healthier, keener due to better nutrition, more protective care and a prosperous cultural environment. And yet troubled children have supplanted the orphans in our institutions, near anarchy breaks out in our juvenile population, and there is an alarming increase in mental illness among the very young. What is the impact of the economic factors of complexity and abundance?

An abundant economy can stimulate an artificial want. The satisfaction of possession beckons to the young as well as to their elders. Possession can compensate for psychological insecurity. It gives status. It makes for significance and even power within one's peer group. Yet the satisfactions offered by abundance require money in a way different from those of an earlier day. The old swimming hole required no cash (and often no towel or Jantzen swim suit). A ride to the beach does; so does a movie, or even a coke. And with more money around, there seems less excuse, in youth's eyes, for not having it. The young can get it through a part-time job, outside the family circle, with proceeds jealously reserved as "mine alone." Or they can wheedle it from parents, with irritating toll in domestic tension. Actually, the period of familial dependence has been prolonged by the abundant economy itself. A highly organized technology has no need nor worthwhile opportunity for the very young. Schools take on a custodial role and the resulting frustration is directed toward the system which has given the abundance.

Ever more directly, the complexity of our highly organized economy can instill a sense of helplessness and insignificance. The system dwarfs the person. He is troubled at his incapacity to understand the structure within which he lives and works. He is frustrated by his personal inability to direct it in any way, to repair it if it fails, to substitute something else for it. All too easily contemporary man may conclude that his

own reactions do not really count, and he may thus lose the consciousness of being master of his own destiny, which is at the root of moral greatness. For youth and for adults alike, each step away from self-reliance, through the subsidizing influence of family, or state, or economic system, is a step toward personal insecurity and anxiety.

This, then, I conceive to be a basic impact of our economy: the feeling of uselessness of personal reaction and responsibility. Some fundamental values are here at stake. The comforts of abundance are means, not goals. True personal fulfillment is still of the spirit. Abundance can be a flabby goal begetting discontent or a means of freeing energy for the more human satisfaction of personal achievement and social good. As for the complexity of our economic life, this does not change the nature of personal fulfillment but only alters its expression. Fulfillment still lies in doing, with noble motive, what is in one's power. Complexity does not limit one's power; it expands it. Youth is called, today as yesterday, to concern for man out of love for God. But today in the wider regions of society both complexity and abundance can make this concern more effective. Competent, intelligent, generous, cooperative action with and through organized society can help more people reach fulfillment than ever before. Yesterday's sharing of one loaf of bread has become today's opportunity to work with others for a better life for whole populations, abroad or right here at home. Our common submergence in a complex economy demands not less but more social responsibility. It has been well said that today's hero (like today's saint) must be an organization man. And this is a vision that I think youth will understand and accept, with all the discipline and sacrifice that it entails—if we adults accept it first.

THE IMPACT OF SOCIAL FACTORS

It is not strange that in a complex, technological economy our human living should become highly organized too. In our generation the impact of organization on our social relations is the central social factor. We are quickly approaching the period of "urban man," man of the crowded and quickly changing neighborhood, man of many disparate associations,

man with a specialist at his elbow day and night. In the basic social unit, the family, life is no longer the simple routine of the young boy consciously maturing by sharing with grownups the occupations of farm or shop. Life is no longer the secure enjoyment of relatives, neighbors, and friends in a small part of the world, where a person has a sense of belonging, where the meaning of life and experience is made clear by generations of tradition. Nowadays a child in the city street may interact with more human beings in an hour than a frontiersman did in half a year.

The separate "conjugal" family has lost not only the physical, psychological, social, and economic support of a group of kinsmen as it has become independent and small and free from ties and responsibilities. Because of its mobility, it has also become isolated from community bonds and even from its own adult members, except when the proximity of parents or in-laws makes baby sitting mutually convenient. Even the family's domestic functions have become more and more professionalized. We have the obstetrician, the pediatrician, the specialist in child development. The teacher who saw four grades of children in front of her for a whole day has yielded to the child who sees four teachers before him in a single morning. It is the Blue Cross for health, the labor union for work, Channel 2 for recreation, social security for old age, and the funeral parlor for death. Outside the home there is the rapid movement of a restless world, giving little time for more than passing impression, demanding a skill of quick adjustment that no previous society has had to face. Gone is the stable community, guardian of tradition, teacher of values that have been tested by generations, wise counsellor assuring us that what we do today must be correct because it has been done for centuries. Within the home the family, once youth's all-embracing world, finds itself isolated, on the fringes, almost bereft of functions.

And yet not quite, because the family still offers the one social relationship which can give the human person a sense of the complete life in the presence of today's fragmented experience: it alone can endeavor to sift out of new and conflicting values a set of norms and principles that can be reliable guideposts on our human journey. The fragmentation of youth's contact with adults belonging to many different groups

leads inevitably to a confusion of values because he has no single source, no single voice to help him become inner-directed. And this is the one important function left to the family in the compartmentalized social relationships of our time. It alone can give youth a sense of identity, a unity of concept and a singleness of purpose. It alone can do this, and no professional agency can, because this function, of its very nature, involves love, affection, and the security of respect.

Never before was the challenge of personal responsibility presented so clearly to men. They can no longer rely on social systems to provide them with tried and tested values. In this context the central role of the family becomes clear. Far from being less important, it becomes more important in our highly specialized world. Our nation's strength will derive from a strong cohesive family life, providing the example and the security of unity and devotion, the firm direction which authority joined with love can give to free the young from inner conflict, a clear knowledge of the difference between good and evil, sound patterns for rising above the difficulties of environment, a respect for authority, and a sense of personal responsibility for one's own acts. This alone the family can do—give youth a sense of personal identity in an impersonally organized world, a clear sense of values in a society which no longer provides them for us.

To do all this in 1960 the family needs help. We are faced on the one hand with the fact that in our economy 32 percent of the labor force consists of women and 30 percent of all women with children under the age of eighteen are working mothers. We are faced on the other hand with the realization that the family is more central to the development of the human person in our society than it has been in any other. It seems clear that a primary, social task of America in the 1960s must be to provide the helps, the services, the guidance the family needs in order to fulfill its essential function in contemporary life. To achieve this will not be easy. Indeed, this task of strengthening family life is, I believe, so difficult that it can be accomplished only by deepening the moral and spiritual climate of our whole nation, through our churches, our schools, and all our social institutions.

THE IMPACT OF CULTURAL FACTORS

There would seem to be a definite causal connection between an increasingly complex economy, with its compartmentalized social relationships, and an accelerated tempo of cultural change. At any rate, the most striking characteristic about our contemporary culture seems to be constant change at a steadily increasing tempo in almost every area. Those of us alive early in the century grew up in a world where there was no television, sputnik, nuclear armament, no selective military service or Cold War or sirens reminding us of the threat of mass destruction. Most of the cultural patterns we knew in our teens our parents knew in theirs. They have all undergone changes and are still in flux. The bitter joke about our new weapons—"If they work, they're obsolete"—might also be the motto for much of our cultural experience today.

There is a basic overall difficulty of living in our culture which affects the young especially, though it affects us all: it is the difficulty of achieving inner stability and basic principles while actively participating in a culture whose keynote is constant change. In a situation of this sort, a young person cannot easily attain any vision of clear-cut goals. To discover or establish his personal identity is harder for him than it was for his father when external institutions and social patterns in family and work were more stable over longer periods of time. Today there seem to be no stable models to imitate, no patterns to follow or firm principles to serve as guide lines. All seems to shift kaleidoscopically, continually dissolving and regrouping differently. For youth in quest of identity, this tends to produce uncertainty and a diffuse anxiety.

Having no stable institution or group or way of living with which to identify in the face of a culture of constant change, there are two facile and extreme solutions to the problem of personal survival. One is simply to withdraw from active participation in the culture. The other is to be swept along by a current of other-directed conformism, assenting dumbly to the goals of whatever group enfolds one. For adult or youth either solution is violent. Withdrawal in its extreme form is madness and is death to aspiration and to action. Conformism, in the sense of a

surrender of personal initiative, creativity and responsibility, is damaging at any time and peculiarly so for young people. For it means that they cannot live out the special drama of adolescence, that they cannot assert and define themselves as distinct individuals with a personal realization of life and value. They are torn between surrendering their attempt to achieve conscious selfhood and enduring the disfavor which greets strong manifestations of individuality in large sectors of our society and the guilty feelings which such disapproval arouses.

Our common task then is clear and terrifyingly difficult. We cannot make our culture static and would not if we could. Yet we must enable youth to succeed in its quest for identity and inner stability while actively participating in a culture of constant change. In brief, we face again the basic problem of how to obtain the fulfillment of the human person in our increasingly complex day.

And what, basically, is this human fulfillment that we seek? What powerful factor is it that effects an integrated personality, that maintains an inner unity and provides life with its form and focus? It is surely not a set of techniques or a repertoire of reactions built up through simple mimicry of current custom. Rather, the healthy integration of personality is effected by a strong and operative sense of fixed and comprehensive purposes—purposes which transcend the teeming manifold of experience and can, therefore, give it pattern and unity; purposes lofty and inclusive enough to dominate without impoverishing the flow of life with its endless wealth of knowledge and impressions, its desires and its strivings, its opportunities and perils.

In brief, I think our task is to restore in the 1960s a national consciousness of those real and abiding purposes and values which provide a vital inner personal stability and are valid in the most diverse and changing contexts. One such value is an esteem and appreciation of the individual person who remains a fixed center of reference even in an age of chaotic change. For the human person has a constant destiny which cannot be shaken and in a changing world he is obliged more imperatively than ever to exercise responsibility for the fulfillment of that destiny. To achieve this, he must derive his personal, moral, and spiritual responsibility not from contemporary mores but from transcendent

values personally understood: man's origin, his destiny, God's Providence, His love, His sanctification of this world by His presence in it. In this way the value of the individual, so traditional in our American concepts of equality of opportunity for education, for employment, for choice of personal fulfillment, will be more deeply understood as the permanent abiding image of God in each youth, no matter where or when.

A CLIMATE OF COMMITMENT

Abram L. Sachar

THE TEMPTATION to characterize the intellectual currents of one's time is always strong; at the start of a new decade it becomes irresistible. Some characterizations have caught the popular imagination more firmly than others. We all remember the "lost" generation of the 1920s, in Hemingway's expatriate heroes and heroines, drinking themselves into unconsciousness in the cafés of the Left Bank; or Scott Fitzgerald's "beautiful and damned" flappers of the Jazz Age who became the accepted stereotypes of a generation of Americans. Many of that generation, however, had never heard of the Latin Quarter and would have fled in discreet revulsion from a bullfight. And yet the adjective "lost" was not purely a literary invention. It caught something of the disillusionment and the defeatism of the period immediately after World War I.

What of the youth coming of age after World War II? What of your time, our time? It has already acquired its quota of tags and identifications which, if accurate, are profoundly disquieting. Some have described it as the "silent" generation, others as the "angry" generation. Yet, even the angry young men of the British and American literary revolt are not rebels or dreamers. Their anger is sullen, a sign of withdrawal and not of protest.

Perhaps the best way to describe the contemporary state of mind is to label it as "uncommitted." It is not a lost generation. If anything, it is too much unlost. It is withdrawn. Its restlessness is not a product of con-

Abram L. Sachar is President of Brandeis University.

cern; it is a product of lack of concern. The retreat into a private world, the lack of commitment to larger issues that exceed purely individual pains and satisfactions, are reflected by our younger writers. In their narcissistic exploration of the psyche of the hero, their concentration on childhood experience before the bonds with society are established, their drift to fantasy, we perceive indications of an awareness of the self, *selfish* rather than social.

The poet Yeats lamented,

> The *best* lack all conviction, while the *worst*
> Are full of passionate intensity.

Today we might subscribe to the first half of the poet's bitter comment. The "best" in the intellectual sense do, indeed, appear to lack conviction, but even the "worst" are characterized by cynicism and cold malice rather than by any "passionate intensity." In the old days we used to worry about the reckless idealism of young people, their impetuousness and impatience. They no longer appear to require the restraining cautions and admonitions of their elders. It seems superfluous in most instances to urge them to be sensible and practical. They share the national obsession with personal happiness; they are an integral part of the cult of gratification at all costs. Corruption in politics, rigged TV shows, payola are alarming in themselves, but even more alarming is the good-natured acceptance of such developments with a kind of cynical affection. There can be no commitment to social needs when there has been such a marked shift from what an M.I.T. professor has termed the Courage Culture that America used to be to the Creature Comfort Culture that it has now become.

How is one to explain this lack of commitment among our young people? One cause may lie in a kind of edge-of-disaster psychology when a whole generation is threatened by vast and incalculable disaster. Any day the robot of technology may push the last button and obliterate all of us in a mechanical apocalypse. The individual, therefore, feels dwarfed and helpless. What can he do except construct his private shelter, make it as comfortable as possible, equip it with every gadget and luxury which our material wealth permits, and not bother about problems and ques-

tions outside of immediate concern. "To Hell With It" then becomes the compelling credo.

Yet the argument from despair is not wholly convincing. Recorded history is full of periods of menace, admittedly not as total as the present, because man's conquest of the physical universe has never before reached so baleful a degree, but periods of menace equally dangerous to the individual. Yet men built again on the ruins, not only efficiently, but with a generous faith for a future which transcended their individual destinies. The supreme scientific and technological miracle of our era, the harnessing of the atom, was achieved, as any account of the project will indicate, not by dispassionate calculators but by men like Arthur Compton, and Fermi and Szilard and Bohr, men aglow with a dream of liberation.

The blame for our unspiritual climate then can be laid only partly to the fear of cosmic annihilation. Surely, this generation's unprecedented regard for pension plans and guaranteed security programs is a curious way of expressing terror of sudden death. One of my department heads told me recently that he was startled when young Ph.D.'s fresh from graduate school, not yet twenty-five, inquired about the University's retirement system when applying for instructorships. Such prudence is no doubt commendable, but one cannot help wondering at the view of life of a youth who must see every pavingstone in place before he ventures on so long a road. This is why I say that the argument from despair is not a true explanation. One must look for other factors to understand our cool and uncommitted young. Has their education, in the wider sense, been at fault?

It is fashionable to point an accusing finger at the familiar villains of the piece—John Dewey and Sigmund Freud. Is not Dewey responsible for the undisciplined uninhibited bundle of appetites we call a child? Did not Freud with his "pleasure principle" and his exorcism of "repressions" compound the damage? Quite recently President Eisenhower, who before assuming the Presidency of the United States was, we should recall, the President of Columbia University, strictured John Dewey in no uncertain terms. In a letter to *Life* Magazine (March 15, 1959) President Eisen-

hower wrote: "Educators, parents and students must be continuously stirred up by the defects of our educational system. They must be induced to abandon the educational path that, rather blithely, they have been following as a result of John Dewey's teachings." The charge is that our youth, the end product of Dewey's theories, is not only ignorant, but selfish and irresponsible as well. In addition to being woefully deficient in the traditional three R's, he emerges from the Dewey chrysalis with no concern for the fourth R—responsibility for the welfare of his world.

In truth, this is quite unfair to John Dewey. In his body of teachings he advocated no such escape from discipline and responsibility. The trouble lies in the fact that he has often been torn from context. He has suffered almost as much at the hands of some of his disciples as from his traducers. His original educational theories have been vulgarized, his precious coinage has been debased, and all about us now we have the ill effects of this debasement.

Dewey was right to shift from traditional formal education, with its emphasis on particular subjects and disciplines, to an emphasis on the personality of the student. He brought us a stimulating and potentially fruitful revaluation. But the trouble began when regard for the child's individuality was erroneously interpreted as a need to pander to the child's whims and caprices. How far is the distance between the "child-centered" school and the self-centered individual? The student educated to believe that his impulses and desires are sacrosanct, and that they constitute the sole meaningful standard for his mental and moral life, is not likely to accept with adequate seriousness the prime obligations of service in the modern world. The youngster taught that there are no absolute sanctions is often likely to reject their validity altogether. Who is not familiar with the pious horror of our students as they shrink from making value judgments? They say, "Who is to presume to praise or condemn? Who really knows what is right or wrong? Why claim ethical merit for a going value when it is merely a matter of opinion?"

Well, it is a short step from this kind of ethical relativism to complete cynicism, to the repudiation of all values which have come out of the Judeo-Christian heritage. Neither Dewey nor Freud, nor the forerunners

of progressive education, nor the pioneers of psychoanalysis proposed such ethical nihilism. They insisted that the test of the free intelligence lies, not in its negation of values, but in its ability to choose wisely among values. But these cautions were often forgotten in the heady wine of revolt. The cult of gratification, the fear of "inhibiting" personality, was bound to bring us to this sorry pass. All too many young people so nurtured have lost their concern for whatever is beyond themselves. They are flabby in aspiration and hence there is no enduring fiber in their social concern.

Studies of the Korean War have shown that American soldiers taken prisoner by the enemy cracked more quickly under the stress of adverse conditions than prisoners of other nationalities. Why? Did their comparative softness result from the greater ease and comfort of life in America? Was it because they were less familiar with hardship and privation than soldiers of less fortunate countries? I think not. Was it not rather that, although they were courageous soldiers in the heat of battle, they were morally unprepared for long-term fortitude? Military authorities are so persuaded that this is the basic difficulty that they have begun studies in depth to determine appropriate solutions.

None of this is meant to imply that life in America should become less abundant or less satisfying than we know it. I do not demean our comforts and our advantages. I love them and enjoy them as everyone does. We are blessed with a happy lot as citizens of a prosperous and powerful democracy. But we may well consider whether our morale is equal to our blessings.

I recently read in the current issue of a national monthly an interesting exchange of correspondence between Adlai Stevenson and John Steinbeck. Steinbeck had just returned from two years of work in England on a play dealing with the Knights of the Round Table. He confronted an America that he had not seen for quite some time. He was very much troubled by what he found, "a creeping all-pervading nerve gas of immorality which starts in the nursery and does not stop before it reaches the highest offices, both corporate and government." He asked what is wrong with Americans today. Is it not that they have too many things? "They spend their hours and money on the couch searching for a soul.

What a strange species we are. We can stand anything God and Nature can throw at us save only plenty. . . . If I want to destroy a nation, I would give it too much, and I would have it on its knees, miserable, greedy, and sick." Steinbeck grieves over the deterioration of a once noble Courage Culture that is now so concerned with creature comforts.

I return to the problem of commitment. If the relativism of much current thinking, a relativism which hesitates to affirm or deny, is at fault, then as educators we have tougher problems than exploding population and spiraling costs. We have the overwhelming task, on every level, from the elementary school to the university, of challenging an intellectual position which condones moral neutrality, which encourages an escape to the Ivory Tower. Some readers will remember Archibald MacLeish's magnificent little volume, *The Irresponsibles*. He was evaluating the tragedy that engulfed the Germany of the Weimar Republic. In the early days when Hitler was still a barroom hooligan whose appeal was mainly to rowdies and bullies, it was possible for the decent elements in society to contain the plague. But most of the professors in the universities, the writers, the philosophers, the intellectuals—most of these felt that this was not their responsibility. It was the concern of the politicians. They had no commitment to the hurly-burly of current issues. Their objectivity might be jeopardized if they took sides! They were so antiseptic in their neutrality that they became sterile. Only Thomas Mann and a few courageous spirits insisted upon commitment. Even Hauptmann, the brilliant interpreter of Goethe, would not besmirch his academic garments by passing judgment on evils which were then still no larger than a man's hand and had not yet became a black and all-consuming cloud.

In our sensitively balanced world, we have learned that we cannot afford the laxity of spirit which searches for the comfortable port for one's self, which sedulously avoids the problems that batter at one's private peace. A time comes when we, too, must enter the fray. If we cannot rely on the men and women who are the custodians of our educational system, upon whom can we rely? If they remain armchair critics, or Monday morning quarterbacks, if they merely sit in the seats of the scorners, who will take up the cudgels? Let me remind you of the mag-

nificent words of Milton, no mean excoriator himself, but always first among the doers: "I cannot praise a fugitive and cloistered virtue, un-exercised and unbreathed, that never sallies out and seeks her adversary, but slinks out of the race where that immortal garland is to be run for, not without dust and heat." How wise the poet was, and how thoroughly he understood the struggle for the immortal garland. Certainly the dour Puritan could never be charged with compromise or opportunism. But he knew that virtue is meaningless if it is cloistered, and that the world of action in which the race is run is not without dust and heat. It is a great poet's way of saying, pay for your convictions with service. You must all remember the ignominious spot to which Dante committed the neutrals, those whom both Heaven and Hell disdained. Contemptuously the Italian poet placed them just outside the gate in the antechamber of his Inferno, always outside and eternally damned.

Of course, commitment is not easy. It means aggravation, discomfort, sacrifice. But what good are the reservoirs of idealism unless they are channelled to enrich and fructify community life? What good are high-sounding, noble ideals that are encysted in a vacuum? Good intentions must be linked with stamina. Unless our most knowledgeable and most sensitive are willing to fight for their convictions, to slug it out, toe to toe, with the primitives and the Neanderthal men, their well-phrased in-tentions will survive only to mock and shame them. Real progress can-not come from the flashy verbalizers who speak brave words, but whose timidity and impatience in relation to the tedious techniques of fulfill-ment lead in the end to futility and impotence.

Educators today are in a strategic position to raise such a flag in their areas of influence. We count on them, not just for idealism, but for par-ticipation, not just for precept, but for example. They do not always have to win. Indeed, they will surely not always win. William James well said: "The difference between a good man and a bad one is the choice of the cause." The best of the past and the present count on all of us to salvage the future.

NOTES AND REFERENCES

THE YOUNG ADULT
by Margaret Mead

1. Symonds, Percival M. "Almost Everything about Adolescence," *Contemporary Psychology*, III: No. 5:132–39, May, 1958.
2. Johnson, E. W. *How to Live through Junior High School*. New York, Lippincott, 1959. Stone, L. J. and Joseph Church. *Childhood and Adolescence*, New York, Random House, 1957.
3. Mead, M. "Thinking Ahead: Why Is Education Obsolete?" *Harvard Business Review*, 36: No. 6:23–30, November–December, 1958.
4. Riesman, D. "The Found Generation," *American Scholar*, 25: No. 4:421–36, Autumn, 1956. Mead, M., "Our Documentary Culture," *American Scholar*, 25: No. 4:401–9, Autumn, 1956.
5. Riesman, D. and N. Glazer. "Intellectuals and the Discontented Classes," *Partisan Review*, XXII: No. 1:47–72, Winter, 1955.
6. Mead, M., "Our Documentary Culture," *American Scholar*, 25: No. 4, Autumn, 1956.
7. Ehrmann, W. *Premarital Dating Behavior*. New York, Holt, 1959.
8. Mead, M. "Higher Education for Men and Women." (To be published by Editorial Projects for Education, University of Arkansas Alumni Association, as a syndicated article for alumni magazines.)
9. Lipton, L. *The Holy Barbarians*. New York, Messner, 1959. Ginsberg, A. *Howl*. San Francisco, City Lights Book Shop, 1956. Trilling, D. "The Other Night at Columbia," *Partisan Review*, XXVI: No. 2:214–30, Spring, 1959.
10. Erikson, E. "Identity and the Life Cycle: Selected Papers," *Psychological Issues Monograph Series*, I: No. 1. New York, International Universities Press, 1959. World Federation for Mental Health. *Identity:* Introductory Study No. 1. London, World Federation for Mental Health, 1957. Wheelis, A. *The Quest for Identity*. New York, Norton, 1958.
11. Erikson, E. "On the Sense of Inner Identity," in Knight, Robert, ed., *Clinical and Theoretical Papers, Austen Riggs Center*, I, 351–64. New York, International Universities Press, 1954.

12. Remmers, H. H. and D. H. Radler. *The American Teenager*. Indianapolis–New York, Bobbs-Merrill, 1957. Jacobs, P. E. *Changing Values in College*. New York, Harper, 1957.

13. Strang, Ruth M. *The Adolescent Views Himself: a Psychology of Adolescence*. New York, McGraw-Hill, 1957. Symonds, "Almost Everything about Adolescence," *Contemporary Psychology*, III: No. 5:132–39, May, 1958.

14. Allport, G. and James M. Gillespie. *Youth's Outlook on the Future: a Cross-National Study*. Garden City, N.Y., Doubleday Papers in Psychology, No. 15, 1955.

15. Spiegel, L. A. "A Review of Contributions to Psychoanalytic Theory of Adolescence," *The Psychoanalytic Theory of Adolescence*, 6:375–93. New York, International Universities Press, 1951. Mead, M. "Cultural Contexts of Puberty and Adolescence," *Bulletin of the Philadelphia Association for Psychoanalysis*, IX: No. 3:59–79, September, 1959.

16. Freud, A. "Adolescence," *Psychoanalytic Study of the Child*, 13:255–78. New York, International Universities Press, 1958.

17. Ginsberg, *Howl*. Trilling, "Other Night at Columbia," *Partisan Review*, XXVI: No. 2, Spring, 1959.

18. Pollack, J. H. "What Makes Happy Families Happy?" *This Week*, Sept. 13 and Sept. 20, 1959. [A report on a study by C. C. Zimmerman and L. F. Cervantes, "Successful American Families" to be published by the Public Affairs Press, Washington, D.C.]

19. Jones, H. E. *Motor Performance and Growth*. Berkeley and Los Angeles, University of California Press, 1949. Shuttleworth, F. K. "The Physical and Mental Growth of Girls and Boys Age Six to Nineteen in Relation to Age at Maximum Growth," *Monographs of the Society for Research in Child Development*, 14: No. 1, 1949.

20. Spiegel, "A Review of Contributions," *Psychoanalytic Theory of Adolescence*, 6:375–93.

21. Inhelder, Bärbel and Jean Piaget. *The Growth of Logical Thinking from Childhood to Adolescence*, trans. by Anne Parsons and Stanley Milgram. New York, Basic Books, 1958. Tanner, J. M., and Bärbel Inhelder. *Discussions on Child Development*, p. 3. Proceedings of the Third Meeting of the World Health Organization Study Group on the Psychological Development of the Child, Geneva, 1955. London, Tavistock, 1958.

Additional References

Blos, P. *The Adolescent Personality*. New York, Appleton-Century, 1941.
—— "Prolonged Adolescence: The Formation of a Syndrome and Its Therapeutic Implications," *American Journal of Orthopsychiatry*, 24: No. 4:733–42, October, 1954.
Devereux, G. *Therapeutic Education*. New York, Harper, 1956.
Erikson, E. *Young Man Luther*. New York, Norton, 1958.

Frank, L. K. and Mary Frank. *Your Adolescent at Home and in School.* New York, Viking Press, 1956.

Gesell, A., F. Ilg, and L. Ames. *Youth: The Years from 10–16.* New York, Harper, 1956.

Glueck, S. and E. Glueck. *Unraveling Juvenile Delinquency.* New York, The Commonwealth Fund, 1950.

Hollingshead, A. B. *Elmtown's Youth: The Impact of Social Classes on Adolescents.* New York, Wiley, 1949.

Mead, M. and R. Metraux. "Image of the Scientist among High-School Students," *Science,* 126: No. 3270:384–90, August 30, 1957.

"A Nationwide Poll of Your Hopes, Plans, and Fears for the Decade Ahead," *Look,* January 5, 1960.

Roe, A., Series of articles, 1946–1949, on personality studies of scientists, technicians, painters, etc., appearing in *Quarterly Journal of Studies in Alcohol, Analytical Psychologist,* etc.

Salisbury, H. *The Shook-up Generation.* New York, Harper, 1958.

Samuels, G. "Visit to a California Work Camp," *New York Times Magazine,* p. 16. October 4, 1959.

Shippee-Blum, E. M. "The Young Rebel: Self Regard and Ego-Ideal," *Journal of Consulting Psychology,* 23: No. 1:44–50, February, 1959.

CHANGING SEXUAL MORES
by Winston Ehrmann

Grateful acknowledgement is made to Mr. and Mrs. Charles L. Robbins, Mrs. Catherine Clark, the Colorado State University Research Foundation, the Department of Economics and Sociology of the Colorado State University, and the Department of Sociology and Anthropology of the University of Florida for assistance and material support in the preparation of this paper.

1. Murdock, George Peter. *Social Structure.* New York, Macmillan, 1949. Ford, Clellan S. and Frank A. Beach. *Patterns of Sexual Behavior.* New York, Harper and Hoeber, 1951.

2. Cavan, Ruth Shonle. *The American Family,* pp. 367–95. New York, Crowell, 1953. Kirkpatrick, Clifford. *The Family,* pp. 97–118, 311–35. New York, Ronald Press, 1955.

3. Ogburn, William F. and Meyer F. Nimkoff. *Technology and the Changing Family,* pp. 49–55. Boston, New York, Houghton Mifflin, 1955.

4. Ehrmann, Winston. *Premarital Dating Behavior,* chapter I and "Introduction" by Margaret Mead. New York, Holt, 1959.

5. Ehrmann, Winston. "Some Knowns and Unknowns in Research into

Human Sex Behavior," *Marriage and Family Living,* XIX: No. 1:16–22, February, 1957.

6. Kinsey, Alfred C., Wardell B. Pomeroy, and Clyde E. Martin. *Sexual Behavior in the Human Male.* Philadelphia, Saunders, 1948.

7. Kinsey, Alfred C., Wardell B. Pomeroy, Clyde E. Martin, and Paul H. Gebhard. *Sexual Behavior in the Human Female.* Philadelphia, Saunders, 1953.

8. Gebhard, Paul H., Wardell B. Pomeroy, Clyde E. Martin, and Cornelia V. Christenson. *Pregnancy, Birth and Abortion.* New York, Harper and Hoeber, 1958.

9. Locke, Harvey J. *Predicting Adjustment in Marriage: A Comparison of a Divorced and a Happily Married Group.* New York, Holt, 1951.

10. Burgess, Ernest W. and Paul Wallin. *Engagement and Marriage.* Chicago, Philadelphia, New York, Lippincott, 1953.

11. Ehrmann, *Premarital Dating.*

12. Exner, Max Joseph. *Problems and Principles of Sex Education.* New York, Association Press, 1915.

13. Davis, Katharine B. *Factors in the Sex Life of Twenty-two Hundred Women.* New York and London, Harper, 1929.

14. Hamilton, Gilbert V. *A Research in Marriage.* New York, Albert and Charles Boni, 1929.

15. Terman, Lewis M. *Psychological Factors in Marital Happiness.* New York and London, McGraw-Hill, 1938.

16. Bromley, Dorothy Dunbar and Florence Haxton Britten. *Youth and Sex.* New York and London, Harper, 1938.

17. Landis, Carney et al. *Sex in Development.* New York, London, Hoeber, 1940.

18. Kinsey et al., *Human Male,* p. 192; *Human Female,* pp. 101–31.

19. Kinsey et al., *Human Male,* pp. 193–217; *Human Female,* pp. 510–64.

20. Kinsey et al., *Human Male,* pp. 531–46; *Human Female,* pp. 173–77.

21. Kinsey et al., *Human Male,* pp. 259–61; *Human Female,* pp. 446–501.

22. Kinsey et al., *Human Male,* pp. 536–46; *Human Female,* pp. 227–81. See Ehrmann, *Premarital Dating,* p. 36, for a summary of the findings.

23. Kinsey et al., *Human Male,* pp. 547–62; *Human Female,* pp. 282–345. See Ehrmann, *Premarital Dating,* pp. 32–36, for a summary of the findings.

24. Ehrmann, "Some Knowns and Unknowns in Research into Human Sex Behavior," *Marriage and Family Living,* XIX: No. 1:16–22, February, 1957. Ehrmann, *Premarital Dating,* chapter 1.

25. Ehrmann, *Premarital Dating,* pp. 56, 82–84, 268.

26. Ehrmann, *Premarital Dating.* Reiss, Ira L., "The Double Standard in Premarital Sexual Intercourse: The Neglected Concept," *Social Forces,* 32:224–30, 1956.

27. See Ehrmann, *Premarital Dating,* pp. 231–32, for a summary of the findings.

28. See Ehrmann, *Premarital Dating*, pp. 89–93, for a summary of the findings.

29. Kinsey et al., *Human Male*, pp. 453, 456; *Human Female*, pp. 246, 303.

30. Hohman, Leslie B. and Bertram Schaffner. "The Sex Lives of Unmarried Men," *American Journal of Sociology*, 52:501–7, 1957. Gebhard et al., *Birth and Abortion*, pp. 153–57. Simpson, George Eaton and J. Milton Yinger. *Racial and Cultural Minorities*, pp. 81–85, 261–71, 542–45, 554–55. New York, Harper, 1958.

31. Kinsey et al., *Human Male*, pp. 394–417; *Human Female*.

32. Ehrmann, *Premarital Dating*, pp. 143–54; for a summary of findings see pp. 154–56.

33. Hollingshead, August B. *Elmtown's Youth*, pp. 232, 240. New York, Wiley, 1949.

34. Kinsey et al., *Human Female*.

35. See Davis, *Factors in Sex Life*; Hamilton, *Research in Marriage*; Bromley and Britten, *Youth and Sex*; Ehrmann, *Premarital Dating*; Burgess and Wallin, *Engagement and Marriage*; Kinsey et al., *Human Female*; and especially Terman, *Factors in Marital Happiness*.

36. Ehrmann, *Premarital Dating*, pp. 132–43; also chapters V, VI, and VII.

37. For example, Salisbury, Harrison E., *The Shook-up Generation*, pp. 31–32. New York, Fawcett World Library, 1958.

38. Gebhard et al., *Birth and Abortion*.

39. Planned Parenthood Federation of America. Mary Steichen Calderone, ed. *Abortion in the United States*, p. 180; also pp. 3–5, 50–69, 162–77. New York, Hoeber, 1958.

40. Shapiro, Sam. "Illegitimate Births, 1938–47," *Vital Statistics—Special Reports 33, 5*, pp. 72, 73, and 84. Federal Security Agency, National Office of Vital Statistics, February 15, 1950.

41. *Children in a Changing World*, 1960 White House Conference, p. 22.

THE CHANGING AMERICAN CHILD
by Urie Bronfenbrenner

1. Bronfenbrenner, U. "Socialization and Social Class Through Time and Space," in Macoby, E., T. M. Newcomb, and E. L. Hartley, eds., *Readings in Social Psychology*. New York, Holt, 1958.

2. Bronson, W. C., E. S. Katten, and N. Livson. "Patterns of Authority and Affection in Two Generations," *Journal of Abnormal and Social Psychology*, 58:143–52, 1959.

3. Sears, Macoby, and Levin. *Pattern of Child Rearing*. Evanston, Ill., Row, Peterson, 1957. Miller and Swanson. *The Changing American Parent*. New York, Wiley, 1958. Miller and Swanson. *Inner Conflict and Defense*. New York, Holt, 1960.

4. For a summary of findings on social class differences in children's behavior and personality characteristics, see Mussen, P. H. and J. J. Conger, *Child Development and Personality*. New York, Harper, 1956.

5. Bronfenbrenner, U. "Some Familial Antecedents of Responsibility and Leadership in Adolescents," in Petruello, L. and B. M. Bass, eds., *Studies in Leadership* (tentative title). In press.

6. Schachter, S. *The Psychology of Affiliation*. Stanford, Stanford University Press, 1959.

7. See Kohn, M. L., "Social Class and Parental Values," *American Journal of Sociology*, 44:337–51, 1959. Bronfenbrenner, 1960, *op. cit.*

8. These shifts in sex difference with a rise in class status are significant at the 5 percent level of confidence (one-tailed test).

9. Strikingly similar conclusions were reached almost 15 years ago in a provocative essay by Arnold Green, "The Middle Class Male Child and Neurosis," *American Sociological Review*, 11:31–41, 1946. With little to go on beyond scattered clinical observations and impressions, Green was able to detect many of the same trends which we have begun to discern in more recent systematic empirical data.

10. Bandura, A. and R. H. Walters. *Adolescent Aggression*. New York, Ronald Press, 1959. Mussen, P. and L. Distler. "Masculinity, Identification, and Father-Son Relationships," *Journal of Abnormal and Social Psychology*, 59:350–56, 1959.

11. Bach, G. R. "Father-Fantasies and Father-Typing in Father-Separated Children," *Child Development*, 17:63–79, 1946. Sears, R. R., M. H. Pintler, and P. S. Sears. "Effects of Father-Separation on Preschool Children's Doll Play Aggression," *Child Development*, 17:219–43, 1946. Lynn, D. B. and W. L. Sawrey. "The Effects of Father-Absence on Norwegian Boys and Girls," *Journal of Abnormal and Social Psychology*, 59:258–62, 1959. Tiller, P. O. "Father-Absence and Personality Development of Children in Sailor Families," *Nordisk Psykologis Monograph Series*, 9, 1958.

12. Papenek, M. *Authority and Interpersonal Relations in the Family*, doctoral dissertation on file at the Radcliffe College Library, 1957.

13. Kohn, M. L. and J. A. Clausen. "Parental Authority Behavior and Schizophrenia," *American Journal of Orthopsychiatry*, 26:297–313, 1956.

14. Miller and Swanson, *Changing American Parent; Inner Conflict*.

15. Gold, M. and C. Slater. "Office, Factory, Store—and Family: a Study of Integration Setting," *American Sociological Review*, 23:64–74, 1958.

16. Miller and Swanson, *Changing American Parent*.

17. Strodtbeck, F. L. "Family Interaction, Values, and Achievement" in McClelland, D. C., A. L. Baldwin, U. Bronfenbrenner, and F. L. Strodtbeck, eds., *Talent and Society*. Princeton, N. J., Van Nostrand, 1958. Rosen, B. L. and R. D'Andrade. "The Psychosocial Origins of Achievement Motivation," *Sociometry*, 22:185–217, 1959.

18. Baldwin, A. L., J. Kalhorn, and F. H. Breese. "The Appraisal of Parent Behavior," *Psychological Monographs*, 58: No. 3 (Whole No. 268), 1945.

Baldwin, A. L. "Socialization and the Parent-Child Relationship," *Child Development*, 19:127–36, 1948. Haggard, E. A. "Socialization, Personality, and Academic Achievement in Gifted Children," *The School Review*, 65:388–414, 1957. Winterbottom, M. R. "The Relation of Need Achievement to Learning Experiences in Independence and Mastery," in Atkinson, J. W., *Motives in Fantasy, Action, and Society*. Princeton, Van Nostrand, 1958. Rosen and D'Andrade, "Psychosocial Origins of Achievement Motivation," *Sociometry*, 22:185–217, 1959.

19. Cold democracy under female administration appears to foster the development of achievement not only in the home but in the classroom as well. In a review of research on teaching effectiveness, Ackerman reports that teachers most successful in bringing about gains in achievement score for their pupils were judged "least considerate," while those thought friendly and congenial were least effective. Ackerman, W. I. "Teacher Competence and Pupil Change," *Harvard Educational Review*, 24:273–89, 1954.

20. Baldwin et al., "Appraisal of Parental Behavior," *Psychological Monographs*, 58: No. 3 (Whole No. 268), 1945. Baldwin, "Socialization and Parent-Child Relationship," *Child Development*, 19:127–36, 1948. Haggard, "Socialization, Personality, and Academic Achievement, etc.," *School Review*, 65:388–414, 1957.

HIGHER EDUCATION
by Richard G. Axt

1. "Illustrative Projections of the Population of the United States, by Age and Sex, 1960 to 1980," *Current Population Reports*, Series P-25, No. 187. Washington, D.C., Bureau of the Census, 1958.

2. Lindquist, Clarence B. *College and University Faculties*, p. 2. Washington, D.C., U.S. Government Printing Office, 1959.

3. *Parents' College Plans Study*. Elmo Roper and Associates, 1959.

4. Tyler, Ralph W. "Educational Objectives of American Democracy," in Eli Ginzberg, ed., *The Nation's Children*. New York, Columbia University Press, 1960.

5. Frankel, Charles, ed. *Issues in University Education*, p. 157. New York, Harper, 1959.

6. *The Pursuit of Excellence*, p. 22. Special Studies Project V, Rockefeller Brothers Fund. New York, Doubleday, 1958.

7. Lindquist, *College and University Faculties*, pp. 3–4.

8. *Projection of Earned Degrees to 1969–70*. Washington, D.C., Office of Education, September, 1959.

9. "Freedom and Diversity," a statement issued by the State Universities Association, the American Association of Land-Grant Colleges, and the association of American Colleges in December, 1959.

10. Based on data in *Education Directory, 1959–60, Part 3: Higher Education*. Washington, D.C., U.S. Government Printing Office, 1959.

11. Ostheimer, Richard H. *Student Charges and Financing Higher Education*, pp. 38 ff., 198 ff. New York, Columbia University Press, 1953.

12. *General Education in a Free Society*, p. 65. Report of the Harvard Committee. Cambridge, Harvard University Press, 1946.

13. McGrath, Earl J. and Charles H. Russell. *Are Liberal Arts Colleges Becoming Professional Schools?* p. 10. New York, Columbia University, Teachers College, 1958.

14. *Better Utilization of College Teaching Resources—A Summary Report*. The Fund for the Advancement of Education, 1959.

15. Eells, Walter Crosby. *College Teachers and College Teaching*, An Annotated Bibliography. Atlanta, Southern Regional Educational Board, 1957.

16. Blaesser, Willard W. and Burns B. Crookston. "Student Personnel Work—College and University," *Encyclopedia of Educational Research*, pp. 1415–27. New York, Macmillan, 1960.

17. *Teacher Supply and Demand in Universities, Colleges, and Junior Colleges, 1957–58 and 1958–59*, pp. 11–12. National Education Association of the United States, 1959.

18. Axt, Richard G. *Research on Graduate Education*. Report of a Conference held at the Brookings Institution on Feb. 27, 1959. Washington, D.C., Brookings Institution, 1959.

19. Office of Education memorandum, January 4, 1960.

20. Farwell, Elwin D., Paul A. Heist, and T. R. McConnell. "Colleges and Universities—Student Population," *Encyclopedia of Educational Research*, p. 294. New York, Macmillan, 1960.

21. *Who Should Go to College?* Boulder, Colo., Western Interstate Commission for Higher Education, 1959.

22. Iffert, Robert E. *Retention and Withdrawal of College Students*. Bulletin 1958, No. 1. Washington, D.C., U.S. Government Printing Office, 1957.

23. Keezer, Dexter M., ed. *Financing Higher Education 1960–70*, pp. 35–36. New York, McGraw-Hill, 1959.

24. Ruml, Beardsley and Donald H. Morrison. *Memo to a College Trustee*. New York, McGraw-Hill, 1959.

25. McConnell, T. R. "The Diversification of American Higher Education: A Research Program," *The Educational Record*, 38: No. 4:300–315, October, 1957.

26. Keezer, *Financing Higher Education*, pp. 35–36.

THE SIGNIFICANCE OF RELIGIOUS DEVELOPMENT
by Earl A. Loomis, Jr., M.D.

1. Wach, Joachim. *Types of Religious Experience*. Chicago, University of Chicago Press, 1951.

2. Stone, Lawrence J. and Joseph Church. *Childhood and Adolescence,* p. 137. New York, Random House, 1957.

3. Winnicott, D. W. *Collected Papers.* London, Tavistock, 1958.

COMMUNITY ORGANIZATION
by Lester B. Granger

Dunham, Arthur. *Community Welfare Organization.* New York, Crowell, 1958.

McMillen, Wayne. *Community Organization for Social Welfare.* Chicago, University of Chicago Press, 1945.

Migratory Labor in American Agriculture: Report of the President's Commission on Migratory Labor. Washington, D.C., 1951.

Robinson, Reginald. *Serving the Small Community; The Story of the UCDS.* New York, Association Press, 1959.

Ross, Murray G. *Community Organization: Theory and Principles.* New York, Harper, 1955.

Social Work Year-Book. New York, National Association of Social Workers, 1957.

JUVENILE DELINQUENCY
by Norman V. Lourie

1. United Nations. *Comparative Study of Juvenile Delinquency,* Part I: North America. New York, 1958.

2. Kvaraceus, William C. and Walter B. Miller, with collaborators. *Delinquent Behavior.* Washington, D.C., National Education Association, 1959.

3. Perlman, I. Richard. "Delinquency Prevention: The Size of the Problem," *Annals of the American Academy of Political and Social Science,* March, 1959.

4. Witmer, Helen L. and Edith Tufts. *The Effectiveness of Delinquency Prevention Programs.* U.S. Children's Bureau.

5. *Annals of the American Academy of Political and Social Science,* issue of March, 1959: *Prevention of Juvenile Delinquency.*

6. Lander, Bernard. *Toward an Understanding of Juvenile Delinquency: A Study of 8464 Cases of Juvenile Delinquency in Baltimore.* New York, Columbia University Press, 1954.

7. Community Research Associates. "Reorientation for Treatment and Control," *Public Welfare,* April, 1958. Also: "Reorganizing to Prevent and Control Behavior," *Mental Hygiene,* April, 1958.

8. National Probation and Parole Association. *Standard Juvenile Court Act,* Revised 1959.

9. U.S. Children's Bureau. *Facts About State Training Schools for Juvenile Delinquents,* Statistical Series.

10. Elias, Albert. "Highfields After Five Years," *The Welfare Reporter,* January, 1958.

11. U.S. House of Representatives, Committee on Education and Labor, Subcommittee on Special Education. *Hearings,* 86th Congress.

PORNOGRAPHY AND YOUTH
by Herbert B. Warburton

1. Roth v. United States, 352 U.S. 476 (1957).
2. 5 Stat. 566, 567 (1842).
3. (1857) 20 & 21 Vict. c. 83.
4. L. R. 3 Q. B. 360 (1868).
5. 13 Stat. 504 (1865).
6. 17 Stat. 598 (1873).
7. 18 U.S.C. 1461 (1956).
8. *Tariff Act of 1939,* 46 Stat. 688, 19 U.S.C. § 1305(a) (1952).
9. United States v. One Book Entitled *Ulysses* by James Joyce, 72 F. 2d 705 (2d Circ. 1934).
10. L. R. 3 Q. B. 360 (1868).
11. J. C. N. Paul and M. L. Schwartz, *Obscenity in the Mails: A Comment on Some Problems of Federal Censorship,* Pa. L. R., 106: No. 2:217 (1957).
12. United States v. Kennerley, 209 Fed. 119, 121 (S.D.N.Y. 1913).
13. 352 U.S. 380 (1957).
14. 352 U.S. 962 (1957).
15. 352 U.S. 962 (1957).
16. 352 U.S. 476 (1957).
17. Sunshine Book Co. v. Summerfield, 128 F. Supp. 564, 249 F. 2d 114 (1957); One, Inc. v. Olesen, 241 F. 2d 772 (1957).
18. 237 F. 2d 796 (2d Circ. 1956).
19. Paul and Schwartz, *Obscenity in the Mails.*

YOUTH AND THE AUTOMOBILE
by Ross A. McFarland and Roland C. Moore

1. Riesman, D. and E. Larrabee. "Autos in America," in Clark, L., ed., *Consumer Behavior-Research on Consumer Reactions,* pp. 69–92. New York, Harpers, 1958.
2. *Accident Facts,* 1959 edition. Chicago, National Safety Council, 1959.
3. *Physical and Mental Requirements for the Driver's License.* New York, New York University Center for Safety Education, 1959.
4. Commission on Juvenile Delinquency, Adult Crime, and Corrections. "Safer Driving by Juveniles in Minnesota." Report to the 1959 Legislature, State of Minnesota, 1959.

5. King, G. F. "The Age Characteristics of Michigan Drivers," East Lansing, Michigan, Michigan State University Highway Traffic Safety Center, Oct. 31, 1958.

6. "16–20 years old operators involved in accidents and arrested, July 1955–June 1956." Special report, Connecticut Motor Vehicle Department, Hartford, Connecticut, Aug. 22, 1956 (mimeo).

7. Lefeve, B. A. "Speed Habits on a Rural Highway," Proceedings of the 33d Annual Meeting of the Highway Research Board, 409–28, January, 1954.

8. Lauer, A. R. "A Sampling Survey of Drivers on the Highways for the 24-Hour Period," pp. 15–25 in Driver Characteristics and Accidents, Highway Research Board Bulletin, No. 73. Washington, D.C., 1953.

9. Weiland, J. H. "The Adolescent and the Automobile," Chicago Review, IX: No. 3:61–64, 1955.

10. Murray, J. M. "Emotional Problems in Relation to Driving," in Action Achievement Report, 8th Annual Massachusetts Governor's Highway Safety Conference. Boston, May 25, 1954.

11. Bauer, J. "The Teenage Rebel and His Weapon—the Automobile," Traffic Safety, LI: No. 5:10–13, 55, November, 1955.

12. Neavles, J. C. and G. Winokur. "The Hot-Rod Driver," Bulletin of the Menninger Clinic, XXI: No. 1:28–35, 1957.

13. Sharp, S. "The Automobile and Pupil Driver Adjustment," Clearing House, XXXII: No. 2:83–85, October, 1957.

14. Vital Statistics of the U.S., 1957, Vol. II, Mortality Data. Washington, D.C., U.S. Department of Health, Education, and Welfare, Public Health Service, 1959.

15. McFarland, R. A. "Health and Safety in Transportation," Public Health Reports, LXXIII: No. 8:663–80, August, 1958.

16. Lauer, A. R. "Characteristics of the Driving Population with Respect to Age, Sex, Driving Habits, and Accident Involvement," Proceedings of the Iowa Academy of Science, LXI: 89–98, 1954.

17. "Motor Vehicle Accident Experience by Age of Driver," Public Safety Memo No. 51, Chicago, National Safety Council, 1957.

18. 1956 Annual Statistical Report. Sacramento, State of California, Department of California Highway Patrol, 1957.

19. "Off the Roadway Accidents, 1955–1956," State of Wisconsin, Wisconsin Motor Vehicle Department, Safety Department, 1957.

20. Bletzacher, R. W., R. F. Baker, and T. G. Brittenham. "A Study of One-car Accidents." Columbus, Ohio, Engineering Experiment Station, College of Engineering, Ohio State University, 1957.

21. Garwood, F. and G. O. Jeffcoate. "The Influence of the Age of Drivers on Various Human Factors Contributing to Accidents and on the Severity of Injury." Road Research note No. RN/2522/FG.GOJ. Hammondsworth, England, Road Research Laboratory, June, 1955.

22. McFarland, R. A., R. C. Moore, and A. B. Warren. Human Variables in

Motor Vehicle Accidents—A Review of the Literature. Boston, Harvard School of Public Health, 1955.

23. Allgaier, E. "Human Behavior and Traffic Accidents," *International Road Safety and Traffic Review* (London) V: No. 3:19–36, 1957.

24. Rainey, R. V., J. J. Conger, and B. A. Walsmith. "Personality Characteristics as a Selective Factor in Driver Education." Paper presented at the Annual Meeting of the Highway Research Board, January, 1960. (In press, 1960.)

25. Tillmann, W. A. and G. E. Hobbs. "Accident-Prone Automobile Drivers: Study of Psychiatric and Social Background." *American Journal of Psychiatry,* CVI: 321–71, 1949.

26. Dunlap, J. W. et al. "Research on the Analysis and Prevention of Motor Vehicle Accidents to Off-Duty Military Personnel," in *Annual Report of the Commission on Accidental Trauma, Armed Forces Epidemiological Board.* Washington, D.C., Department of Defense, 1957–1958.

27. Gaskill, H. S. "Final Report, Survey of Personal and Interpersonal Factors in Driving," in *Annual Report of the Commission on Accidental Trauma, Armed Forces Epidemiological Board.* Washington, D.C., Department of Defense, 1960.

28. Rommel, R. C. S. "Personality Characteristics and Attitudes of Youthful Accident Repeater Drivers," *Traffic Safety Research Review,* III: No. 1:13–14, 1959.

29. Mann, W. A. "Driver Education and the Teenage Driver." East Lansing, Michigan State University Highway Traffic Center, Michigan State University, October, 1958.

30. "A Critical Analysis of Driver Education Research." Prepared by the NEA Research Division in collaboration with the NEA National Commission on Safety Education. Washington, D.C., National Education Association, 1957.

31. Chalfant, M. W. "The Effectiveness of Driver Improvement Procedures." East Lansing, Michigan State University Highway Traffic Safety Center, Michigan State University, March, 1958.

32. Reference 29, above. See also, Nothelfer, G. A., "An Experiment in Reorienting Driver Attitudes in Teenage Drivers," *Traffic Safety Research Review,* II: No. 1:22–23, March, 1958.

INTERGROUP RELATIONS
by Hilda Taba

1. Dodson, Dan W. "The North, Too, Has Segregation," *Educational Leadership,* November, 1955.

2. For description of programs of intergroup education see Taba, Brady, and Robinson, *Intergroup Education in Public Schools,* American Council on Education, Washington, D.C., 1952.

3. Bettelheim, Bruno. "Segregation: New Style," *The School Review*, XVI: No. 3:271–72. Autumn, 1958.

4. Davis, Allison. *Social Class Influences on Learning*. Cambridge, Harvard University Press, 1945. *Harvard Review of Education*, "Class Structure and American Education," Special Issue I and II, 23: No. 3, Summer, 1953.

5. See, for example, the summaries of research on "Human Relations and Education," *Review of Educational Research*, XIX: No. 4, October, 1959.

NEGRO YOUTH ON DEMOCRACY'S GROWING EDGE
by Frederick D. Patterson

1. Embree, Edwin R. "Negroes and the Commonwealth," *Survey Graphic*, November, 1942.

2. Southern Education Reporting Service, "Status of School Segregation—Desegregation in the Southern and Border States," p. 2.

3. McCauley, Patrick, and Edward D. Ball, eds. *Southern Schools: Progress and Problems*, p. 114. Nashville, Southern Education Reporting Service, 1959.

4. The Atlanta Committee for Cooperative Action, *A Second Look: The Negro Citizen in Atlanta*.

5. *The Washington Post and Times-Herald*, February 25, 1960.

6. Medical Fellowships, Inc. is an organization formed in 1940 to secure financial assistance and school placement for Negro medical students.

7. *Where Shall We Live?*, Report of the Commission on Race and Housing, Berkeley and Los Angeles, University of California Press, 1958.

CREATIVE DISCIPLINE
by Kenneth B. Clark

1. Sheviakov, George V. and Fritz Redl. *Discipline for Today's Children and Youth*. Association for Supervision and Curriculum Development of the National Education Association, 1944; revised 1956.

2. Wolf, Katherine M. *Controversial Problems of Discipline*. Child Study Association of America (pamphlet), 1953.

3. Martin, Mildred H. "Some Reactions of Pre-school Children to Discipline," *Nervous Child*, IX: No. 2:125–30, 1951.

4. Watson, Goodwin. "Some Personality Differences in Children Related to Strict or Permissive Parental Discipline," *Journal of Psychology*, 44:227–49, 1957.

5. Baruch, Dorothy W. "How to Discipline Your Children," *Public Affairs Pamphlet No. 154*, 1949.

6. Baruch, Dorothy W. *New Ways in Discipline*. New York, McGraw-Hill, 1949.

7. Redl, Fritz. "What Makes Children Misbehave," *McCall's Magazine.* Reprinted by U.S. Department of Health, Education & Welfare.

8. Bakwin, R. and H. Bakwin. "Discipline in Children," *Journal of Pediatrics,* 39:623–34, 1951.

9. Havighurst, Robert J. "Functions of Successful Discipline," *Understanding the Child,* XXI: 35–38, 1952.

10. Lourie, Norman V. "Discipline: A Consistent Nonpunitive Concept," *Child Welfare,* XXX: No. 9:3–6, 1951.

11. Colm, Hanna. "Help and Guidance as Discipline for Preadolescents," *Nervous Child,* IX: 131–38, 1951.

12. Senn, Milton J. "Permissiveness in the Early Years," *Child Study,* XXVI: No. 3:67–68, 1949.

13. Edgar, Robert W. "Discipline and Purpose," *Teachers' College Record,* 57:8–14, 1955.

14. Skard, Ose Gruda. *Barn och Disciplin* (Child and Discipline). Stockholm, 1956.

15. Schmideberg, Melitta. "Training for Responsibility," *Phi Delta Kappan,* XLI: No. 3:90–93, 1959.

16. New York *Times,* May 26, 1954, p. 34. Report of a speech by Margaret Mead before the National Congress of Parents and Teachers, and the *National Parent-Teacher,* December, 1956, pp. 11–12.

17. Adorno, T. W., Else Frenkel-Brunswik, D. J. Levinson, and R. Nevitt Sanford. *The Authoritarian Personality.* New York, Harper, 1950.

18. Clark, K. B. *Prejudice and Your Child.* Boston, Beacon Press, 1955.

19. Frazier, E. Franklin. *Negro Youth at the Crossways.* American Council on Education, 1940.

20. Clark, K. B. "Color, Class, Personality and Juvenile Delinquency," *Journal of Negro Education,* XXVII: No. 3:240–51, 1959.

21. *Nervous Child,* IX: No. 2:111–213, 1951. Entire issue devoted to "Basic Views on Discipline."

22. DuBois, Franklin S. "Security of Discipline," *Mental Hygiene,* XXXVI: 353–72, 1952.

A SOCIOLOGIST'S VIEW
by Talcott Parsons

1. Burns, Eveline. "The Government's Role in Child and Family Welfare," in Ginzberg, Eli, ed., *The Nation's Children,* vol. 3. New York, Columbia University Press, 1960.

2. Glick, Paul Charles. *American Families.* New York, Wiley, 1957.

3. Bernert, Eleanor. "Demographic Trends and Implications," in Ginzberg, Eli, ed., *The Nation's Children,* vol. 1. New York, Columbia University Press, 1960.

CERTAIN of the contributions contain lines of poetry. The editor is grateful to the following for giving their kind permission to quote these passages: The Macmillan Company for the lines from William Butler Yeats's "The Second Coming," on page 318; *The New Yorker* Magazine and Richard Wilbur for the lines from Wilbur's "Advice to a Prophet," on page 292; and Scott, Foresman and Company for the lines by Emily Dickinson on page 300.

Values and Ideals of
American Youth